G000165564

LONDON BUS HANDBOOK

Capital Transport

Twenty-second edition 2002

ISBN 185414 252 6

Published by Capital Transport Publishing
38 Long Elmes, Harrow Weald, Middlesex

Printed by CS Graphics, Singapore

Front cover The first new double-deck design for nearly four years was launched onto the scene during 2001. The Wright Eclipse Gemini (the name Gemini – the twins – referring to the concept of a twin-deck development of the existing Eclipse single-deck design) was first shown in public at the UITP Exhibition in London in May 2001, and is certainly a most striking machine. The launch customer is Arriva London, who is taking fifty for north London routes, mainly the 102, 121 and 141, although they will also appear on the 29, 144, 221, 329 and W3 at times as well. VLW 4 is seen here on Hendon Way on 22nd September. *Geoff Rixon*

Title page upper During 2001, several routes were exchanged between operators to bring economies of operation. As part of the run-down of London Buslines, their route 490 was swapped with T-GM's route U3, and the Optare Excels formerly in Capital Connections red, white and black livery adopted T-GM's standard fleet colours. They are habitually used on route 490 but, until a new blind set could be made, destination displays for other routes had to be adapted by blanking out some points. Announcing its attributes is Excel R990 EWU at Feltham in July 2001. *Colin Brown*

Title page lower First Group's London companies were officially re-branded as First London in 2001, but the application of the name has been very slow in practice. The first group of buses to arrive new with the revised name were the seventeen Plaxton bodied Dennis Tridents for route 105, and the last of this batch, TN 1000, pauses on the Bath Road near Heathrow on 3rd July 2001. The 105 is one of several routes that have seen double-deckers restored after a period of single-deck operation, and this trend is set to continue. *Colin Brown*

Rear cover upper The UK's much heralded new registration system took effect on 1st September 2001. The first two letters indicate where the vehicle is registered (e.g. London's are LA–LY), then the age identifier (e.g. 51 is September 2001 to February 2002), followed by a random three letters. On the first day, Armchair had eight of the ubiquitous Dart SLFs with 10.1m Plaxton Pointer 2 bodywork in service, for the conversion of route 117 from older standard floor Darts. Armchair has used Reading office for its registrations, and RX51 FNS is approaching Feltham on the first day. *Geoff Rixon*

Rear cover lower Route 60 has gone down in the history books in the past three years as one with probably the most operators and vehicle types to be seen in a short time. More recently, though, it had settled to DAF low-floor buses, latterly operated by Arriva but now transferred within London Buses to Sovereign. On 1st September 2001 Connex Bus took over the route and has purchased seventeen Tridents for the purpose. On the first day, TA 43 with its new Sheffield registration, calls at South Lodge Avenue, Pollards Hill. *Geoff Rixon*

Contents

One of the most unexpected events in London in recent times was the purchase back by London Buses of many standard RMs that had long gone from the Capital. They have been refurbished both inside and out, and fitted with new engines and automatic gearboxes. Sovereign's route 13 was the first recipient, where twenty-one of them replaced nineteen orange-liveried RMLs in the summer of 2001. Initially at least, and in some cases indirectly, the rest of the 'Marshall' RMs are being used to provide extra resources on existing Routemaster routes rather than to convert more routes to such vehicles. *Geoff Rixon*

INTRODUCTION

This book gives details as at September 2001 of buses that operate London Buses contract services. We acknowledge the assistance given by some of the operating companies. The fleet information is extracted principally from the records of the London Omnibus Traction Society (LOTS) and readers needing regular updated information are recommended to membership of LOTS or the PSV Circle.

Since the last edition of this book in February 2000, various changes of nomenclature have taken place, parallel to the lead-up to and election of a new Mayor for London, who was to assume much responsibility for London's transport systems. On 1st April 2000, London Transport Buses (LTB) became London Bus Services Ltd (LBSL), trading publicly as 'London Buses' (LB). There seemed to be a determined effort to expunge all reference to the name 'London Transport', perhaps to free the name for re-use at a later date. The whole set-up falls within the remit of TfL (Transport for London) which became fully operational from 3rd July 2000, following the election of Ken Livingstone as Mayor in May 2000.

In this book, reference to 'LB' is to London Bus Services Ltd (or 'London Buses') which now controls the bus service network in Greater London, and offers and awards route tenders. Part of the Mayor's strategy is to improve bus service quality and, since 28th April 2001, some new route contracts in London have been let on a 'Quality' basis, with stricter requirements for reliability. TfL made it known that they were to seek new sites for bus garages in London, with space being leased to potential operators. In any case, TfL already own existing garages such as Ash Grove and Edgware, each of which is used by two operators, as well as the former Streatham Garage, which has been leased out for non-bus use for some years but could be returned to bus operation fairly easily.

During 2000, East Thames Buses was born out of the former Harris Bus operation, and now provides the sight of London Buses' own London SW1 address on the legal lettering panel after many years of its absence. A predominately all-red livery was adopted, and very quickly applied to the whole fleet. Here East Lancashire bodied Olympian No.345 awaits departure from Becontree Heath Bus Station in June 2001. *Geoff Rixon*

Changes in the industry in the past eighteen months have seen First Group's subsidiaries in London coming closer together under the First London banner, with a common management. This brought it into line with similar arrangements at Arriva, Go-Ahead and Stagecoach. During 2001, First London Buslines was gradually wound down as all its routes were transferred to other garages or other operators. On 21st March 2000, Delgro, the Singapore-based international transport group, purchased Metroline. On 7th August 2000, Travel London was sold to Independent Way Ltd, whose other bus operation was Limebourne. This took the National Express group out of local bus operation in London (except for route H30 at Heathrow), and they continued to concentrate on express and airport-related services. The year also saw the launch of a new corporate image for Stagecoach and a new name, Stagecoach in London, which incorporated both East London and Selkent operations.

Early 2000 saw the effective take-over of the former Harris Bus operation by London Buses Ltd, who obtained an Operator's Licence in their own name after a lapse of several years. After Harris Bus had been in receivership for some time but had no likely bidders, LBL took on the running of the services. Eventually the period of poor service was reversed, buses were repainted all red and the trading name East Thames Buses was adopted, from the formal date of 25th March 2000. A year later, TfL announced that ETB would be a permanent feature. Its routes would not be re-tendered in the normal way, and even ETB, as TfL's own in-house bus company, might be used to take on any other operation in the event of "operator failure, excessive high bidding or un-remedied poor performance".

On 7th July 2001 Connex Bus purchased the bus operating assets of both Limebourne and Travel London, which had been in common ownership under Independent Way Ltd. TfL had alleged that these operations had been the worst performing services in London, and hoped that the new owners would improve the service. Nevertheless, there was little outward sign of any change of ownership in the next few months. Limebourne had been running route C3, as well the G1 on behalf of Arriva, but Connex soon secured more permanent LB contracts on both routes in their own right.

Stagecoach introduced a new corporate livery late in 2000, but the London version took some time to make itself felt. It was not until the volume deliveries during the summer of 2001 that new buses came to London in the '80%-red' version. As with all new double-deckers in 2001, the new-style blinds have a much larger destination but a shallower 'number/via point' display. By the end of 2001, 70% of all Stagecoach London's double-deck fleet were Alexander bodied Tridents. TA 361 is in London Road, Barking on 22nd June. *Geoff Rixon*

London Buses' 80%-red rule for the central Zone 1 is now almost universal, with recent entrants Connex Bus and Durham Travel Services adopting red from the start. East Thames Buses has adopted an unrelieved red livery, while Crystals and Epsom Buses have painted some buses into red. The RMs and DAFs that are leased by London Buses to Sovereign for routes 13 and 114 are also in red. This left just around 12% of buses on LB services that are not red, and these are largely confined to the outer reaches of London. Corporate identities of the major groups continued to be evident, although all have adapted their national styles to the standards of London Buses.

London Buses has always maintained that it wants more competition, but new entrants to route tendering have been few, and instead some operators have consolidated their position. Connex Bus first came onto the scene in February 2000 on route 3, and have successfully bid for several more routes, while Durham Travel Services (trading as 'London Easylink') was the unexpected winner of route 185 from February 2001. Mitcham Belle, Thorpe's and Tellings-Golden Miller all expanded their portfolios of LB services during 2000/01 and all three needed to move into new premises to cope with the increase in work.

Driver shortages continued to present a problem. As had happened in recent times on routes 60, 127 and C1, it was Blue Triangle who were able to provide their 'drivers aid package' to come to the rescue of other operators. At various times during 2001 they operated routes 367, 492 and C10 on behalf of the incumbent operator, although all such work had ceased by the end of September. The policy of The Mayor and London Buses to improve frequencies and extend periods of operation continued to be implemented and, while undoubtedly in theory good for passengers, cases of service cuts due to staff shortages or of curtailments due to congestion, have been evident. Eventually, the Mayor arranged for a pay bonus to be paid to all drivers and conductors from April 2001, and this went some way toward improved recruitment.

Changes of operator in mid-stream of a contract have been a feature of London bus operation for some years, usually due to staffing reasons. The most recent of these occurred on 28th April 2001 when routes 263, 490 and U3 changed hands, while the 315, already run by Connex Bus on sub-contract from Arriva, was assumed by Connex

A possible rival to the dominance of the Dart SLF in the single-deck market is the DAF SB120, so far only fitted with the Wright Cadet body. Although some other operators outside London purchased a few, Arriva London only had a solitary example (CW 1) on test for nearly a year. Then from August 2001, they took their first production batch, with twenty-two – forming the DWL class – for route 319 running from Brixton Garage. More similar buses were due to follow for Arriva's outer London routes 256 and 346. DWL 1 at Wandsworth Common displays this striking advert, something it carried for a few weeks when new. *Geoff Rixon*

in its own right. Arriva had ran out of space to accommodate vehicles on route 263, so First Capital, having just lost route 67 to Stagecoach, kept its buses and drivers to take on route 263 for its last year prior to being re-tendered. Tellings-Golden Miller, running route U3 into Uxbridge from Fulwell Garage, swapped it with route 490. The 490 ran close to Fulwell but was worked by First London Buslines from its distant Southall Garage. In turn, the U3 was more sensibly and economically thence worked by First London from Uxbridge Garage. Less unremunerative dead running was the result, saving fuel, needing fewer drivers and complying with the new emphasis on giving a better quality of service.

A feature of 2000/01 has been the surrender of certain commercial routes running within Greater London under the 'section 3/2' (or London local service agreement) system. These are whereby LB allow the routes to operate in their area, but pay an amount to the operator to compensate for having to charge the LT fare scale. Operators on routes such as 166, 363, 405, 406 and 517 gave them up, and LB took over with routes of their own under the LB system. This has gone some way to increasing the overall vehicle requirement in London as a whole. Nevertheless, some operators maintain a fair number of commercial (LLSA) routes, notably Metrobus in the Bromley and Beckenham area.

Since the last edition of this book, around 1900 new buses have entered service, or were about to do so. Around 60% were double-deck, all fully accessible low-floor models, made up of Dennis Trident, Volvo B7TL and DAF DB250LF chassis. Except for just two East Lancs bodied buses, all were fitted with Plaxton President or Alexander ALX400 bodywork. In late summer 2001, delivery commenced of the first brand-new double-deck design for three years. This was the Wright Eclipse Gemini, of which fifty had been ordered for Arriva London on Volvo B7TL chassis. The other 40% of the new buses were single-deck, of which over 700 were Dennis Dart SLFs, and well over half had the ubiquitous Plaxton Pointer 2 body. Nevertheless, a fair proportion had Alexander or Marshall bodywork, a mere four with East Lancs, while the first examples appeared of the new Caetano Nimbus, a design that seemed to be gaining a fair custom. Just seven Optare Solos, five Volvo B6BLEs and seven B10BLEs and one DAF SB120, broke the dominance of the Dart SLF. The SB120 was a new midibus design, mounted with a Wright Cadet body, and was evaluated by Arriva London. The test period of an evaluation example was rewarded by an initial order of twenty-two for Arriva's route 319. By autumn 2001, around 4000 low-floor buses were in service in Greater London, and the needs of passengers are being ever more embraced by London Buses and the operators.

The effects of the DDA (Disability Discrimination Act) have been many, but since 1st September 2000 all new double and single-deck buses have had to have wheelchair access, and indeed many older vehicles have been so retro-fitted. A more controversial item was that new buses in build at or after 1st January 2001 had to have a revised destination blind display and alternative interpretations of the rules were adopted by different operators. Examples of this altered lettering and number style will be seen in the pictures in this book on vehicles new during 2001.

The merger of Dennis, Alexander and Plaxton into a combine named Transbus International initially saw no changes. However, in summer 2001, Transbus announced that it was to close, but later to just reduce, production at Plaxton's Scarborough factory. Nevertheless, the Pointer 2 body, almost exclusively built on Dennis Dart SLF chassis, was henceforth to be built instead at Alexander's plant in Scotland, and the first examples built there were delivered to Metrobus in London in August 2001. Simultaneously, Marshall's of Cambridge sold off its bus division and this was to be moved to a new site. Meanwhile, the trend in London had imperceptibly started to veer in favour of double-deckers being specified on several newly awarded contracts at the expense of single-deck operation, for example routes 79, 105 and 191. This was partly due to an undeniable rise in passenger numbers throughout London, following from improvements to vehicle quality and frequencies, not to mention an increasingly reasonable fares structure. As each new route tender was awarded, it became almost routine that an increased frequency, greater running time or recovery time, and thus a higher vehicle requirement, was specified.

During 2000/01 it became evident that London Buses was specifying new low-floor buses in just about every case for new route contracts, even for routes that already had them, or which had modern buses (for example, Olympians) thereon. The knock-on effects of this were soon being felt elsewhere in Britain. In the most prominent example, the Stagecoach 2001 orders for London totalled 287 buses (177 Tridents and 110 Dart SLFs), but only ninety single-deckers for the rest of the UK combined. Plenty of step-entrance Darts, plus Scania and Olympian double-deckers, all only a few years old, were cascaded from London to provincial Stagecoach companies. In 2001 even the earliest Dennis Dart SLFs, new only in 1996/97, started to depart from London. Arriva and FirstGroup have indulged in similar exercises though on a lesser scale, but a policy of vehicle replacement before they are life-expired could have a different effect on those without the pool of group companies to cascade buses towards.

An inevitable consequence of the enormous intake of new buses is the disposal of older vehicles. Metrobuses and Titans, the standard buses of the 1980s, are now almost all gone from the mainstream fleets. The single-deck Lance, Lynx and National, and MetroRider and StarRider minibuses are down to a mere handful of examples.

Until now, we have not mentioned the best-loved London bus of all – the Routemaster. After over forty years of service, anyone would have concluded that its last days would not be far away. The Mayor made no secret of his regard for the vehicle, and TfL even announced that they would like a lot more conductors on buses in central London. The first step in this quest was a surprising one: – London Buses bought up as many standard RMs as they could lay their hands on, including some from Reading Mainline and others from preservationists. After some months in storage, in February 2001 Marshall's of Cambridge was given the contract to perform a complete makeover on these buses. They were fitted with new Cummins engines and automatic Alison gearboxes, while the bodies received new seating, flooring, heating and lighting, hopper windows, as well as internal CCTV fitment. The first refurbished example appeared back on the road in June, and the majority are now at work on route 13 with Sovereign as the contractor. In turn, this enabled RMLs displaced from route 13 to bring RML routes with other companies up to strength. Furthermore, the increase in Sunday service provision generally has put such pressure on the doored fleet on that day. Consequently, during 2001 Routemasters have made a return to eight routes on Sundays. A different sort of conversion is of route 55 from October 2001, with conductors added onto low-floor doored Tridents, partly to see how it would affect boarding and journey times on such vehicles.

In autumn 2001, the world of London's buses was being enhanced by Arriva's new Wright Eclipse Gemini, and First London had borrowed six articulated buses for trial use along route 207 on the Uxbridge Road. The Red Arrow services were to gain 18-metre articulated buses in spring 2002, while Mercedes-Benz Citaros are on order by First London for a new central London service. Plans are afoot to produce a successor to the Routemaster, the so-called 'Q Master' project. It looks like it might have front, centre and rear doors, and an engine under the staircase, in the position pioneered in the 1930s with the AEC Q type for London Transport.

Not everything in London's bus world can possibly be contained in this one volume, and we have only covered buses and companies engaged on local bus work in Greater London, almost all of it under various types of contract to London Buses. Several of the companies herein, notably Blue Triangle, First London and Metroline, engage part of their fleet on private contract, school services or rail replacement work, and this is supplemented by large numbers of buses from private operators from within and outside London as is required. We do not generally cover the London area coach fleets, sightseeing buses, airport-related coach services, commuter coach and Green Line services, as all of these are outside the remit and control of London Buses. The book represents the fleet situation as it was at the beginning of November 2001, together with details of buses known to be on order.

November 2001   David Stewart and Colin Lloyd

Destined to be the last of Stagecoach's vast fleet of Titans in London is the first one of all, T 1. Although still being used in service at Romford in September 2001, it is being kept by Stagecoach in its original 1978 style of livery for special duties. Seen here at one such special occasion, on its first public airing in its new colours, it was at the annual Cobham bus gathering in April 2001. *Colin Brown*

AirLinks, mainly responsible for coach links and airport-related contract services, does operate just one LB route, the H30. It is unusual in that it operates entirely within the Heathrow free-fare zone, mainly supported by BAA and British Airways. Dart SLF T71 WWV departs from Hatton Cross on its circuitous journey around the south, west and north sides of the Airport. *David Stewart*

AIRLINKS

AirLinks the Airport Coach Company Ltd, 682 Armadale Road, Feltham, Middlesex, TW14 0LW

A large operator of coach and contract services at all the London airports, together with inter-airport services, mostly branded as Speedlink, Jetlink and Airbus. The latter brand was added, following the purchase from London United of their Airbus branded Alexander Royale bodied Volvo Olympians, together with the routes, in February 2000. There is just a brief mention here of the operation of six buses on a LB/British Airways joint contract route H30 at Heathrow Airport. The company is part of the National Express Group, and operates six dedicated buses for the H30 from its Feltham coach base.

ARMCHAIR

Armchair Passenger Transport Co. Ltd, Armchair House, Commerce Way, Brentford, Middlesex, TW8 8LZ

After ventures in Surrey and Berkshire, Armchair has been moderately successful with London tendering. The bus fleet is now concentrated entirely on LB work, routes operated being all fairly local to their base; indeed two of them (E2 and E8) actually terminate at the Depot. The three batches of Olympians are mixed on routes 65 and 237, the P-registered Dart SLFs are on routes E2 and E8 and the Alexander bodied Dart SLFs on route 209. The newest and shortest Dart SLF is usually to be found on route 485, while the remaining standard Plaxton Darts on routes 117 and 190 were being replaced by new SLFs in autumn 2001. LB routes operated are the 65, 117, 190, 209, 237, 485, E2, E8 and school journeys on routes 371 and 609. The fleet carries orange and white livery, in varying proportions, and is housed at Commerce Way, Brentford. There is also a large coach fleet that covers private hire, sightseeing and a number of daily commuter services.

Armchair's double-deck fleet is composed almost entirely of Olympians, in three batches with three different bodywork styles, and is utilised on routes 65 and 237. An example of the seventeen Leyland-bodied examples, H549 GKX, is pictured here on route 65, travelling along Brook Street, Kingston in company with one of the Alexander bodied examples. *Geoff Rixon*

The short route 209 between Hammersmith and Mortlake, terminating at the point where the late-lamented Mortlake Bus Garage used to stand, is a very busy and frequent service. Carrying another full load down the unusually named Castelnau in Barnes is T148 AUA, one of the thirteen Alexander ALX200 Dart SLFs invariably to be found on this route. *Geoff Rixon*

ARRIVA LONDON group

(all trading as Arriva serving London)
Arriva London North Ltd, Arriva London North East Ltd and Arriva London South Ltd,
16 Watsons Road, Wood Green, London N22 7TZ

The *Arriva serving London* group is a combination of the former Leaside Buses, South London Transport and Grey-Green companies. Leaside had been purchased by the Cowie Group on 29th September 1994. Cowie followed this up by buying South London Transport on 10th January 1995, the last of the London Buses companies to be sold. In the autumn of 1995, the red livery was modified with a double yellow 'flying sash' at the rear, and even in 2001 some buses survive in this condition. Grey-Green had been the Cowie Group's original bus operating company but retained its separate identity for a while. However, in late 1997 Cowie re-branded itself as Arriva London North (Leaside), ... South (South London) and ... North East (Grey-Green).

Arriva also introduced a new corporate colour scheme, but in London the full version fell foul of the '80%-red rule' and, after a few single-deck buses were repainted with a full cream front, was modified to red with the so-called 'cow horns' cream relief. Vehicles of the three companies are now indistinguishable, hence the combination of the fleet details in this book. Garages of London North are at Clapton, Edmonton, Enfield, Palmers Green, Tottenham and Wood Green, London North East has one base at Barking, while London South operates from Battersea, Beddington Farm, Brixton, Norwood, South Croydon and Thornton Heath. The group maintains a separate unit as *Leaside Travel* at Edmonton Garage. This unit uses an unusual maroon, blue and white livery, carried by its Metrobuses and coaches on school and contract work.

The company was the first in London to introduce low-floor double-deckers into service – on route 242 in November 1998. These were DAF DB250LFs and just under 400 have followed into stock. A break with this practice occurred in 2001, with the company being the launch customer with an order for fifty Volvo B7TLs with the revolutionary Wright Eclipse Gemini bodywork, and these buses started to enter service in September 2001.

The new standard type within Arriva London is the DLA class; the Alexander ALX400 bodied DAF DB250LF. Three years after being the first low-floor double-deck type to enter service in London, Arriva has 321 of them in stock and DLA 234 at Herne Hill on route 468 is a typical example. The earliest DLAs had a longer wheelbase and central stairs, but later ones (such as this) have all been shorter examples with forward stairs but with no loss of seating capacity. *Geoff Rixon*

Arriva's older standard bus is rapidly in decline. However, in spite of the influx of DLAs and DLPs, Arriva remains an operator of the Metrobus. In autumn 2001, examples could still be found here and there, especially on routes around Wood Green and Enfield. M 939 passes Alexandra Palace on the normally DLA-operated route W3. *Stephen Madden*

Still on a DAF DB250LF chassis, but after twenty with Plaxton President bodywork had been delivered during 2000, another thirty-six DLPs came in 2001. The latter are all allocated to Wood Green Garage for route 29 and DLP 51 rounds Trafalgar Square on 14th September. Note the large yellow nearside mirror, which is also fitted to some of the new VLW class. *Geoff Rixon*

Many of Arriva's standard Routemasters have had refurbishments and repaints during 2000/01. On 28th July 2001, RM 1593 provided a sparkling sight rounding Marble Arch on route 137. This is one of the eight routes to revert to Routemasters on Sundays in 2001. Note the yellow handrails on the platform.
Geoff Rixon

Many of Arriva's RML's used on routes 19, 38 and 73 carry slogans to advertise Sadler's Wells Theatre in Rosebery Avenue. RML 2574 passes Hyde Park Corner on a short journey on the 19, and has a somewhat non-standard application of the stock number! Although route 19 works from the Battersea outstation, most of its buses actually carry the BN code of its parent garage, Brixton.
Stephen Madden

The central London operations of Kentish Bus were progressively transferred to other group companies. The forty-three Northern Counties bodied Olympians bought when Kentish Bus was jointly owned with Northumbria, moved over to Arriva, both North and South, and latterly some to North East as well. Those in the south run from Norwood Garage, like L 542 on the 176 on Waterloo Bridge.
Stephen Madden

A type conversion during 2001 by default was the Sunday service on route 73. With a major intake of DLAs into Tottenham Garage for routes 41 and 243, and the loss of the Metrobus allocation, the DLA inevitably became allocated to the route. The last few deliveries had the DDA-compliant blinds, shown here on DLA 309 in Oxford Street on 29th July. *Colin Brown*

The 1986/87 delivery of ECW-bodied Leyland Olympians was a substantial investment by the then London Buses. Latterly, most had lost their sparkle, and the 'tag artists' have since defaced virtually every bus in south and southeast London. Route 130 was intended for withdrawal once the Croydon Tramlink began, but survived – in a reduced form – after all. The Croydon area remains a stronghold of the type and L 153 pauses in Dingwall Road. *Colin Brown*

Forming a 'batch of one' is the former London & Country L 611, turning into West Croydon Bus Station on route 403 on 27th April 2001. A remarkable survivor, and in spite of its L class-code, it is actually a Volvo B10M with an astonishing 88 seats in its East Lancashire bodywork. *Geoff Rixon*

The former Grey-Green operation, re-christened Arriva London North East, retained its separate identity, albeit with standard Arriva London red colours. However, a small element of individuality survives on many buses with the use of 'Grey-Green' fleet numbers, in spite of attempts to re-classify them. One of the unusual 1992-bodied East Lancs buses, rebuilt onto 1985 vintage Volvo B10M coach chassis, is here performing on the 103 in Romford. *Colin Stannard*

Once all in Grey-Green colours and dating from 1988/9, the high-floor Volvo B10Ms with Alexander bodywork are still mainly to be found on routes 24, 125 and 275. They are nominally classified VA, but not all yet carry that class code. VA 130 works on route 275 in Barkingside.
Colin Stannard

Arriva London has a lot of class codes for its Darts, with seven different variations on the Plaxton Pointer, all meaning something slightly different! However, the DP is basically identical to the DRL. DP 163 in central Croydon is one of four transferred within Arriva from its former country cousin Londonlinks/ London & Country, and betrays its origin with its three-track route number blind.
Colin Brown

This view sees a refugee from the large contingent of Northern Counties Paladin bodied Dennis Darts which were delivered to Kentish Bus in 1994. One of KB's routes, the 225, was worked for a short while by Grey-Green, but after they in turn surrendered it (to Selkent), the five Darts used thereon gravitated to Arriva London North, by then under common management. Hence the rather unlikely appearance of DRN 122 for use on route 192, seen here at Edmonton Green.
Colin Brown

Grey-Green had seventeen Dart SLFs with the then new Alexander ALX200 bodywork delivered in 1997 for routes 20 and 167. These have since been repainted to Arriva red, and the parent company has taken more, classifying all as the ADL class. Seven of them are used on route 444, on which ADL 5 is seen at 'The Cambridge' Edmonton, although the route is due to be diverted away from here past the nearby North Middlesex Hospital once road layout problems are resolved. *Colin Brown*

In spite of the minuscule class differences of earlier Dart classes, the PDL code has been used for two different lengths and three different seat layouts. In 2001, route W4 was taken over from Metroline and the short Dart SLFs used thereon restored a single-deck allocation to Tottenham Garage after very many years as a purely double-deck garage. The one-liner on the blind of PDL 43 belies its tortuous routeing. *Colin Lloyd*

A break from the diet of red can be seen on weekdays in the Waterloo, Westminster and surrounding areas. Arriva London has three 8.8m twenty-one seat Dart SLFs on a contract for DSS staff travelling between their various premises and offices. PDL 16 calls at Elephant & Castle on another lunchtime 'shuttle' service. *Colin Brown*

A most unusual livery which bears little relationship to Arriva, is that of Leaside Travel. They even retain the swan emblem of Arriva's forebear Leaside Buses. Most of their Metrobuses carry this livery, and can be seen on a fair range of school-bus services for London Buses in north London and look like being retained in service for some time to come. *Colin Lloyd*

Just a mere handful of Arriva's buses in London remain in the first version of 'London' livery. Originally the national corporate scheme was adopted with red merely replacing the blue, but with the fuller fronted cream area. This fell foul of LT's 80%-red ruling, and those so treated are gradually reverting to the standard 'cow horns' style. Late summer 2001 saw DRL 158 still at work in Croydon. *Colin Brown*

Arriva's new baby, the Wright Eclipse Gemini bodied Volvo B7TL, cuts an impressive image, and provides a major upgrade to some north London routes. This is especially true on a route such as the 102, which has seen nineteen years of continous Metrobus operation. The very first of the type to work the route was VLW 3 on 20th September 2001, here at East Finchley turning from The Bishops Avenue onto the A1. *David Stewart*

Arriva's national blue and cream livery enters Greater London at relatively few places nowadays. The Shires' No.5123 (formerly LR 93) is one of a batch of fifteen Leyland bodied Olympians dating from 1989/90 that are to be found on routes 142 and 340. *Capital Transport*

ARRIVA THE SHIRES & ESSEX group

Arriva the Shires Ltd and Arriva East Herts & Essex Ltd, 487 Dunstable Road, Luton, Bedfordshire, LU4 8DS

Arriva serving the Shires & Essex is controlled from Luton and includes the buses based at Watford and High Wycombe garages in this book, running into Greater London on routes 142, 340, 350, H18 and U9. Luton also controls the former County Bus fleets (some still in cream and green and with Townlink, Lea Valley or Thameside names), operating from bases at Debden, Grays, Harlow and Ware. The only buses in the fleet listed in this book are those regularly used on routes 256, 310, 311, 324, 327, 346, 348, 370, 373, 397, W13, W14, these being services operated under various LB contracts or arrangements. Other vehicles may be seen on occasions.

The group is the descendant of Luton & District, London Country North West and County Bus, and has expanded widely, controlling as it does Arriva services in Colchester and Southend. The group has a common numbering system, and most vehicles are now mostly repainted to the national version of Arriva livery of turquoise and cream (officially called aquamarine and light stone), with appropriate fleetnames (officially known as strap-lines). Even so, some buses still sport pre-Arriva colours.

Nineteen 9.4m Dart SLFs with Alexander ALX200 bodywork were the surprise purchase by Arriva East Herts and Essex for a group of newly-won LB routes in north-east London during 2000. They have dual-door bodywork, and No.3465 travels along Wanstead High Street on the W14. Unusually, these buses carry small Arriva names above the cab, rather than the more usual large side fleetnames. *Mark Lyons*

To the north of London, an Arriva 'country' service utilises red and cream buses, this being more historical, as red had been originally used for a marketing exercise between two companies (the then County Bus and MTL London Northern) along the Lea Valley corridor. Gradually during 1999, former Arriva London Metrobuses had been passed on, after refurbishment, to Arriva East Herts & Essex, for route 310 (Enfield & Hertford). No.5363, still carrying its former London number of M 233, calls at the new Waltham Cross Bus Station. *Colin Lloyd*

Every bus of Arriva Kent Thameside that works into Greater London is in Arriva livery, the company being among the first in the Group to complete its repaint programme, admittedly aided by many new buses coming in 1998/99. Most of its LB routes are worked by the Plaxton Pointer 2 bodied Dart SLF, and those used regularly on LB routes have single-piece, rather than three-track, number blinds, as exemplified by No. 3279 in Dartford. *Laurie Rufus*

ARRIVA SOUTHERN COUNTIES group

Arriva Southern Counties Ltd, (t/a Arriva serving Kent Thameside, Kent & Sussex, Surrey & West Sussex), Invicta House, Armstrong Road, Maidstone, Kent, ME15 6TY

Arriva Southern Counties at Maidstone controls the fleets of Kent Thameside and Kent & Sussex, as well as the 'Surrey & West Sussex' fleet. London Buses contracts run by the Kent fleets are routes 126, 286, 402, 428, B11, B13, R5, R8 and school buses on 132 and 601. Garages of the group running buses into London are Dartford, Northfleet and Tunbridge Wells. The companies are the former Kentish Bus and Maidstone & District operations. What remains of the former London & Country companies all trade as *Arriva serving Surrey & West Sussex* but, after severe cutbacks in 2001, now only two routes (418 and 470) penetrate into London as far as Kingston, operated from garages at Guildford and Woking. Only the buses from the Kent fleets operating into Greater London are included in this book. The bus fleets are all in corporate turquoise and cream livery.

Blue Triangle vehicles have been well-known to enthusiasts in and around London for several years, mostly because of their predilection for vintage buses, as well as their frequency of operation on rail replacement work. On 1st May 1999, their first London Buses route began, the 474 (Canning Town & East Beckton) and, after some months of MCW Metrobus operation, new Dennis Tridents eventually appeared from October. This view of DL 907 at North Woolwich clearly shows the interior layout and the bonded glazing treatment. *Laurie Rufus*

Blue Triangle is one of the increasing number of operators to buy the Caetano Nimbus bodywork mounted on Dart SLF chassis. One wonders how many of their passengers realise that the fleetname originated with the emblem used on AEC buses in past times? Of the eight in the batch, DN 181 alone has gold fleetnames (the others have white). Turning at Chadwell Heath on route 368, it shows off its 11-metre length. *Colin Stannard*

BLUE TRIANGLE

Blue Triangle Buses Ltd, Denver Trading Estate, Ferry Lane, Rainham, Essex, RM13 9BU

The company has been around for some seventeen years, working on contract, rail replacement and certain bus routes in Essex. From 1999, it branched out into emergency service coverage, helping out London Buses on routes 1, 60 and 127 when the incumbent operators were unable to fully cover all the services. This aspect of the business continued onto routes 185, 367, 492 and C10 over various periods in 2001, although such work has finished for the present. It was not until 1st May 1999 that it began its first LB contract route, the 474 (Canning Town & East Beckton), in its own right. Nine East Lancs bodied Dennis Tridents soon took over, and another fourteen assumed route 248 (Romford & Cranham) during autumn 2001. The Caetano bodied Dart SLFs operate on route 368 (Barking & Chadwell Heath). Metrobuses and Titans continue to form a large part of the fleet, and are extensively used on rail replacement services all over London. These older buses are also used on schoolday services in the Romford area, as well as Essex route 565 into Romford and commercial route 204 in Loughton. Furthermore, a handful of vintage ex-London buses is used on special occasions.

CONNEX BUS

Connex Bus UK Ltd, Unit 10 Beddington Cross, Croydon, Surrey, CRO 4XH

Connex is a recent entrant into the London tendered route arena, beginning with the award of routes 3 and N3 from 5th February 2000. The company had never operated buses in Britain before, although members of its parent group operated in continental Europe. However, in less than two years, the total bus fleet had already reached 100 vehicles. Dennis Tridents were ordered for the 3/N3, and plans for an operating base at Selhurst rail depot were soon supplanted by the opening of more suitable premises at Beddington Cross. Route 322 was then won, followed later by the 315, both from Arriva, with short Dart SLFs entering the fleet for these routes. The shut-down of services worked by Arriva in east Surrey caused London Buses to take over control of route 405 (Croydon & Redhill) and Connex Bus won this from 21st April 2001. This route utilised longer Plaxton bodied Dart SLFs. During 2001, more Tridents arrived when route 196, and then the 60, were successfully won from London General and Arriva respectively, and yet another seventeen will be needed in December 2001 with the assumption of route 157.

Aside from these expansions in its own right, on 7th July 2001 Connex Bus purchased the bus operating assets of Independent Way Ltd, covering the buses, staff and the Silverthorne Road, Battersea, base of both Limebourne and Travel London. These companies had a turbulent recent history. The Q-Drive group, whose local bus operation traded as Limebourne, had gone into receivership in October 1998, and on 20th November 1998, its local management staged a buy-out of the bus business using the name Independent Way Ltd. The existing fleet was re-possessed by finance companies; replacement buses had to be hired, but it soon obtained thirty-four Caetano bodied Dart SLFs and bought other second-hand Darts. Already running LB routes 42, 156, C3 and C10, route 344 was soon added. The C10 was notable, in that in May 1996 its vehicles were the first by a contract operator to adopt the 80% red scheme as was then being laid down by LB for buses operating contracts within Central London Fare Zone 1. Since August 1999, Limebourne had been running Arriva's route G1, using some of Arriva's Darts, to assist with their driver shortages. Conversely, during April 2001 Limebourne handed over route C10 to Blue Triangle due to alleged poor performance.

Meanwhile on 7th August 2000, Independent Way bought the Travel London operations from the National Express Group. It had won two LT contract routes C1 and 211 from June 1998, using Optare Excels on the 211 and Optare Solos on the C1. Its depot had fallen foul of local authority planning regulations, and the inability to resolve this problem was a major factor in the sale, and buses moved to join Limebourne at Silverthorne Road.

Becoming a major operator in south London in such a short time was not all, as local bus services had also been developed in Sussex in 2000, operated by Darts based at Lewes Railway Station, although the base moved to Newhaven in summer 2001. Additionally, and to provide replacement bus services for Connex's own rail network, a few Metrobuses, Olympians and Darts are kept in the fleet. Taking together Connex's indigenous fleet, its Sussex and acquired operations, and those buses still expected, the fleet total was intended to reach around 200 by the end of 2001.

Opposite top The first new bus operator in London in 2000 was Connex Bus, and they have since expanded considerably, with more routes won on tender and by acquisition. The first route was trunk route 3, for which a batch of Alexander ALX400 bodied Tridents with central staircases was purchased. Outwardly a normal red London bus, but the colours used on Connex trains are evident with the narrow yellow stripe and blue skirt. *Stephen Madden*

Opposite bottom The first Tridents had rather small fleetnames, but the latest Dart SLFs taken into stock in 2001 had much larger names. Bearing traditional-style white fleet numbers, garage code and running number, DA 16 looks every inch a London bus, in spite of it being owned by a very new company. It had just arrived at the Cheviot Road terminus of route 315, as since transfer from Arriva, the route can no longer terminate in the nearby Norwood Bus Garage. *Geoff Rixon*

On 7th July 2001, Connex Bus took over all the operations of Limebourne and Travel London. It was three months before any change started to be made to the vehicle fleet, the livery or the fleetnames. In September the very first vehicle received all-red livery with a Connex name. Other than this, the travelling public would hardly have been aware of the ownership change baring the change of legal lettering. One of thirty-four Caetano Compass bodied Dart SLFs, No.414, carries the Limebourne name at Vauxhall. *Mark Lyons*

The abandonment by Arriva of its entire network in east Surrey during early 2001 saw route 405 between Croydon and Redhill taken on by London Buses, tendered and awarded to Connex Bus. Thus, brand-new Dart SLFs now charge a £1 fare right out to Redhill, in contrast to the much higher fare on Arriva's motley collection of Metrobuses and Volvo B6s. *Colin Brown*

It might say *Travel London* on the bus, but it has been a Connex vehicle since July 2001. As with all of Travel London's vehicles, it used to have an additional slogan to tell that it was part of the National Express group. Twenty-one Optare Excels maintain route 211 between Hammersmith and Waterloo, and No. 422 (not yet carrying its Connex 'XL' coding) at Victoria is an example. *Colin Brown*

Crystals has been well known for their fleet of accessible minibuses, although they do operate a handful of outer London bus routes. In recent years they have used a turquoise colour scheme, but are now adopting a red livery. Six Optare Solos entered stock in spring 2001, five of them to cover a major enhancement of route B14. The fleetname on Y294 PDN is indistinct on the all-red in Bexleyheath. *Laurie Rufus*

CRYSTALS

C.J. Springham, 127 Dartford Road, Dartford, Kent, DA1 3EN

Starting life as a taxi firm in 1970, Crystals bought their first minibus in 1972. The company was one of the first operators of LT tendered routes when route 146 was taken over in August 1985, although the contract was lost in 1993. The company has since gained two minibus routes (R2, R7) at Orpington and another (B14) at Bexleyheath, together with a range of Mobility Bus routes right across south London from Putney to Bexleyheath and from Southwark to Croydon. Vehicles on routes R2 and R7 carry a livery of turquoise, while those employed on Mobility Bus routes are in red with yellow relief. However, a change occurred in May 2001 when five new Optare Solos were put onto route B14, these being all-over red. Vehicles are now all kept at the address above, which is located midway between Dartford and Crayford.

Amongst its many Olympians, East Thames Buses operates a handful of DAF DB250s to provide a bit of variety. No. 381 is in Woolwich in its unrelieved red, a far cry from the unusual blue and lime green of its previous owner, Harris Bus of Grays. *Laurie Rufus*

Gone is the route branding on this Excel, a feature of Harris Bus, but frequently made irrelevant by the use of buses on the 'wrong' route. New blinds are also an improvement over the customary use of the 'Welcome to Harris Bus' display! No. 372 pauses in Blackfen. *Laurie Rufus*

EAST THAMES BUSES

London Buses Ltd (t/a East Thames Buses), 172 Buckingham Palace Road, London SW1W 9TN

A major hiatus occurred during the turn of 1999/2000 when Harris Bus of West Thurrock went into receivership. During this period, its bus operation was decimated due mainly to the exodus of driving staff. In February 2000, LT Buses took over the day-to-day running of the operation, following the failure to sell the company. A new Operators Licence in the name of London Buses Ltd was soon granted, and LBL thus returned to local bus operation in their own right. It re-opened Ash Grove Garage at Cambridge Heath in east London to work three of the routes (128, 129 and 150), while retaining the 108, 132, 180 and 661 at the former Harris Bus base at Crabtree Manor Way in Belvedere. The fleetname East Thames Buses was adopted, and Harris' unusual pale green and blue livery gave way to all-over red within a few months.

The 'Quality Line' branding on Epsom Buses began with the delivery of Mercedes-Benz Varios in 1998, mostly to upgrade commercial routes K9 and K10 between Epsom and Kingston. Both UVG and Plaxton bodied vehicles arrived, and an example of the latter marque, S453LGN, calls at Cromwell Road in Kingston. During late summer 2001, the company began to repaint these smart buses into a red livery. *Stephen Madden*

Suddenly in the summer of 2001, Epsom Buses treated their fleet used on LB routes to an all-over red livery, albeit retaining the 'Quality Line' fleetname. Compared with their company colours of cream and maroon, the effect is quite plain. Dart SLF S465 LGN travels along Cannon Hill Lane in Lower Morden on route 413, a service due to pass to London General at the end of 2001. *Geoff Rixon*

EPSOM BUSES

H.R. Richmond Ltd, Blenheim Road, Longmead Estate, Epsom, Surrey, KT19 9AF

Epsom Buses is the trading name for the local bus work undertaken by Epsom Coaches, founded in 1920 by Mr H.R. Richmond. Bus work started in 1986 with one minibus route, but blossomed with several former London Country routes assumed at deregulation in October 1986. Subsequently, there have been several adjustments to the network, with a mix of commercial and Surrey County Council routes operated. London Buses work began when routes 413 and S1 were taken over from London General during the autumn of 1997, and routes 404, 463, S3, S4 and S5 have followed. Other routes in the Epsom and Kingston area are E5, E9, K9, K10 and 408, although the 166 was transferred to Arriva in July 2001. For some years, the fleet livery for buses has been cream with maroon relief, applied in different proportions, and all are based at the Blenheim Road address. Having said that, from August 2001 the Dart SLFs used on LB services were treated to an all-red livery, while maintaining the company's *Quality Line* branding. There is also an extensive coach operation, which is not included in this publication.

FIRST CAPITAL

First Capital North Ltd and First Capital East Ltd, Macmillan House, Paddington Station, London W2 1TY

The origin of this large fleet came when Ensignbus of Purfleet gained LT route 145 from 21st June 1986, and a blue and silver livery was used. Many more routes and vehicles followed until the business was sold to the CNT group of Hong Kong on 29th December 1990. By then, the Capital Citybus name was used, and a new yellow livery was introduced, initially featuring Chinese characters in the fleetname. The company was bought back by a management-led team on 21st December 1995, and a revised fleetname style started to appear on vehicles following the breaking of ties with its former owner. With a remarkable twist, Ensignbus re-emerged in 1999 with a short-lived bus operation, again using the blue and silver colours. Considerable success with London Buses tendering has been a feature of the company's recent history, and by 1997 three depots were being used, at Dagenham (Chequers Lane), Hackney (Waterden Road) and Northumberland Park (Marsh Lane).

The company was sold to the First Group on 8th July 1998, with buses soon acquiring the group's logo as well as the 'First Capital' trading name. The formal company title of Capital Citybus was kept for a time, although it was re-named to First Capital North (for Hackney and NP depots) and East (Dagenham depot) in March 2000. A red livery with yellow relief had been introduced in 1997, initially for buses running into central London, but later adopted universally. Even so, the halting of routine repaints in 2000 meant that, by the summer of 2001, around seventy-five buses in the fleet still carried the former livery of yellow with red relief. During the late summer of 1998, most of Thamesway's LT routes and their buses were assimilated, together with the Ponders End (Morson Road) depot. Buses soon started to be repainted into Capital's red and yellow livery, though a handful of buses remained in Thamesway's yellow and mauve colours in 2001. During this year, Ponders End was reduced to an outstation, reserve and training base.

The First corporate image gradually became more common, and in 1999 a yellow and off-white wavy stripe was adopted, but only on new buses. At the same time, the company came closer to its sister company CentreWest, with a common fleet numbering scheme adopted, but these were only carried on new vehicles. During late 2001, the 'First London' name should gradually supplant the 'First Capital' titling but, even so, examples of all former liveries and names can still be seen around the territory in north and east London. The company is the first in the London area to order the Mercedes-Benz Citaro, eleven of which are due to operate on a special Central London service early in 2002.

Opposite top Several changes of plan regarding the numbering of the First Capital and CentreWest fleets resulted in the Dennis Tridents being in a common sequence, using Capital's numbers and CentreWest's letter prefixes. All of the longer Alexander bodied versions went to Capital and run on route 25. TAL 942 in Ilford displays the weekday 'via Bank' notification – unusually for a London bus route, it runs a different way at weekends, 'via Tower'. *David Stewart*

Opposite bottom Capital received the majority of the eighty-seven Tridents delivered in 1999, and here TN 803 operates route 1 at Waterloo. The blind is so detailed that the route number has unfortunately been almost pushed off the edge and can be difficult to discern. *Stephen Madden*

The 80%-red livery was first developed by Capital Citybus for buses on routes that ran into the Central London fare zone 1. The colour scheme has been subsequently adopted for the whole fleet, even though a number of yellow buses remained in service in late 2001. A batch of Alexander (Belfast) bodied Olympians was bought in 1997 for route 91, and here No. 227 is seen arriving at Trafalgar Square. *Stephen Madden*

Northern Counties bodied Olympians arrived in 1996 for route 67, and were all in the then standard yellow livery. Most are now red, and in April 2001 moved to route 263, a route taken on for just a year in an exchange with Arriva. No. 241 descends Barnet Hill. *Colin Stannard*

Long wheelbase Dennis Arrows with East Lancs Pyoneer bodywork are the main fare on route 369, and were the first of their body styling to appear on Capital's routes in 1997. Several are still in their original yellow colours, such as No. 424 in Barking in June 2001. *Colin Brown*

The small Dennis badge on the front of No. 410 in Ilford identifies the bus as one of the Dennis Arrows with the stylish Northern Counties Palatine II bodywork. They are mostly used on route 179, although on this day in May 2001 it was on route 369. *Colin Brown*

Optare Excels are allocated to route 396 between Ilford and Goodmayes. No. 702 is found at King George Hospital in Goodmayes, with a destination of Ilford Broadway, the only route to actually terminate there, not marked on any map but locally regarded as the junction of High Road and Ilford Lane. *Colin Brown*

In summer 1998, seven former DW class Darts were transferred from First CentreWest. After working several services, they can now usually be found on route 462 where they have replaced smaller former Thamesway minibuses. No. 642, fitted with new-style DDA-style blinds, heads out through Barkingside to Hainault. *Colin Stannard*

The link with CentreWest, who had patronised Marshall bodywork for some years, resulted in Capital taking several batches of the marque. As with CentreWest, they have come in 8.9m (DMS), 9.3m (DM) and 10.2m (DML) lengths. Most of the DM variants are dual-doored examples, but those bought for route W6 are single-door, like DM 778 pictured in leafy Southgate. *Colin Stannard*

The Dennis Dominator has never been a common type in London, but Capital has operated the type for many years. Many have since departed, but the 1991 batch remains intact for the moment. Earlier in 2001, No. 266 powers down South Street Romford on route 248. This route passed to Blue Triangle in September, but the Dominators were re-allocated to other Capital services. *Colin Stannard*

Clearly showing the step-entrance characteristics of the standard Dennis Dart is Capital's No.695 in Ilford in May 2001. This bus is one of several transferred within First Group from Thamesway and previously carried their yellow and purple livery. Now a short London Buses service, route W19 is the last remnant of longer Thamesway services (251/551) that used to run through from Walthamstow well out into Essex and Southend. *Colin Brown*

FIRST CENTREWEST

First CentreWest London Buses Ltd, Macmillan House, Paddington Station, London W2 1TY

CentreWest was purchased from London Buses by a management-led team on 2nd September 1994, the fleet already including a large proportion of midibuses. In December 1995, CentreWest branched out to the far side of London when it won some LT contract routes in the Orpington area. Then in March 1996, the holding company of CentreWest purchased both Bee Line and London Buslines, which consequently resulted in some interchanging of vehicles between the fleets. On 26th March 1997 the CentreWest group was sold to First Bus (renamed to First Group in November 1997). Subsequently, under First Group ownership, Bee Line passed to the control of First Hampshire whilst London Buslines was integrated into the parent company, although it did retain its separate yellow livery with red skirt.

Otherwise, traditional London red livery continued to be carried by most of the fleet, although buses gained yellow relief and fleetnames, and lost the grey skirt inherited from LBL. The group's *f* logo and First names precede the local marketing names which have been used by buses based at Acton Tram Depot and Uxbridge (Uxbridge Buses), Alperton (Challenger), Greenford (Ealing Buses), Orpington (Orpington Buses) and Westbourne Park (Gold Arrow). Having said that, as with First Capital, the 'First London' name is likely to gradually supplant all the local fleetnames, although all were still in use in autumn 2001.

London Buslines was gradually wound down during 2001. Routes 203 and 285 were lost to other operators on re-tendering, routes 105 and 258 and the mobility buses were transferred to mainstream CentreWest Garages on revised LB contracts, and the 490 passed over to Tellings-Golden Miller. In exchange for the latter, the U3 was swapped back, but is operated by Uxbridge Garage. All this meant that it was possible to close London Buslines' Southall base, which had some doubt over security of tenure, on 31st August 2001. Nevertheless, the yellow livery continued to be seen as the still-modern fleet was transferred into various CentreWest Garages and used on 'red' routes, until a repaint programme could be mounted. London Buslines was an historic operation, as it was a pioneer in the tendered route arena when it won route 81 (Hounslow & Slough) under Len Wright's ownership in July 1985, in the very first round of LT tendering.

Substantial patronage of Marshall bodywork has been evident in recent years, and Darts so bodied have been used to oust earlier and smaller midibuses, many of the latter being cascaded to Beeline. During 1999, First CentreWest's fleet numbering sequence was integrated with that of First Capital, but the concept was a compromise between the two systems and so far has only been adopted in respect of new vehicles, with Dart and Trident fleet numbers intermixed between the two fleets. The application of First-style stripes on vehicle sides has not been adopted as widely as with Capital. The company's management also covers the Croydon Tramlink operations, and the Orpington Depot operates two of the dedicated feeder services (T31, T32) to trams in New Addington. The Darts used thereon are in a red and white livery to match the trams.

An experimental fully air conditioned Volvo B7TL with East Lancs Vyking bodywork was taken for evaluation in December 2000 and was used spasmodically for about a year on route 207. The same route was to see an evaluation of 18-metre Volvo articulated single-deck buses from October 2001, the testing period expected to last about four months.

Opposite top Just one Volvo B7TL with an East Lancashire air-conditioned body has been trialled on route 207 for a year since December 2000. VE 953 was the first bus to carry the First London fleetname, and is seen here calling at the RAF camp at Uxbridge during its second month of operation. *Colin Brown*

Opposite bottom The Uxbridge Road corridor is home to a large fleet of buses on the 207 and 607, and is due to see trials with articulated buses, and maybe even trams, in the future! TNL 924 is one of the forty-three long wheelbase Tridents for the 207, but it has escaped in this view to the parallel 607 Express service. *Stephen Madden*

Once the two companies were in common ownership, the double-deck buses of London Buslines were gradually absorbed into the CentreWest fleet, and the Buslines routes went over to all-Dart operation. Many of these buses have since moved on to Capital and Eastern Counties, but a few remain for route E1 and schoolday journeys on route 282. LN 31 is seen in Ruislip Road in Greenford, by now having lost its complement of homebound school-children. *Colin Brown*

The limited stop route 607 between Uxbridge and Shepherd's Bush is a very popular service, and fifteen Volvo Olympians with a distinctive white band are employed. However, two buses are spare each day, and often turn out on other local routes from Uxbridge Garage where they are all based. V 42 arrives back home in the local High Street in May 2001. *Colin Brown*

In spring 1999, the company purchased twenty (of the twenty-two) stock-built Volvo Olympians for route 83, which were the last new standard-floor double-deckers for London. Suffering something of an identity crisis, fleet numbers VN 888–907 were allocated to follow on from Capital and CentreWest Tridents TN 801–887, but were later altered to VN 88–107. Still with its *Challenger* branding, VN 89 departs from Golders Green. *Colin Brown*

Legends extolling the benefits of route 23 adorn the sides of RML 2498 at Aldwych. Note the large driver's duty number in the cab window – several years ago these replaced traditional London running numbers with CentreWest. *Geoff Rixon*

Medium length Dart SLFs took over the 28, 31 and 328 by the summer of 1999 from the smaller DW class. In turn, the DWs had earlier replaced the even smaller MA class a few years before – which had replaced RMs accompanied by some disquiet! The routes were, and indeed still are, very busy and seventy-seven of these DMs are allocated for the three routes. Kensington Church Street is the location of DM 278. *Mark Lyons*

First CentreWest also operates a network from Orpington, a long way from its more familiar home territory. As part of this allocation, a number of Marshall bodied Dart SLFs carry this red and white livery, to work on routes T31 and T32, which connect – with through ticketing – with trams of the Croydon Tramlink at Addington Interchange. DML 380, with non-matching registration, is at the Vulcan Way terminus at New Addington. *Colin Stannard*

'Heathrow Fast' is a livery designed by *Best Impressions* on a route supported by the British Airports Authority and Stockley Park. The batch was repainted in summer 2001, but retained the striking livery style as shown on Dart SLF L 3 at RAF Uxbridge. *Stephen Madden*

The former London Buslines Dart SLFs now with CentreWest were treated to an upgrade from late summer 2001, with wheelchair ramps added and a red livery adopted. These were some of the first examples of vehicles to receive the new 'First London' identity, as shown on DML 635 in Uxbridge on 4th September. Route 331 itself was due to receive yet more new Marshall bodied Dart SLFs in October, which would carry former RM registrations. *Colin Brown*

Thamesway passed most of its London routes to Capital some years ago, but still retain route 193 and some Mobility Bus services in east London. Marshall bodied Dart SLF No. 854 is seen on the latter network approaching Barking. *David Stewart*

FIRST THAMESWAY

First Essex Buses Ltd, Stapleford Close, New Writtle Street, Chelmsford, Essex, CM2 0SD

In July 1990, the LT routes and other south and west Essex operations of Eastern National passed to the new Thamesway Company. Since then, the LT operations expanded and many new Mercedes-Benz minibuses and Dennis Darts were acquired. From 1st December 1995, the Company was re-united with Eastern National to become Essex Buses Ltd, but both retained their individual names within the FirstGroup. When Capital Citybus passed to FirstGroup in July 1998, Capital then took on the operational control of Thamesway's London Buses' routes and, within three months, also took over most of the vehicles. The only mainstream LB contract route now operated by Thamesway in its own right is the 193 which is operated from the new Romford Depot at Bryant Avenue, Harold Wood. The minibuses on the 193 are to be replaced by new Optare Solos in 2002, and these are expected to carry red livery. Meanwhile, Basildon depot continues to run Mobility Bus routes in the Romford area, as well as providing some Lynxes for LB school route 646 (Noak Hill & Cranham).

Caetano Nimbus bodywork can be seen in central London, on Hackney Community Transport's Dart SLF operated route 153 (Finsbury Park – Liverpool Street). After having done a tour of the back streets of Holloway and Barnsbury, HDC 6 emerges into Upper Street in Islington. *Colin Stannard*

HACKNEY COMMUNITY TRANSPORT

Hackney Community Transport, 2 Hertford Road, Dalston, London N1 5SH

The large group of Mobility Bus services in north and east London, formerly worked by Arriva, were taken over from 26th June 1999. A fleet of four Fiat Ducato tri-axle minibuses operates the routes, undoubtedly the most unusual vehicles on any London Buses service. From 3rd February 2001, LB route 153 (Finsbury Park & Liverpool Street) was won utilising a fleet of Caetano Nimbus bodied Dart SLFs. This expansion meant that the bus fleet outgrew its Dalston base resulting in the LB fleet having to move into Ash Grove Garage, housed alongside East Thames Buses vehicles. However, HCT's indigenous community bus fleet and the maintenance base remains at Dalston. Another new service was the 394, beginning in September 2001 between Islington and Cambridge Heath via Hoxton. Of interest is that HCT is one of the first customers of the new Optare Alero, indeed the first real low-floor minibus to go into production in the UK, though these should only be used on community bus services.

Early in 2001, Durham Travel Services, trading in London as London Easylink, (though the word 'London' is not very easy to read!), took over route 185 between Victoria and Lewisham. They were one of the first operators to display the new DDA-compliant destination blinds on their twenty Volvo B7TLs. VP 171 calls at the foot of Dog Kennel Hill at East Dulwich, once the location of a four-track tramway. The 185 is the present-day successor to tram route 58. *Colin Brown*

LONDON EASYLINK

Durham Travel Services Ltd, Transco Gas site, 709 Old Kent Road, London SE15 1JZ

DTS is an operator based in County Durham, although prior to its arrival in London, its only Metropolis experience was the operation of National Express services to the Capital. It was the surprise winner of the tender for route 185 (Victoria & Lewisham) and twenty Volvo B7TLs were acquired. After a short delay from the intended start date, their buses took over on 13th February 2001, and operate in an all-red livery, using the London Easylink fleetname.

LONDON CENTRAL and
LONDON GENERAL

London Central Bus Co. Ltd, and London General Transport Services Ltd, 25 Raleigh Gardens, Mitcham, Surrey, CR4 3NS

The Go-Ahead Group purchased London Central on 18th October 1994. The basic bus livery has remained traditional London red with white relief, accompanied by a stylised fleet logo based on a Thames clipper ship. Meanwhile, London General had been purchased by a management-led team on 2nd November 1994 and, with a total of 636 vehicles, was the largest fleet of any of the privatised London Buses companies. Traditional London livery of red with white relief was retained, accompanied by a white and orange fleetname incorporating a vertical orange stripe and a thin yellow band. Although the original privatisation logo, a B-type bus from the General of the First World War era, has now been largely abandoned, a small handful of buses carries a traditional pre-war style of livery and retains this emblem.

Then in May 1996, London General was purchased by the Go-Ahead Group, and rationalisation with London Central soon took place, with most management functions being combined. In practice, London Central's head office functions gradually moved from Camberwell to the existing Mitcham offices of London General between 1997 and 1999. London Central's livery was modified with a thin yellow band above the grey skirt, this being a London General influence. The combined fleets do retain their individual fleetnames, but are within a common fleet numbering sequence; hence buses are often switched between companies as required. London Central buses operate from garages at Bexleyheath, Camberwell, New Cross and Peckham, whilst the London General buses run out of garages at Merton, Putney, Stockwell, Sutton and Waterloo.

During the 1990s, new bus deliveries consisted of large batches of Olympians and Darts, but late in 1999, both companies received the first examples of two new types. Seventeen DAF single deckers with East Lancs Myllennium bodies were used on high profile services to the Millennium Dome from 1st January 2000, but were later re-allocated to local route 486. They also became the first companies in London to receive the new Volvo B7TL low-floor double-decker, Alexander bodied examples arriving for routes 45 and 63, and many others with Plaxton President bodywork, which soon became familiar over the whole operating areas of both companies. By summer 2001, almost 300 were in stock, causing the large fleet of Metrobuses and Titans to be reduced to a relative handful. Coincident with the AVL and PVL introduction, a darker grey, almost black, skirt colour was adopted which has been applied to repaints for most of the older types. Spring 2002 is due to see a major change on the Red Arrow services 507 and 521, with replacement of the ageing Greenways by a batch of thirty-one 18-metre articulated Mercedes-Benz Citaro G buses, equipped with three doors.

Opposite top Typifying the link between London General and Central, the DPL class of Darts were transferred from General's routes 200/201 when they were lost to another operator, most going onto Central's P12 at Peckham. Since this picture was taken of DPL 6 at Peckham Rye, the batch went back to General again and can now be found at Putney Garage on routes 39 and 239! *Colin Stannard*

Opposite bottom A unique class to London Central is the batch of seventeen DAF SB220s with East Lancs Myllennium bodywork, bought for special services to the Dome in 2000. They still go there, even though the Dome is now closed and the route (486) is a different one. MD 11 passes through the new Retail Park at Charlton en-route for the Jubilee Line connection at North Greenwich. *David Stewart*

All the National Greenways are with London General on the Red Arrow network, now down to three routes. It will soon reduce to two, but with new 18-metre articulated vehicles. The route number destined to disappear will be the 501, displayed here on GLS 443 at Holborn. Repainting of the skirt panels on many buses of both fleets into dark grey has featured in recent years.
Colin Brown

RM 782 on route 36 at Victoria appears at first glance to have two lots of route branding – until you look closer, that is! Most of London Central's standard RMs have undergone differing forms of refurbishment, and many have received the hopper windows, rather detracting from the traditional appearance of the vehicle. *Colin Brown*

A visitor to Hyde Park Corner will see ten (of the twenty) Routemaster routes in London. One of these is London General's route 14, even after curtailments at the northern end, still plying between central London and Putney, a course it has undertaken since the days of the original LGOC 'General'. RML 899 is one of the original 1961 delivery of the class and wears its forty years well.
Stephen Madden

The two companies maintain a handful of 'specials' in differing but traditional livery styles. One of these is Metrobus OM 420, seen here in September 2000 visiting London United's Hounslow Garage Open Day, going out on a local sightseeing tour around Heathrow.
Stephen Madden

Titan T 1129 is one of the 'special duties' fleet and during 2000 was used on a link between the Tate Gallery's sites in central London. This is a typical sort of use for this vehicle, unusual in London fleets in being single-door, and second-hand (originating from West Midlands Travel).
Stephen Madden

The majority of the VC class of Volvo Citybuses are used on route 133 from Stockwell Garage. However, the first six (VC 1–6) are on 'special duties', which includes an operation for Surrey County Council on route 293 between Morden and Epsom. VC 1 heads along Stonecot Hill at the 'Woodstock'. *Colin Stannard*

Late in 1997, a batch of twenty-seven Olympians with Northern Counties Palatine II bodywork with coach type seating came into the fleet to provide a somewhat unexpected touch of luxury for passengers on route 74. NV 166 at Hyde Park Corner shows the limited side route branding. *Stephen Madden*

The first London operator of the Volvo B7TL low-floor double-decker was London Central, who took their first batch of forty-six early in 2000 for routes 45 and 63. The first examples were Alexander bodied and formed the AVL class, and AVL 43 rounds the Elephant & Castle on route 63. However, there are insufficient to cover the full peak hour requirements on the route, and a handful of Titans still remain. *Stephen Madden*

With the speedy withdrawal of Stagecoach's Titan fleet in summer 2001, London Central looks set to be the last mainstream operator of the type in London. Their last twenty examples were soldiering on as spare vehicles to the main fleets at three garages, and T 954 is one of a handful that have remained working from Bexleyheath Garage since the influx of PVLs in 2000. They can be found on any relevant double-deck route, such as here on the 229 in Station Road, Sidcup on 10th August 2001. *Laurie Rufus*

The initial delivery of fifty-five PVLs, the Plaxton President bodied version of the Volvo B7TL, were all allocated to Bexleyheath Garage. They had central staircases and few upper-deck opening windows, unsuitable features that have been rectified on some later deliveries. PVL 8 is seen in its home town, after a long journey from North Greenwich on the 422. *Laurie Rufus*

At the time of publication of this book, 249 examples of the PVL had been delivered with a little over half of them going to General garages. Early in 2001, a few had these single-line destination blinds, which attracted much criticism, and later buses have had the new DDA styling. PVL 205 travels through Streatham on route 118, recently won from Arriva. *Gerald Mead*

The small Dennis badge on the front of PDL 6 gives this away as one of the small batch of thirteen Tridents with London General. Based at Stockwell Garage alongside a number of PVLs, they are usually to be found on route 88, now extended across central London to Camden Town. The bus is at the traditional terminus in the middle of the road at Old Town, Clapham Common.
Colin Brown

The Dart SLFs on routes 155 have been moved back and forth between Merton and Stockwell Garages to suit staffing levels in recent times. Plaxton Pointer LDP 118 is at Elephant & Castle, carrying a Merton code, still current at September 2001. Both companies' low-floor single-deckers have a thick white band on the sides of the roof to distinguish them at a distance.
Stephen Madden

Although some companies have many different variations of class code, in London Central and General the LDP class covers all low-floor Plaxton bodied Dart SLFs, thus far coming in four lengths and in both single and dual-door versions. The smallest examples are five 8.8m buses at Putney Garage for route 424, a new service in 2001 that replaced part of the old C4. Route 424 restored a link to the Telegraph Inn on Putney Heath, a point that LDP 160 has just left.
Colin Stannard

London United is arguably one of the most distinctive bus fleets in London, with a different type of livery to most, and a selection of small classes of vehicles. One of Arriva's routes to be passed over to other operators in 1999 due to garage closures and staff shortages, was the 85 between Kingston and Putney Bridge. London United, together with the route, took twelve of the Arriva DAF DB250s, and all were repainted into London United livery. Numerically the first, DN 1 is seen in Kingston in April 2001. *Geoff Rixon*

LONDON UNITED

London United Busways Ltd, Wellington Road, Fulwell, Middlesex, TW2 5NX

London United was purchased by a management-led team on 5th November 1994, and the traditional London red livery was soon adapted to a new style with silver grey roof, grey upper-deck window-surrounds, and a thin white band above the grey skirt. Routemasters received grey (instead of white) relief, with yellow used for external transfers such as fleet numbers and garage codes. In September 1995, the holding company of London United purchased Stanwell Bus, better known as Westlink, from the National Express Group. Then in the summer of 1997 Transdev, a French-based holding company, purchased the London United group. Gradually, Westlink's own livery and fleetname were eliminated, and the separate Operator's Licence was surrendered on 15th August 2000. The company's Airbus services between Heathrow Airport and Central London were scaled-down during 1999, and sold to National Express from 5th February 2000, together with the nineteen coach-seated Olympians and the 'Airbus' marketing name.

London United has always been prominent in London bus operation with regard to its marketing, and has adopted route branding in some measure, although an earlier use of a 'Harrier' logo on Darts was abandoned as buses were repainted. Bolder branding is incorporated on a batch of all blue Darts on routes 555/6/7, whilst a red, blue and orange livery is used on another batch of Darts for the T123 express service between Feltham Station and Heathrow Central Terminals. This latter service was due to be withdrawn late in 2001 and the buses re-deployed onto normal services. More restrained branding is evident with the use of slogans and various designs on buses on routes 57, 94, 111, 216 and 371. The company does not operate only in London, but also has several routes in north-west Surrey, partly on contract to that county.

The former Westlink base at Hounslow Heath remains in use, and indeed has been expanded, while the rest of the London United fleet is kept at garages at Fulwell, Hounslow, Shepherd's Bush and Stamford Brook. This latter garage had been kept 'in reserve' for some years, and also houses the company's driver training buses and maintenance facilities as well as being used to store delicensed vehicles. The historic Kingston Garage, inherited from Westlink, closed on 13th May 2000 and the site was re-developed. Buses were then parked on a nearby open area until a new garage could be opened at Tolworth in late 2001.

With delivery of fifty-four buses during 1996/7/8, the Volvo Olympian and Alexander bodywork combination became London United's standard double-decker. They are now the mainstay of routes 57, 131 and 281 in the Kingston area, those on the 57 and 281 carrying forms of branding. However, in August 2001 VA 1 received a fine repaint ready for a new career on other routes as the 131 was to receive new Tridents in late 2001. Here it is at Hampton Court Station on route 411. *Geoff Rixon*

Yellow fleet numbers and garage codes, plus a flake grey relief band, distinguish the main Routemaster fleet with London United. Many of those used on route 94 now carry route branding for the service, which became the first to revert to RML operation on Sundays on 1st April 2001. RML 2519 is seen in Regent Street in May. *Geoff Rixon*

Recently repainted, but back into its traditional style of livery to recall an earlier era of London United Tramways, RML 880, displaying what was its original short-lived number in 1961 (ER 880), calls at a stop in Oxford Street on 23rd July 2001. *Geoff Rixon*

After none had been dealt with for some time, several of the Metrobuses still in old London Buses livery were treated to standard company livery from autumn 1999. Many remain in service two years later, though not for much longer. M 203 was one so treated, and is seen on route 406, a route taken up as a London Buses service after the surprise abandonment by Arriva Surrey & West Sussex. *Geoff Rixon*

London United has at least three different liveries for training buses, the contrast in design and colour meaning to indicate to other road users to 'watch out'. One of those with orange crescents is M 157, cornering carefully at Hampton Court.
Geoff Rixon

When London United lost route 140 in the September 1999 re-tendering process, most of the ECW bodied Olympians were sold. However, nine were kept and are normally used on route 116 (until the end of 2001 at least), as well as some routes just into north-west Surrey in the Ashford area. L 305 is doing a short working on route 216, normally a single-deck service.
Stephen Madden

Route branding is quite a feature of some London United routes, and the 111 is no exception. The Boeing 747 nose is not quite like the real BAC One-Eleven aircraft of the 1960s, but never mind! This Alexander bodied Volvo B7TL VA 103 is on the Bath Road at Heathrow North.
Stephen Madden

The company bought three Dennis Tridents with outwardly similar ALX400 bodies to the VA class. However, they can be distinguished at a distance by the forward staircase position as shown on TA 203 on the Ruislip Road near Yeading. The three TAs were due to move to Fulwell Garage in autumn 2001 and be joined by another twenty-two for service on routes 131 and 267. *Colin Brown*

All of the large operators in London are now in possession of low-floor double-deckers, with bodywork split principally between the Alexander ALX400 and Plaxton President, but with a few East Lancashire Lolynes added in. The models of chassis have also been split, with London General, London United and Metroline buying from both Dennis and Volvo. VP 106 is one of London United's Volvo B7TLs with Plaxton President bodywork, seen at Hyde Park Corner. It is on route 9, one of the routes that operated with Routemasters during the week but driver-only on Sundays. During 2001, eight routes were re-converted back to Routemaster operation on Sundays, although route 9 was not yet one of them. *Mark Lyons*

The LLW class of Dennis Lances dating from 1993/4 show how long low-floor buses have been around, although at the time they were only experimental, and were indeed often temperamental. Since route 120 was double-decked, London United's ten examples moved to route H91 and most have been repainted. At Hounslow West Station, LLW 7 shows the new style, and unlike most vehicles has a centrally positioned side fleetname.
Stephen Madden

Two small classes, of six Optare Excels and eight MAN/Optare Vectas, share route 371. This is the 'pretty route', connecting Kingston and Richmond, criss-crossing picturesque Ham and Richmond Hill on the way. Like MV 3, all carry different slogans to attract people to the route.
Geoff Rixon

Quite a number of the older Plaxton Pointer bodied Darts are still around, although some were in the act of being replaced over the turn of 2001/2. One route that still sees them is the 283, on which DR 102 traverses Shepherd's Bush Green. The Wetland Centre at Barnes sponsors the route to its off-road site, and suitable legends are carried on some of the DRs so used.
Colin Lloyd

London United invested heavily in the Plaxton Pointer 2 bodied Dart SLF from 1999, with 203 due for delivery by the end of 2001. Many of them, though not all, carry the Easy Access logo and designs on the sides. DP 35 is one of these and is seen on route H98 arriving in Hounslow. *Gerald Mead*

London United won route 285 from London Buslines from 30th June 2001, and yet more Dart SLFs with Plaxton Pointer 2 bodywork have been added to the fleet. DPS 543 is crossing Kingston Bridge on 25th July, showing the first DDA-style blinds used by the company. It is expected that a new and special colour scheme will be introduced at a later date for route 285. *Geoff Rixon*

Eleven of the DP-class Darts (23–33) carry all-over blue livery, and carry various sorts of branding for the group of routes (555/6/7) that connect Heathrow with the Sunbury and Walton area. The roof sides carry lettering for the cross-airport facility that these buses also provide, with support from the BAA to give free travel on this section. *Stephen Madden*

The Mini-Pointer-Dart has been taken in some numbers by Metrobus with the latest examples completed by Alexander's of Falkirk. A representative of the last pure Plaxton-built bus in 2000 is No.353, pictured in Dingwall Road, East Croydon on 14th August. *Colin Brown*

METROBUS

Metrobus Ltd, Oak Farm, Farnborough Hill, Green Street Green, Orpington, Kent, BR6 6DA

Following the collapse of the tiny Orpington & District Bus Company in February 1981, operations were taken over by the Tillingbourne Bus Company from 2nd March 1981, and a local company was formed, Tillingbourne (Metropolitan) Ltd. New routes were developed in the area between Orpington and Croydon on roads never before served by London Transport services. Metrobus Ltd was born in a management-led buy-out on 24th September 1983. Further commercial routes were developed in the Bromley and Beckenham areas, more LT contracts were won and routes were taken on as other operators surrendered them. During 1997, the buses and routes of East Surrey Buses of South Godstone were acquired, and further expansion took the company to Brighton and Newhaven with another base at Lewes.

On 3rd September 1999, the company passed into the Go-Ahead Group, but with the existing management, fleet, bases and livery being retained unaltered. Both before and after this date, considerable investment in new buses has been evident, supplemented by purchases of relatively modern second-hand Darts. After Arriva Surrey & West Sussex made it known that it wanted to close down its services based in east Surrey and Crawley, and initial attempts to sell part of the operation failed, Metrobus stepped in. Metrobus introduced a commercial town network in Crawley from 31st March 2001, and then from 21st April followed up by winning almost all the former Arriva routes when offered to tender by Surrey and West Sussex County Councils. Eighteen buses released from the loss of LB routes 181 and 284 in March were moved south later joined by Darts and London NV-class Olympians transferred from fellow Go-Ahead companies. Metrobus thus became the dominant bus operator from the London borders beyond Bromley and Croydon through Surrey and Sussex to the South Coast.

Bus routes operated on LB contract or with LB agreement are 64, 119, 138, 146, 161, 233, 246, 261, 320, 336, 351, 352, 353, 356, 358, 359, 367, 409, 464, 494, 630, 654 and T33. The fleet carries a blue and yellow livery. The majority of those for LB contracts are kept at Green Street Green, although those on routes 146, 246, 409 and 464 come from the South Godstone base. The fleet list in this book covers only the buses normally used on services within Greater London, although occasionally buses from the 'country' garages at Crawley, Lewes and South Godstone may be seen.

Two batches of Volvo Olympians with East Lancs Pyoneer bodywork have been taken into stock, the 1997 intake of fifteen being for route 64 and thirteen 1998 deliveries for the 119. One of the latter is No. 849, seen in central Croydon. Note that Metrobus are now applying small white fleet numbers to the lower front panel. *Colin Brown*

The first London operator of the East Lancs Lolyne bodywork, here on a Dennis Trident chassis, was Metrobus, who introduced fifteen onto route 161 in the late summer of 1999. The family resemblance with the earlier Pyoneer body design is evident. A sixteenth was delivered in 2001, and No. 416 is here unusually working on route 119. *Colin Brown*

Thirty-eight standard Alexander bodied Volvo Olympians were acquired new by Metroline. The first batch was to replace acquired Titans on route 52, but these have since moved to be the normal daily allocation on routes 260 and 266. The familiar setting of Brent Cross sees AV 16 leaving on another long trip to Hammersmith. *Colin Brown*

METROLINE

Metroline Holdings plc, (Metroline Travel and Metroline London Northern),
118–122 College Road, Harrow, Middlesex, HA1 1DB

A management-led team purchased Metroline Travel on 7th October 1994. On 28th November 1994, Atlas Bus was acquired from the Pullmans Group, together with route 52 and its twenty-six Leyland Titans, these soon moving to nearby Willesden Garage. The Brents Travel Group of Watford was purchased in October 1995, and a few coaches have remained in Brent's mainly white livery within Metroline ever since. Parallel to these events, on 26th October 1994 MTL Trust Holdings of Liverpool purchased London Northern. MTL then took over R&I Tours in October 1995, whilst by 1996 London Suburban Bus had come into MTL ownership by virtue of the take-over of its parent company Liverbus in Liverpool. By June 1996, both sets of acquired buses were absorbed into the MTL London fleet, and MTL's allover unrelieved red livery was soon adopted. In June 1997, Metroline Holdings plc (as, by then, it had become) was floated on the Stock Exchange. The new plc then acquired the enlarged London Northern business on 2nd July 1998, being ratified by 17th August. Within a matter of a couple of months, the Highgate offices were closed and the whole combined operations were run from Harrow. However, on 18th February 2000, Metroline Holdings was acquired by Delgro, a Singapore-based transport group, this being ratified by 21st March. In late 2000, a former Singapore Olympian came to the UK but, to date, remains unique in the Metroline fleet, being usually to be found on route 260 from Willesden Garage.

Metroline's livery is red with a blue skirt but, although repainting of the former MTL fleet started soon after the take-over in 1998, a number of buses were still in unrelieved all-over red without fleetnames even in late 2001. Having inherited an especially large number of elderly Metrobuses, recent investment in Trident and Volvo B7TL low-floor double-deckers has been very necessary. Also, many of the non-standard inherited single-deckers are being rapidly replaced by Dart SLFs. The fleet operates from garages at Cricklewood, Edgware, Harlesden, Harrow Weald, Holloway, North Wembley, Potters Bar and Willesden. Most vehicles in the Contract Services and Brent's fleet are based at Cricklewood. Around two-dozen vehicles from Potters Bar Garage are operated on a mix of commercial and county council contracted routes in southern Hertfordshire.

The purchase of Metroline by the Singapore-based Delgro group has seen an ex-Singapore Volvo Olympian come into stock. Just one has arrived, and fits in fairly well on route 260, although a fair number of detail differences from standard AVs can be easily seen. AV 39 calls at Golders Green in August 2001. *Colin Brown*

The blue skirt livery and white fleetname has made a great improvement to the V class of Northern Counties Palatine II bodied Volvo Olympians, inherited from London Suburban Bus via London Northern. Now in their third livery in eight years of life, the class still carries the hard seats that can be seen in this view of V 215 descending Highgate Hill. *Stephen Madden*

The blue skirt livery styling of Metroline is applied in a somewhat modest way on its Routemasters, as exemplified by RML 2471 turning from Staverton Road, Willesden. The side route branding covers only a small section of route 6, but this is due to the common section shared with route 98, Metroline's other Routemaster service. This vehicle was used as the test-bed for the new Cummins/ Alison engine/ gearbox combination as employed on the Marshall's RM refurbishments in 2001.
Colin Brown

Metroline maintains a handful of standard RMs and just three are at Willesden Garage. RM 1979 is one of the very few RMs still running in London with an AEC engine. Compared with the RML's at Willesden, the route branding omits the word 'Selfridges' which is carried over the central small window on the RMLs.
Colin Brown

Metroline's purchase of London Northern brought with it some commercial routes in Hertfordshire. The Scania double-deckers, a rare type in London, form the main allocation on routes 84 and 242 from Potters Bar Garage. The class can thus be seen entering London at Barnet on the 84, but in this April 2001 view S 14 reaches Waltham Cross.
Colin Lloyd

Metroline bought both long and short Tridents, but then transferred their allegiance to the B7TL. Early in 2001, some of the new B7TLs were used to convert route 43 from Tridents. Thus, Tridents less then two years old converted part of the service on routes 4, 271 and W7 and saw off lots of Metrobuses to the breakers yards. Here, TP 26 comes down Highgate Hill on the 271.
Stephen Madden

Dennis Trident deliveries to Metroline in 1999 reached 117 examples, split roughly equally between Plaxton and Alexander bodywork. The latter went to Cricklewood and Harrow Weald Garages mainly for routes 16, 140 and 182. Cricklewood's route 16 was later converted to the longer TAL version, allowing TAs to convert route 32. Here TA 107 is at Heathrow North on route 140.
Stephen Madden

This is not VPL 197 as it might seem from its registration, but in typical Metroline fashion it is actually VPL 180, although the fleet number is not visible. Route 52, as well as the 82 and 113, were to lose their Metrobuses to the Volvo B7TL/ Plaxton President during summer and autumn of 2001. Rounding Hyde Park Corner, the bus displays what has become the 'normal' DDA-style blind. *Stephen Madden*

The smaller capacity of the TAs was, like the TPs on the 43, a disadvantage on a busy route and, like the 43, route 16 was converted to larger buses, in this case the TAL class. TAL 127 at Victoria represents the longer 10.5m version of the ALX400. *Colin Brown*

Metroline, after its assumption of the businesses of several other operators in recent years, still has around thirty different classes of bus. The Northern Counties Paladin bodied Darts, normally to be found on route 214, are now in Metroline's standard livery, even though four of the class still sport the all-over drab red of London Northern. DNL 114 is at the Angel, Islington. *Colin Lloyd*

Seventy-nine Marshall bodied Dart SLFs of the DMS and DML classes came in 1998, and most were used to upgrade several LTB contract routes or to replace older and smaller midibuses such as the last StarRiders and the MW class of Wright bodied MB811Ds. The last three to arrive were DMLs 533–5 for use on route 317, and 534 is in the newly rebuilt and enlarged Bus Station at Waltham Cross. *Colin Lloyd*

The various lengths of Darts have resulted in bus companies having different ideas over how to classify them. Hence, one outwardly identical bus can have a totally different coding from another. Metroline's 9.8 metre examples became the EDR (extended DR), the DRL code already having been used for the 9 metre version of the 8.5 metre DR. EDR 34 calls at Childs Hill on route 245. *Colin Brown*

The DL (single door), DLD (dual door), DLS (short) and DLM (mini) class letters serve to differentiate the Plaxton Pointer bodied Dart SLFs of Metroline. The majority are DLDs and some of the newest have converted routes 95, 268 and 274 to the type in 2001. Showing another non-matching registration is DLD 187 at Dormers Wells in Southall. *Colin Brown*

The Mini Pointer Dart (DLM class) is so far confined to eleven examples, the first pair (DLM 150/1) being branded for the Potters Bar town service PB1. DLM 150, with modest route branding, links the outlying estates with the shops and Rail Station. *Colin Stannard*

The long-serving and familiar Metrobus should be gone from the fleet by 2002, and one of Metroline's Garages, Cricklewood, was the first to operate the type back in 1978. Here is a last chance to illustrate a type common for over two decades, with Cricklewood's M 1193 on route 112 at Brent Cross. *Colin Brown*

The Volvo B6BLE/ East Lancs Spryte is a very rare beast, as far as London is concerned at any rate. Metropolitan Omnibus, re-christened from London Traveller, has twenty in west London on routes 187 and 487. The yellow stripes of London Traveller have now gone, and an all-red livery with a logo that is the outline of the Greater London county has been adopted. VS 517 at South Harrow shows the immensely detailed destination blind that is employed. *Colin Brown*

METROPOLITAN OMNIBUS

Metropolitan Omnibus Company (London) Ltd, Unit 2 Radford Estate, Old Oak Lane, Harlesden, London, NW10 6UA

This company was formed in summer 1999, assuming three LB routes (187 and 487, as well as school journeys on H12) from 4th September 1999. Metropolitan also assumed various schoolday journeys on LB routes 143, 302, 626 and 643 which had previously been operated by London Traveller, with a fleet of Metrobuses from bases in Neasden and Potters Bar. The London Traveller fleetname and red livery were adopted for a while, pending introduction in late 2000 of yellow METROPOLITAN *OMNIBUS* fleetnames and a logo depicting a stylised London map in silver. Buses were painted in plain red, with the earlier application of yellow striping on some vehicles removed. Fifteen new Volvo B6BLE low-floor buses were purchased at the commencement of operations in September 1999, adding a further five in 2000 when the 187 was extended. There have been further additions to the fleet of used Metrobuses, reflecting additional LB schools and rail replacement contracts.

Mitcham Belle is an old-established south London coach operator that won its first LTB contract route (127) from 10th April 1999, and followed it up with the 200/201 in 2000. All three are local to its home, and two more routes (K5 and 152) were added during 2001. One of the second batch of Dart SLFs is W142 WGT seen here on the 200. *Colin Brown*

Providing a splash of patriotic red, white and blue in south-west London, Mitcham Belle took four Optare Solos into stock in September 2001 for route K5, which they had assumed from T-GM from 30th June. There are no problems with the blinds being DDA-compliant, when fitting in the short 'Ham' destination on this bus! The neat little KX51 UCT travels through Kingston on the first day of operation 7th September. *Geoff Rixon*

MITCHAM BELLE

Wimco Group Coaches Ltd, (t/a Mitcham Belle Coaches), 223 Streatham Road, Mitcham, Surrey, CR4 2AJ

A very old established coach company, which also specialises in transport for disabled people, won its first London Buses contract route with the 127 (Tooting & Purley) from 10th April 1999, and twelve Dart SLFs were obtained to operate it. Then in June 2000 routes 200 and 201 were added, with more Dart SLFs. Route K5 followed a year later, and four Optare Solos, quite a rare type in London, soon arrived to operate it. This expansion outstripped the capacity at the traditional base, and most buses on LB work were moved into a second depot at 87 Beddington Lane. A further route, the 152, is due to be taken over from London General in December 2001 and the bus fleet will then total around 55.

Sovereign has had a presence in Harrow since December 1990, but from 4th September 1999, won more services, mostly at the expense of Metroline. This brought their London operation to a larger size than their whole operation in Hertfordshire. Fifty-seven brand-new Dart SLF/ Plaxton Pointer 2's were bought to serve the new contracts, as exemplified by No. 534 in Stanmore. *Mark Lyons*

SOVEREIGN

Sovereign Bus & Coach Co. Ltd and Sovereign Buses (London) Ltd, Babbage Road, Stevenage, Herts, SG1 2EQ

Sovereign Bus & Coach was established in January 1989, but now forms part of the Blazefield Group, which is divided into several small operating companies. An associated 'Sovereign Harrow' operation was set up in December 1990 for newly won locally based LT contracts, using Mercedes-Benz minibuses. Borehamwood Travel Services (BTS), dating from August 1984, was purchased by Sovereign in August 1994. BTS had operated LT route 292 from 1988 until November 1993 before losing it to Metroline, although Sovereign was to win it back from December 1998. BTS had also gained the contract to operate crew route 13 (Golders Green to Aldwych) using RMLs leased from London Buses, and later the 114 using Olympians. However, by September 1996, the BTS name had been dropped and Sovereign names were applied to the vehicles. In late April 1999, the former BTS depot at Borehamwood, which was on Railtrack owned land, was closed as the site was sold for housing development, and buses were moved to the former London Buses Garage at Edgware.

From 21st August 1999, the separate Operator's Licences for Sovereign Harrow and London Sovereign were replaced by one in the name of Sovereign Buses (London) Ltd, and all LT services were then under the same umbrella. As well as Edgware, part of this fleet continues to operate from the Venture Garage at 331 Pinner Road, Harrow that had already been in use for nearly nine years. However, a maintenance facility was created at Edgware, with Harrow becoming an outstation.

Sovereign's smart blue and cream livery, now universal in Hertfordshire, adorns the fifty-seven Dart SLFs on routes H10, H11, H12, H13, H17 and 183 as well as the Olympians on route 292. By late summer 2001, most of the H-registered Olympians used on route 114 since 1991 were moved to Blazefield's Lancashire operations. These were replaced on the route by a batch of London Buses owned DAF low-floor double-deckers latterly used by Arriva London on route 60 in south London. Sovereign London was the first operator of the RMs bought back by London Buses in 2000, and fully refurbished by Marshalls during 2001. They have new Cummins engines, automatic gearboxes, and many internal changes. These took over on route 13 by late summer 2001, enabling the RMLs, which were the last buses still in BTS's old poppy red livery, to be taken back by LB and re-allocated as support and enhancement to other Routemaster routes around London.

During July 2001 the six DAF/ Optare Spectras used on route 60 in south London were moved to Sovereign's 114, and were followed by the ten DAF/ Presidents off route 60 on 1st September. These vehicles were controlled by London Buses, leased to Sovereign for the duration of the 114 contract, and were kept in the red and black livery worn since they were new in 1999. The black skirt and tinted windows appear to make DLO 28 look darker than it really is, in this view near Ruislip on 14th September 2001. *Colin Brown*

The RMs refurbished by Marshall's for route 13 have been leased by London Buses to Sovereign, again for the duration of the contract from 1st September 2001. A handful began work before this though, and the first to do so, RM 1933, shows off its rear-end treatment at St.John's Wood. Note the revised light clusters, yellow handrails and rebuilt platform. *Stephen Madden*

The VNs and VAs are in a common numbering sequence, referring to the Northern Counties or Alexander bodied Volvo Olympians. Many of the shorter VNs are due to be ousted to provincial Stagecoach companies by the end of 2001, but plenty will still be left in London, for the foreseeable future anyway. Both classes have moved back and forth between East London and Selkent as required, typifying the very common practice of mixing the fleets between the two Stagecoach companies. In this May 2001 shot, VN 154 was still working at Romford. *Colin Brown*

STAGECOACH IN LONDON

East London Bus & Coach Co. Ltd, 2–4 Clements Road, Ilford, Essex, IG1 1BA
South East London & Kent Bus Co. Ltd, 180 Bromley Road, London, SE26 2XA

Both East London and Selkent were purchased together by Stagecoach Holdings on 6th September 1994, taking a total of 1009 vehicles. Major fleet replacement has occurred in the short period since acquisition, with new and acquired buses replacing virtually all of the older types. In July 1997, East London took over control of Docklands Transit following its purchase by Stagecoach Holdings, and full integration took place in October 1997. Fleets of both London companies are integrated under common management, there is a common numbering sequence, and transfers north and south of the River occur quite frequently. East London garages are at Barking, Bow, Leyton, Romford, Stratford and Upton Park, whilst the Selkent garages are at Bromley, Catford and Plumstead.

As buses have been replaced in London, Stagecoach has actively cascaded most of them on to other UK subsidiaries, and this practice continues, giving Stagecoach one of the most modern fleets in London. Indeed, the great influx of new buses in recent times means that, by the end of 2001, the oldest buses (Routemasters aside, of course) in passenger service would date only from 1994. Scania and Titan double-deckers (aside from T 1), Lances and standard Darts were all being removed from stock.

Beginning in 1994/95, vehicles lost their white and grey relief very quickly under Stagecoach ownership, both through full and partial repaints, and gained Stagecoach logos on all red. However, from the end of 1994, East London Routemasters appeared with cream relief bands instead of white plus gold logos, while RMC 1461 has been beautifully restored to its original Green Line colours. A few driver training Titans and Deltas carry white-based corporate Stagecoach national livery. Then in autumn 2000, the Stagecoach group introduced a new corporate national colour scheme, and new area or local fleetnames. In London, the 80%-red rule still applied, and restrained blue and orange striping was added to the all-red. A new logo was adopted and the fleetname 'Stagecoach in London' quickly started to appear on new and repainted vehicles.

Many of the VA class of Alexander bodied Olympians, like most of Stagecoach London's modern double-deckers, are long wheelbase and of high seating capacity. These features are fairly unusual in London, but make it handy when they might be passed on to other provincial Stagecoach companies. Several VAs now used on route 67 have been treated to the latest livery, as seen on VA 74 at Aldgate. *David Stewart*

Deliveries of the Alexander ALX400 bodied Dennis Trident should reach 532 (numbers go to 534 but there are two gaps in the sequence). Early examples entered service in the first months of 1999, and now all nine garages operate the type. TA 338, allocated to Bromley for route 208, is seen in Bexleyheath on route 269 in May 2001, well in advance of official conversion of the route in September. *Laurie Rufus*

The shorter version, the TAS, started to be accepted into the fleet in autumn 2000, as difficulties had arisen with the longer buses on some routes. Indeed, some routes were too restricted for longer buses and route 194 was the first service to receive the new class. Both TA and TAS classes delivered over the winter of 2000/01 came in plain red, many gaining the new livery application here in London. Still in all red is TAS 232 at East Croydon. *Colin Stannard*

Gold fleetnames, and even cream relief, bring a very traditional London Transport air to Stagecoach's Routemaster fleet. The fleet includes three RMCs (including one in the old traditional Green Line colours), five standard RMs and the last RML of all, 2760, still preserved in original condition. All of these 'specials' perform on most weekdays on route 15. However, more typical is RML 2495 seen at Hyde Park Corner on route 8. *Stephen Madden*

Of the three RMCs, 1485 has received the latest style of fleetname, although it remains otherwise in 'traditional' Stagecoach condition. One of few Routemasters in London that passengers cannot jump on and off in the street, it passes Marble Arch on the way to its western terminus at Paddington in May 2001. *Geoff Rixon*

The London Buses 1994 experiment with low-floor buses affected route 101, and the Scania variation (most were on Dennis Lance chassis) survives with East London, even though similar buses with Arriva left London in 1999. Even in July 2001, SLW 21 at Beckton looks little different from when it was new. *Colin Lloyd*

The standard floor Plaxton Pointer Dart has been prolific in Stagecoach London fleets for some years, but in 2000, many were 'cascaded' onward to provincial Stagecoach companies. In turn, low-floor versions have come into the fleet and SLD 140 represents this marque in Barking. Originally with the old, but now with the new fleetname, it is one of many so treated. *Colin Stannard*

Outwardly similar to other Pointers, SLD 226 is one of a batch of thirteen of the longest Dart SLFs in London, the 11.3m 'Super Pointer Dart'. Like their provincial sisters, they have black window surrounds. The short, but busy route 227, has always been single-deck, and older readers may recall the long AEC Renowns (LT class), affectionately known as 'Scooters'. We hear that some staff refer to these SLDs as 'Scooters' too! *Colin Lloyd*

The 2001 intake of SLDs comprised 110 examples, and all were bodied by Alexander, in contrast to the all-Plaxton intake of the 1999/2000 order. The first to arrive were the highest numbered (SLD 328–346), 10.8m dual-door buses mainly for route 145, but frequently used on Barking's other routes. SLD 334 in Barking shows the exceptionally clear blind display of this batch, the latest fleet number application, and the new single-deck livery to its best advantage. *Colin Brown*

The second batch to arrive were the lowest numbered of the series (SLD 237–253), and were the shortest, indeed the first of the 8.9m versions to serve with Stagecoach London. They were intended for routes 124 and 273 at Catford Garage, but in both cases, route restrictions still had to be resolved before they could be used. SLD 250 is in Eltham in August. *Laurie Rufus*

Thorpe's were mainly known in London for their specialised work in the field of accessible transport. They operate the circular Stationlink service, hourly in each direction, SL1 clockwise and SL2 anti-clockwise, linking all main line stations and using fully accessible Optare Excels. The four 1996 models in the fleet were joined by two second-hand buses in summer 2001 and one of these, R846 FWW, is heading up Park Lane in August 2001. *Colin Brown*

Since 26th September 1998, Thorpe's have operated one mainstream LT service, the 210, but added route 70 (Acton- South Kensington) in 2000. Just fourteen of the order for fifteen Dart SLFs arrived, and the fifteenth came some months later. Here it is, DLF 79 heading off from Acton. *Colin Lloyd*

THORPE'S

F E Thorpe & Sons Ltd, Unit 5, Fourth Way, Wembley Stadium Trading Estate, Middlesex, HA9 0LH

Frank E Thorpe & Sons Ltd started as a small private coach company back in 1968, with a fleet of coaches and minibuses on private hire, school and local authority contracts. The company moved into LT work in October 1992 with the winning of the central London inter-station route, marketed as Stationlink. Originally run with three Optare City Pacers, four Optare Excels were bought in 1996, these being the first of the type to appear on the streets of London. LT minibus route C4 was gained from April 1995 but lost in 2001, and in August 1997 Thorpe took over the LT contracts of Javelin Coaches, Wandsworth with a large group of Mobility Bus routes in west and southwest London. A more mainstream service is route 210, taken over from Grey-Green in September 1998 with a new fleet of Dart SLFs, with more following with the gain of route 70 in June 2000. This expansion caused a move from the cramped original base at 272 Latimer Road in North Kensington to Wembley Stadium Trading Estate, though most buses are kept on a nearby parking ground off South Way. Vehicles on the 210 carry a striking red and yellow livery, but some were later repainted with more red, although the Darts used on route 70 were all-over red from new.

After a period of operation on the route through its connection with Capital Logistics, T-GM won route 726 in its own right, and in 2000 bought seven Volvo B10BLEs with Alexander ALX300 bodywork to work the service. These are the only examples of their type on a London Buses service, and W902 UJM shows the company's colours on this flagship route at Kingston. *Geoff Rixon*

TELLINGS-GOLDEN MILLER

Tellings-Golden Miller Ltd, 20A Wintersells Road, Byfleet, Surrey, KT14 7LF

In June 1985, Tellings Coaches of Byfleet took control of the local bus operations of Golden Miller of Feltham. Even so, it was not until April 1995 that the combined Tellings-Golden Miller company returned to LT tendered work in a small way with midibus route S3 in the Sutton area (later surrendered) followed by route 235 from January 1998. However, much change occurred in 1999 following Arriva's closure of their Leatherhead Garage from 1st May, and Hounslow from 3rd July, resulting in several Arriva routes and buses passing to T-GM.

Then on 1st June 1999, Capital Logistics was sold to Tellings-Golden Miller and both then became constituents of the Status Bus & Coach Group. Capital Logistics operated a large fleet of coaches at both Heathrow and Gatwick Airports, mainly for car park, air crew and hotel contracts. The firm had themselves entered LT tendered bus work in a small way in August 1993 with route H26, and in 1998 routes U3, 726 and 60 were gained. However, the 60 was only taken up by Capital in its own right after some months of mayhem, although T-GM soon rid themselves of the unremunerative contract in March 2000. The 726 was later won by T-GM in its own right on re-tender, whilst the U3 was swapped with CentreWest's route 490 (but worked by their London Buslines depot) on 28th April 2001, in the mutual interests of economy.

Capital's Croydon base, as well as the former L&C Hounslow base, were eventually abandoned, and bus operations from the Capital coach depot at West Drayton were moved. The moves of the bus fleet took place over a period of six months from April to September 2000, culminating in the occupation of the eastern part of the old Tram Depot at Fulwell. Once part of the old LUT tram and trolleybus site, it had been separated from what became London United's Fulwell Garage many years earlier, and was once used by London Buses for its sales and disposal stock. By autumn 2001 around 100 buses were based at Fulwell on LB services, leaving the traditional base at Byfleet to work the Surrey routes.

Expansion astride or over the border in Surrey has seen many routes gained. Routes 48, 426, 437, 438, 441, 446, 471, 513, 514, 515, 561 and 564 are currently worked for Surrey County Council in the Staines, Woking, Walton and Kingston areas, as well as services for students at the various Kingston University campuses. Routes operated for London Buses are 203, 235, 465, 490, 726, H20, H21, H26, H28, R62, R68 and R70, all worked from Fulwell, joined by the H25 from November 2001, as another tender win from London United. Dart SLFs have become the standard vehicle in the fleet, in various lengths, but for the H25 seven Caetano Nimbus bodied versions have been ordered instead of the usual Plaxtons. T-GM's normal fleet livery is blue and white with yellow relief, while the three former Capital Logistics' liveries are no longer to be seen on vehicles in the fleet. However, the old London & Country green livery survived on seven Darts in autumn 2001. There is a large luxury coach fleet, which is not featured in this book.

A series of misfortunes to befall the former London & Country operation saw route withdrawals, frequency cuts and garage closures. T-GM has been a main beneficiary and has taken on several of the routes and vehicles. One of the last buses to bear L&C's once familiar green and red colours, Dart SLF P293 FPK carries prominent lettering for its new operator. This batch of buses remains on lease from Arriva for the duration of the present route 465 contract. *Stephen Madden*

The combination of the various T-GM bus operations early in 2000 was characterised by the introduction of a batch of nine 'MPDs' to replace a selection of hired minibuses and some older MB709Ds, and were followed by more. They are mainly allocated to routes H20, H26 and H28, these being one-time London United, Capital Logistics and Arriva (L&C) services respectively. The 'serving the local community' legend on V301 MDP has been used on buses not specifically route branded. *Stephen Madden*

Ten 10.1m Plaxton Pointer bodied Dart SLFs came in 2000 for the take-over from London United of route R68, and the branding that had been applied to LU's Darts was perpetuated on T-GM's vehicles. The fleetname above the windows is now standard on the company's vehicles, to allow either advertising or branding to appear on the sides. W403 UGM travels through Teddington. *Geoff Rixon*

Wing's Buses embarked into London Buses tendering in 1999 with route U7, using three East Lancs Spryte bodied Dart SLFs in an unusual yellow, red and orange colour scheme. This was followed up from 1st April 2000 with the H50, a new route to connect Stockley Park with both Hayes and West Drayton Stations. Four more similar buses arrived, but these were in two-tone green with red relief, to identical shades of the former London & Country – who in earlier years had themselves many buses bodied by East Lancs! W437 CRN at RAF Uxbridge is depicted in H50 livery, but is unusually at work on the U7. *Colin Brown*

WING'S BUSES

Wing's Buses Ltd, West London Bus & Coach Centre, North Hyde Gardens, Hayes, Middlesex. UB3 4QT

The long established coach and minibus firm of Wing's Luxury Travel won its first LB contract route in 1999, taking up the short U7 route from 13th November. A bus subsidiary, Wing's Buses, was set up to operate the route, worked by three East Lancs bodied Dart SLFs in an unusual yellow, orange and red scheme, contrasting with the mainly white coach livery. A second LB route (H50) was won from April 2000, being a link between Hayes and West Drayton via Stockley Park. Four similar buses came to the fleet, but are air-conditioned accessible buses incorporating such refinements as tinted windows and on board audio-visual passenger information. These came in a mainly two-tone green livery, in identical shades to the former London & Country scheme. On 1st April 2001, vehicles moved from the traditional depot at 127 Waterloo Road, Uxbridge, to a new site at Hayes.

Type Totals

Double-Deck Buses

AEC Regent	1
AEC Routemasters	641
DAF/Alexander ALX400	321
DAF/Northern Counties	20
DAF/Optare Spectra	6
DAF/Plaxton President	66
Dennis Arrow/East Lancs	38
Dennis Arrow/Northern Counties	16
Dennis Dominator/East Lancs	38
Dennis Dominator/Northern Counties	24
Dennis Trident/Alexander	781
Dennis Trident/East Lancs	51
Dennis Trident/Plaxton President	291
Leyland Olympian	70
Leyland Olympian/ECW	161
Leyland Olympian/Roe	1
Leyland or Volvo Olympian/Alexander	238
Leyland or Volvo Olympian/East Lancs	36
Leyland or Volvo Olympian/Northern Counties	146
Leyland Titan	61
MCW Metrobus	524
Scania/Alexander	10
Scania/Northern Counties	9
Volvo B10M/East Lancs	9
Volvo Citybus/Alexander	39
Volvo Citybus/East Lancs	7
Volvo Citybus/Northern Counties	36
Volvo B7TL/Alexander	91
Volvo B7TL/East Lancs	1
Volvo B7TL/Plaxton President	414

Single-Deck Buses

AEC Regal	1
DAF/East Lancs Myllennium	17
DAF/Optare Delta	26
DAF/Wright Cadet	23

Dennis Dart/Alexander	323
Dennis Dart/Caetano	55
Dennis Dart/Duple or Carlyle	16
Dennis Dart/East Lancs	20
Dennis Dart/Marshall	495
Dennis Dart/Northern Counties	57
Dennis Dart/Plaxton	1666
Dennis Dart/Reeve Burgess	10
Dennis Dart/Wadham Stringer	1
Dennis Dart/Wright	63
Dennis Lance/Alexander	1
Dennis Lance/Plaxton	1
Dennis Lance/Wright	25
Leyland National	6
Leyland National Greenway	39
MAN/Marshall	24
MAN/Optare Vecta	8
Marshall Minibus	1
Optare Excel	68
Scania/Van Hool	1
Scania/Wright	16
Volvo B6BLE/Wright	3
Volvo B7LA/Wright (artic)	2
Volvo B10LA/Wright (artic)	4
Volvo B10BLE/Alexander ALX300	7

Minibuses

Fiat Ducato	4
Iveco/Marshall	4
LDV/Crystals	3
MCW Metrorider	3
Mercedes-Benz Minibuses (various bodies)	121
Optare MetroRider	26
Optare Solo	23
Optare StarRider	2
Renault	2
Renault-Dodge/Plaxton	3

E748 SKR	MCW Metrobus DR132/11 Ex Stagecoach South, 2001		MCW	H46/31F	1988
F772 EKM	MCW Metrobus DR132/14 Ex Stagecoach South, 2001		MCW	H46/31F	1989

	Leyland Olympian ONCL10/1RZ		Alexander RL	H47/30F	1990
G361 YUR	G364 YUR	G368 YUR	G371 YUR		
G362 YUR	G365 YUR	G369 YUR	G372 YUR		
G363 YUR	G366 YUR	G370 YUR			

	Leyland Olympian ON2R50C13Z4		Leyland	H47/31F	1991
H546 GKX	H550 GKX	H554 GKX	H559 GKX	H564 GKX	
H547 GKX	H551 GKX	H556 GKX	H561 GKX		
H548 GKX	H552 GKX	H557 GKX	H562 GKX		
H549 GKX	H553 GKX	H558 GKX	H563 GKX		

	Dennis Dart SFD412BR5TGD1		Plaxton Pointer 9.8m	B37F	1996
P27 MLE	P29 MLE	P32 MLE	P35 MLE		
P28 MLE	P31 MLE	P34 MLE			

	Dennis Dart SFD412BR5TGD1		Plaxton Pointer 9.8m	B39F	1996
P154 MLE	P157 MLE	P159 MLE			
P156 MLE	P158 MLE	P160 MLE			

	Dennis Dart SLF SFD212BR1TGW1		Plaxton Pointer 10m	B35F	1997
P675 RWU	P680 RWU	P685 RWU	P690 RWU	P695 RWU	
P676 RWU	P681 RWU	P686 RWU	P691 RWU	P696 RWU	
P677 RWU	P682 RWU	P687 RWU	P692 RWU	P697 RWU	
P678 RWU	P683 RWU	P688 RWU	P693 RWU	P698 RWU	
P679 RWU	P684 RWU	P689 RWU	P694 RWU	P699 RWU	

	Volvo Olympian OLY–50		Northern Counties Palatine II	H47/29F	1997/8
R417 SOY	R419 SOY	R780 SOY	R782 SOY		
R418 SOY	R420 SOY	R781 SOY			

	Dennis Dart SLF SFD212BR1WGW1		Alexander ALX200 10.2m	B27D	1999
T140 AUA	T143 AUA	T146 AUA	T149 AUA	T152 AUA	
T141 AUA	T144 AUA	T147 AUA	T150 AUA		
T142 AUA	T145 AUA	T148 AUA	T151 AUA		

Y962 KRX	Dennis Dart SLF SFD612AR11GW1		Plaxton Pointer 2 8.8m	B29F	2001

Y63 LTF	Dennis Dart SLF SFD212BR11GW1		Plaxton Pointer 2 10.1m	B30D	2001

	Dennis Dart SLF SFD212BR11GW1		Plaxton Pointer 2 10.1m	B30D	2001
RX51 FNP	RX51 FNT	RX51 FNV	RX51 FNY		
RX51 FNS	RX51 FNU	RX51 FNW			

On order: A further 8 x Dennis Dart SLF SFD212/Plaxton Pointer 2 10.1m B30D are due for route 190.

AIRLINKS
(LT fleet only)

71–76		Dennis Dart SLF SFD322AR1WGW1		Plaxton Pointer 2 10.7m	B33D	1999
71	T71 WWV	**73**	T73 WWV	**75**	T75 WWV
72	T72 WWV	**74**	T74 WWV	**76**	T76 WWV

ARRIVA SERVING LONDON

(Arriva London North [including Leaside Travel], London North East and London South)

ADL 1	V701 LWT	Dennis Dart SLF SFD212BR1XGW1	Alexander ALX200 10.2m	B27D	1999

ADL 2–8		Dennis Dart SLF SFD212BR1XGW1		Alexander ALX200 10.2m	B30D	2000
ADL 2	W602 VGJ	**ADL 4**	W604 VGJ	**ADL 6** W606 VGJ	**ADL 8**	W608 VGJ
ADL 3	W603 VGJ	**ADL 5**	W605 VGJ	**ADL 7** W607 VGJ		

ADL 9–23		Dennis Dart SLF SFD322BR1XGW1		Alexander ALX200 10.8m	B33D	1999
ADL 9 V609 LGC	**ADL 12** V612 LGC	**ADL 15** V615 LGC	**ADL 18** V618 LGC	**ADL 21** V621 LGC
ADL10 V610 LGC	**ADL 13** V613 LGC	**ADL 16** V616 LGC	**ADL 19** V619 LGC	**ADL 22** V622 LGC
ADL 11 V611 LGC	**ADL 14** V614 LGC	**ADL 17** V617 LGC	**ADL 20** V620 LGC	**ADL 23** V623 LGC

ADL 952–68		Dennis Dart SLF SFD212BR1TGW1		Alexander ALX 200 10.2m	B36F	1997
ADL 952 P952 RUL	**ADL 956** P956 RUL	**ADL 960** P960 RUL	**ADL 964** P964 RUL	**ADL 968** P968 RUL
ADL 953 P953 RUL	**ADL 957** P957 RUL	**ADL 961** P961 RUL	**ADL 965** P965 RUL	
ADL 954 P954 RUL	**ADL 958** P958 RUL	**ADL 962** P962 RUL	**ADL 966** P966 RUL	
ADL 955 P955 RUL	**ADL 959** P959 RUL	**ADL 963** P963 RUL	**ADL 967** P967 RUL	

ADL 969–983		Dennis Dart SLF SLD212BR1WGW1		Alexander ALX 200 10.2m	B27D	1998
ADL 969 S169 JUA	**ADL 972** S172 JUA	**ADL 975** S175 JUA	**ADL 978** S178 JUA	**ADL 981** S181 JUA
ADL 970 S170 JUA	**ADL 973** S173 JUA	**ADL 976** S176 JUA	**ADL 979** S179 JUA	**ADL 982** S182 JUA
ADL 971 S171 JUA	**ADL 974** S174 JUA	**ADL 977** S177 JUA	**ADL 980** S180 JUA	**ADL 983** S183 JUA

CW 1	W218 CDN	DAF DEC12SSB120	Wright Cadet 10.2m	B31D	2000

DBS 14	R213 CKO	DAF DE23RSDB250	Northern Counties Palatine II	H43/24D	1998
		Ex Arriva Southern Counties, 1999			

DBS 15	V715 LWT	DAF DB250RS505	Northern Counties Palatine II	H43/24D	1999

DDL 1–18		Dennis Dart SLF SFD212BR1WGW1		Plaxton Pointer 2 10.1m	B26D	1998
DDL 1 S301 JUA	**DDL 5** S305 JUA	**DDL 9** S309 JUA	**DDL 13** S313 JUA	**DDL 17** S317 JUA
DDL 2 S302 JUA	**DDL 6** S306 JUA	**DDL 10** S310 JUA	**DDL 14** S314 JUA	**DDL 18** S318 JUA
DDL 3 S303 JUA	**DDL 7** S307 JUA	**DDL 11** S311 JUA	**DDL 15** S315 JUA	
DDL 4 S304 JUA	**DDL 8** S308 JUA	**DDL 12** S312 JUA	**DDL 16** S316 JUA	

DI 4†	P754 RWU	DAF DE33WSSB3000	Ikarus 396	C53F	1997
		Ex Arriva EH & E, 1998			

DLA 1–64		DAF DB02RSDB250LF		Alexander ALX 400 10.6m	H45/21D	1998–9
DLA 1 R101 GNW	**DLA 4** S204 JUA	**DLA 7** S207 JUA	**DLA 10** S210 JUA	**DLA 13** S213 JUA
DLA 2 S202 JUA	**DLA 5** S205 JUA	**DLA 8** S208 JUA	**DLA 11** S211 JUA	**DLA 14** S214 JUA
DLA 3 S203 JUA	**DLA 6** S206 JUA	**DLA 9** S209 JUA	**DLA 12** S212 JUA	**DLA 15** S215 JUA

DLA 16 S216 JUA	**DLA 26** S226 JUA	**DLA 36** S236 JUA	**DLA 46** S246 JUA	**DLA 56** S256 JUA
DLA 17 S217 JUA	**DLA 27** S227 JUA	**DLA 37** S237 JUA	**DLA 47** S247 JUA	**DLA 57** S257 JUA
DLA 18 S218 JUA	**DLA 28** S228 JUA	**DLA 38** S238 JUA	**DLA 48** S248 JUA	**DLA 58** S258 JUA
DLA 19 S219 JUA	**DLA 29** S229 JUA	**DLA 39** S239 JUA	**DLA 49** S249 JUA	**DLA 59** S259 JUA
DLA 20 S220 JUA	**DLA 30** S230 JUA	**DLA 40** S240 JUA	**DLA 50** S250 JUA	**DLA 60** S260 JUA
DLA 21 S221 JUA	**DLA 31** S231 JUA	**DLA 41** S241 JUA	**DLA 51** S251 JUA	**DLA 61** S261 JUA
DLA 22 S322 JUA	**DLA 32** S232 JUA	**DLA 42** S242 JUA	**DLA 52** S252 JUA	**DLA 62** S262 JUA
DLA 23 S223 JUA	**DLA 33** S233 JUA	**DLA 43** S243 JUA	**DLA 53** S253 JUA	**DLA 63** S263 JUA
DLA 24 S224 JUA	**DLA 34** S234 JUA	**DLA 44** S244 JUA	**DLA 54** S254 JUA	**DLA 64** S264 JUA
DLA 25 S225 JUA	**DLA 35** S235 JUA	**DLA 45** S245 JUA	**DLA 55** S255 JUA	

DLA 65–123 DAF DB02RSDB250LF Alexander ALX 400 10.6m H45/19D 1999

DLA 65 S265 JUA	**DLA 77** S277 JUA	**DLA 89** S289 JUA	**DLA 101** T301 FGN	**DLA 113** T313 FGN
DLA 66 S266 JUA	**DLA 78** S278 JUA	**DLA 90** S290 JUA	**DLA 102** T302 FGN	**DLA 114** T314 FGN
DLA 67 S267 JUA	**DLA 79** S279 JUA	**DLA 91** S291 JUA	**DLA 103** T303 FGN	**DLA 115** T315 FGN
DLA 68 S268 JUA	**DLA 80** S280 JUA	**DLA 92** S292 JUA	**DLA 104** T304 FGN	**DLA 116** T316 FGN
DLA 69 S269 JUA	**DLA 81** S281 JUA	**DLA 93** T293 FGN	**DLA 105** T305 FGN	**DLA 117** T317 FGN
DLA 70 S270 JUA	**DLA 82** S282 JUA	**DLA 94** T294 FGN	**DLA 106** T306 FGN	**DLA 118** T318 FGN
DLA 71 S271 JUA	**DLA 83** S283 JUA	**DLA 95** T295 FGN	**DLA 107** T307 FGN	**DLA 119** T319 FGN
DLA 72 S272 JUA	**DLA 84** S284 JUA	**DLA 96** T296 FGN	**DLA 108** T308 FGN	**DLA 120** T320 FGN
DLA 73 S273 JUA	**DLA 85** S285 JUA	**DLA 97** T297 FGN	**DLA 109** T309 FGN	**DLA 121** T421 GGO
DLA 74 S274 JUA	**DLA 86** S286 JUA	**DLA 98** T298 FGN	**DLA 110** T310 FGN	**DLA 122** T322 FGN
DLA 75 S275 JUA	**DLA 87** S287 JUA	**DLA 99** T299 FGN	**DLA 111** T311 FGN	**DLA 123** T323 FGN
DLA 76 S276 JUA	**DLA 88** S288 JUA	**DLA 100** T110 GGO	**DLA 112** T312 FGN	

DLA 124 T324 FGN	DAF DB02RSDB250LF	Alexander ALX 400 10.6m Ex demonstrator, 2000	H45/17D	1999
DLA 125 T325 FGN	DAF DB02RSDB250LF	Alexander ALX 400 10.6m Ex demonstrator, 2000	H45/17D	1999

DLA 126–321 DAF DB02RSDB250LF Alexander ALX 400 10.2m* H43/21D 1999–2001
*(DLA 224–321 are H43/20D)

DLA 126 V326 DGT	**DLA 154** V354 DGT	**DLA 182** W382 VGJ	**DLA 210** W438 WGJ	**DLA 238** X438 FGP
DLA 127 V327 DGT	**DLA 155** V355 DGT	**DLA 183** W383 VGJ	**DLA 211** W411 VGJ	**DLA 239** X439 FGP
DLA 128 V628 LGC	**DLA 156** V356 DGT	**DLA 184** W384 VGJ	**DLA 212** W412 VGJ	**DLA 240** X503 GGO
DLA 129 V329 DGT	**DLA 157** V357 DGT	**DLA 185** W385 VGJ	**DLA 213** W413 VGJ	**DLA 241** X441 FGP
DLA 130 V330 DGT	**DLA 158** V358 DGT	**DLA 186** W386 VGJ	**DLA 214** W414 VGJ	**DLA 242** X442 FGP
DLA 131 V331 DGT	**DLA 159** V359 DGT	**DLA 187** W387 VGJ	**DLA 215** X415 FGP	**DLA 243** X443 FGP
DLA 132 V332 DGT	**DLA 160** V660 LGC	**DLA 188** W388 VGJ	**DLA 216** X416 FGP	**DLA 244** X504 GGO
DLA 133 V633 LGC	**DLA 161** V361 DGT	**DLA 189** W389 VGJ	**DLA 217** X417 FGP	**DLA 245** X445 FGP
DLA 134 V334 DGT	**DLA 162** V362 DGT	**DLA 190** W434 WGJ	**DLA 218** X418 FGP	**DLA 246** X446 FGP
DLA 135 V335 DGT	**DLA 163** V363 DGT	**DLA 191** W391 VGJ	**DLA 219** X419 FGP	**DLA 247** X447 FGP
DLA 136 V336 DGT	**DLA 164** V364 DGT	**DLA 192** W392 VGJ	**DLA 220** X501 GGO	**DLA 248** X448 FGP
DLA 137 V337 DGT	**DLA 165** V365 DGT	**DLA 193** W393 VGJ	**DLA 221** X421 FGP	**DLA 249** X449 FGP
DLA 138 V338 DGT	**DLA 166** W366 VGJ	**DLA 194** W394 VGJ	**DLA 222** X422 FGP	**DLA 250** X506 GGO
DLA 139 V339 DGT	**DLA 167** W367 VGJ	**DLA 195** W395 VGJ	**DLA 223** X423 FGP	**DLA 251** X451 FGP
DLA 140 V640 LGC	**DLA 168** W368 VGJ	**DLA 196** W396 VGJ	**DLA 224** X424 FGP	**DLA 252** X452 FGP
DLA 141 V341 DGT	**DLA 169**uW369 VGJ	**DLA 197** W397 VGJ	**DLA 225** X425 FGP	**DLA 253** X453 FGP
DLA 142 V342 DGT	**DLA 170** W431 WGJ	**DLA 198** W398 VGJ	**DLA 226** X426 FGP	**DLA 254** X454 FGP
DLA 143 V343 DGT	**DLA 171** W371 VGJ	**DLA 199** W399 VGJ	**DLA 227** X427 FGP	**DLA 255** X507 GGO
DLA 144 V344 DGT	**DLA 172** W372 VGJ	**DLA 200** W435 WGJ	**DLA 228** X428 FGP	**DLA 256** X508 GGO
DLA 145 V345 DGT	**DLA 173** W373 VGJ	**DLA 201** W401 VGJ	**DLA 229** X429 FGP	**DLA 257** X457 FGP
DLA 146 V346 DGT	**DLA 174** W374 VGJ	**DLA 202** W402 VGJ	**DLA 230** X502 GGO	**DLA 258** X458 FGP
DLA 147 V347 DGT	**DLA 175** W432 VGJ	**DLA 203** W403 VGJ	**DLA 231** X431 FGP	**DLA 259** X459 FGP
DLA 148 V348 DGT	**DLA 176** W376 VGJ	**DLA 204** W404 VGJ	**DLA 232** X432 FGP	**DLA 260** Y451 UGC
DLA 149 V349 DGT	**DLA 177** W377 VGJ	**DLA 205** W436 WGJ	**DLA 233** X433 FGP	**DLA 261** Y461 UGC
DLA 150 V650 LGC	**DLA 178** W378 VGJ	**DLA 206** W437 WGJ	**DLA 234** X434 FGP	**DLA 262** Y462 UGC
DLA 151 V351 DGT	**DLA 179** W379 VGJ	**DLA 207** W407 VGJ	**DLA 235** X435 FGP	**DLA 263** Y463 UGC
DLA 152 V352 DGT	**DLA 180** W433 WGJ	**DLA 208** W408 VGJ	**DLA 236** X436 FGP	**DLA 264** Y464 UGC
DLA 153 V353 DGT	**DLA 181** W381 VGJ	**DLA 209** W409 VGJ	**DLA 237** X437 FGP	**DLA 265** Y465 UGC

DLA 266 Y466 UGC	**DLA 278** Y478 UGC	**DLA 290** Y523 UGC	**DLA 302** Y502 UGC	**DLA 314** Y514 UGC
DLA 267 Y467 UGC	**DLA 279** Y479 UGC	**DLA 291** Y491 UGC	**DLA 303** Y503 UGC	**DLA 315** Y529 UGC
DLA 268 Y468 UGC	**DLA 280** Y522 UGC	**DLA 292** Y492 UGC	**DLA 304** Y504 UGC	**DLA 316** Y516 UGC
DLA 269 Y469 UGC	**DLA 281** Y481 UGC	**DLA 293** Y493 UGC	**DLA 305** Y526 UGC	**DLA 317** Y517 UGC
DLA 270 Y452 UGC	**DLA 282** Y482 UGC	**DLA 294** Y494 UGC	**DLA 306** Y506 UGC	**DLA 318** Y518 UGC
DLA 271 Y471 UGC	**DLA 283** Y483 UGC	**DLA 295** Y495 UGC	**DLA 307** Y507 UGC	**DLA 319** Y519 UGC
DLA 272 Y472 UGC	**DLA 284** Y484 UGC	**DLA 296** Y496 UGC	**DLA 308** Y508 UGC	**DLA 320** Y531 UGC
DLA 273 Y473 UGC	**DLA 285** Y485 UGC	**DLA 297** Y497 UGC	**DLA 309** Y509 UGC	**DLA 321** Y521 UGC
DLA 274 Y474 UGC	**DLA 286** Y486 UGC	**DLA 298** Y498 UGC	**DLA 310** Y527 UGC	
DLA 275 Y475 UGC	**DLA 287** Y487 UGC	**DLA 299** Y499 UGC	**DLA 311** Y511 UGC	
DLA 276 Y476 UGC	**DLA 288** Y488 UGC	**DLA 300** Y524 UGC	**DLA 312** Y512 UGC	
DLA 277 Y477 UGC	**DLA 289** Y489 UGC	**DLA 301** Y501 UGC	**DLA 313** Y513 UGC	

DLP 1–20 DAF DB02RSDB250LF Plaxton President 10.5m H45/19D 1999

DLP 1 V601 LGC	**DLP 5** T205 XBV	**DLP 9** T209 XBV	**DLP 13** T213 XBV	**DLP 17** T217 XBV
DLP 2 T202 XBV	**DLP 6** T206 XBV	**DLP 10** T210 XBV	**DLP 14** T214 XBV	**DLP 18** T218 XBV
DLP 3 T203 XBV	**DLP 7** T207 XBV	**DLP 11** T211 XBV	**DLP 15** T215 XBV	**DLP 19** T219 XBV
DLP 4 T204 XBV	**DLP 8** T208 XBV	**DLP 12** T212 XBV	**DLP 16** T216 XBV	**DLP 20** T220 XBV

DLP 40–75 DAF DB02RSDB250LF Plaxton President 10.6m H45/24D 2001

DLP 40 Y532 UGC	**DLP 48** Y548 UGC	**DLP 56** LJ51 DKD	**DLP 64** LJ51 DKV	**DLP 72** LJ51 DLV
DLP 41 Y541 UGC	**DLP 49** Y549 UGC	**DLP 57** LJ51 DKE	**DLP 65** LJ51 DKX	**DLP 73** LJ51 DLX
DLP 42 Y542 UGC	**DLP 50** LJ51 DJU	**DLP 58** LJ51 DKF	**DLP 66** LJ51 DKY	**DLP 74** LJ51 DLY
DLP 43 Y543 UGC	**DLP 51** LJ51 DJV	**DLP 59** LJ51 DKK	**DLP 67** LJ51 DLD	**DLP 75** LJ51 DLZ
DLP 44 Y544 UGC	**DLP 52** LJ51 DJX	**DLP 60** LJ51 DKL	**DLP 68** LJ51 DLF	
DLP 45 Y533 UGC	**DLP 53** LJ51 DJY	**DLP 61** LJ51 DKN	**DLP 69** LJ51 DLK	
DLP 46 Y546 UGC	**DLP 54** LJ51 DJZ	**DLP 62** LJ51 DKO	**DLP 70** LJ51 DLN	
DLP 47 Y547 UGC	**DLP 55** LJ51 DKA	**DLP 63** LJ51 DKU	**DLP 71** LJ51 DLU	

DP 3† P753 RWU	DAF DE33WSSB3000	Plaxton Premiere 350	C53F	1997
	Ex Arriva EH & E, 1998			
DP 160 M160 SKR	Dennis Dart 9SDL3053	Plaxton Pointer 9m	B35F	1995
	Ex Arriva Southern Counties, 1999			
DP 161 M161 SKR	Dennis Dart 9SDL3053	Plaxton Pointer 9m	B35F	1995
	Ex Arriva Southern Counties, 1999			
DP 162 M162 SKR	Dennis Dart 9SDL3053	Plaxton Pointer 9m	B35F	1995
	Ex Arriva Southern Counties, 1999			
DP 163 M163 SKR	Dennis Dart 9SDL3053	Plaxton Pointer 9m	B35F	1995
	Ex Arriva Southern Counties, 1999			

DP 301–310 *Dennis Dart 9SDL3002 Plaxton Pointer 9m B35F 1991
Ex Arriva EH & E, 1998 *(DP 302–7 are 9SDL3011)

DP 301 J301 WHJ	**DP 303** J303 WHJ	**DP 305** J305 WHJ	**DP 307** J307 WHJ	**DP 309** J309 WHJ
DP 302 J302 WHJ	**DP 304** J304 WHJ	**DP 306** J306 WHJ	**DP 308** J308 WHJ	**DP 310** J310 WHJ

DPL 1† N551 LUA	DAF DE33WSSB3000	Plaxton Premiere 350	C49FT	1996
	Ex Arriva EH & E, 1998			
DPL 2† 398 CLT	DAF DE33WSSB3000	Plaxton Premiere 350	C49FT	1996
	Ex Arriva EH & E, 1998			

DPP 416–431 Dennis Dart SLF SFD212BR1VGW1 Plaxton Pointer 10m B34F 1997
Ex Arriva EH & E, 1998

DPP 416 R416 COO	**DPP 420** R420 COO	**DPP 424** R424 COO	**DPP 428** R428 COO
DPP 417 R417 COO	**DPP 421** R421 COO	**DPP 425** R425 COO	**DPP 429** R429 COO
DPP 418 R418 COO	**DPP 422** R422 COO	**DPP 426** R426 COO	**DPP 430** R430 COO
DPP 419 R419 COO	**DPP 423** R423 COO	**DPP 427** R427 COO	**DPP 431** R431 COO

DRL 38–51 Dennis Dart 9SDL3016 Plaxton Pointer 9m B34F 1992

DRL 38	K538 ORH	DRL 40	K540 ORH	DRL 46	K546 ORH	DRL 48	K548 ORH	DRL 51	K551 ORH
DRL 39	K539 ORH	DRL 41	K541 ORH	DRL 47	K547 ORH	DRL 50	K550 ORH		

DRL 147–158 Dennis Dart 9SDL3024 Plaxton Pointer 9m B34F 1993

DRL 147	L247 WAG	DRL 151	L151 WAG	DRL 154	L154 WAG	DRL 157	L157 WAG
DRL 148	L148 WAG	DRL 152	L152 WAG	DRL 155	L155 WAG	DRL 158	L158 WAG
DRL 149	L149 WAG	DRL 153	L153 WAG	DRL 156	L156 WAG		

DRL 201–209 Dennis Dart 9SDL3053 Plaxton Pointer 9m B34F 1995
Ex Arriva Southern Counties, 1999

DRL 201	N701 GUM	DRL 203	N703 GUM	DRL 206	N706 GUM	DRL 209	N709 GUM
DRL 202	N702 GUM	DRL 205	N705 GUM	DRL 208	N708 GUM		

DRL 210–212 Dennis Dart 9SDL3053 Plaxton Pointer 9m B34F 1995

DRL 210	N710 GUM	DRL 211	N711 GUM	DRL 212	N712 GUM

DRL 213–218 Dennis Dart SFD212BR5TGD1 Plaxton Pointer 9m B34F 1996

DRL 213	P913 PWW	DRL 215	P915 PWW	DRL 217	P917 PWW
DRL 214	P914 PWW	DRL 216	P916 PWW	DRL 218	P918 PWW

DRN 115–124 Dennis Dart 9SDL3034 Northern Counties Paladin 9m B35F 1994

DRN 115	L115 YVK	DRN 117	L117 YVK	DRN 119	L119 YVK	DRN 124	L124 YVK
DRN 116	L116 YVK	DRN 118	L118 YVK	DRN 122	L122 YVK		

DVH 5† G905 TYR DAF MB230LB615 Van Hool Alizee H C53F 1990
Ex Arriva London North East, 1998
DVH 6† G906 TYR DAF MB230LB615 Van Hool Alizee H C53F 1990
Ex Arriva London North East, 1998
DVH 7† G907 TYR DAF MB230LB615 Van Hool Alizee H C49FT 1990
Ex Arriva London North East, 1998
DVH 8† G908 TYR DAF MB230LB615 Van Hool Alizee H C49FT 1990
Ex Arriva London North East, 1998

DWL 1–22 DAF SB120 Wright Cadet 10.2m B31D 2001

DWL 1	Y801 DGT	DWL 6	Y806 DGT	DWL 11	LJ51 DDU	DWL 16	LJ51 DEU	DWL 21	LJ51 DFF
DWL 2	Y802 DGT	DWL 7	LJ51 DDK	DWL 12	LJ51 DDV	DWL 17	LJ51 DFA	DWL 22	LJ51 DFG
DWL 3	Y803 DGT	DWL 8	LJ51 DDL	DWL 13	LJ51 DDX	DWL 18	LJ51 DFC		
DWL 4	Y804 DGT	DWL 9	LJ51 DDN	DWL 14	LJ51 DDY	DWL 19	LJ51 DFD		
DWL 5	Y805 DGT	DWL 10	LJ51 DDO	DWL 15	LJ51 DDZ	DWL 20	LJ51 DFE		

L 4–259 Leyland Olympian ONLXB/1RH Eastern Coach Works H42/26D 1986–7
Ex London Buses, 1994

L 4	C804 BYY	L 24	C24 CHM	L 41	C41 CHM	L 65	C65 CHM	L 146	D146 FYM
L 5	C805 BYY	L 25	C25 CHM	L 45	C45 CHM	L 66	C66 CHM	L 147	D147 FYM
L 6	C806 BYY	L 26	C26 CHM	L 46	C46 CHM	L 78	C78 CHM	L 148	D148 FYM
L 8	WLT 807	L 27	VLT 27	L 47	VLT 47	L 79	C79 CHM	L 149	D149 FYM
L 13	VLT 13	L 31	C31 CHM	L 49	C49 CHM	L 99	C99 CHM	L 150	D150 FYM
L 14	C814 BYY	L 32	C32 CHM	L 50	C50 CHM	L 102	C102 CHM	L 151	WLT 751
L 16	WLT 916	L 33	330 CLT	L 52	C52 CHM	L 113	C113 CHM	L 152	D152 FYM
L 17	C817 BYY	L 35	C35 CHM	L 56	C56 CHM	L 135	D135 FYM	L 153	D153 FYM
L 20	C820 BYY	L 36	C36 CHM	L 58	C58 CHM	L 139	D139 FYM	L 154	WLT 554
L 21	C21 CHM	L 37	C37 CHM	L 59	C59 CHM	L 140	D140 FYM	L 155	D155 FYM
L 22	C22 CHM	L 38	C38 CHM	L 63	C63 CHM	L 143	D143 FYM	L 156	656 DYE

L 157	D157 FYM	L 178	D178 FYM	L 199	D199 FYM	L 220	D220 FYM	L 241	D241 FYM
L 158	D158 FYM	L 179	D179 FYM	L 200	D200 FYM	L 221	D221 FYM	L 242	D242 FYM
L 159	D159 FYM	L 180	480 CLT	L 201	D201 FYM	L 222	D222 FYM	L 243	D243 FYM
L 160	D160 FYM	L 181	D181 FYM	L 202	D202 FYM	L 223	D223 FYM	L 244	VLT 244
L 161	D161 FYM	L 182	D182 FYM	L 203	D203 FYM	L 224	D224 FYM	L 245	D245 FYM
L 162	D162 FYM	L 183	D183 FYM	L 204	D204 FYM	L 225	D225 FYM	L 246	D246 FYM
L 163	D163 FYM	L 184	D184 FYM	L 205	D205 FYM	L 226	D226 FYM	L 247	D247 FYM
L 164	D164 FYM	L 185	D185 FYM	L 206	D206 FYM	L 227	D227 FYM	L 248	D248 FYM
L 165	D165 FYM	L 186	D186 FYM	L 207	D207 FYM	L 228	D228 FYM	L 249	D249 FYM
L 166	D166 FYM	L 187	D187 FYM	L 208	D208 FYM	L 229	D229 FYM	L 250u	D250 FYM
L 167	D167 FYM	L 188	D188 FYM	L 209	D209 FYM	L 230	D230 FYM	L 251	D251 FYM
L 168	D168 FYM	L 189	D189 FYM	L 210	D210 FYM	L 231	D231 FYM	L 252	D252 FYM
L 169	D169 FYM	L 190	319 CLT	L 211	D211 FYM	L 232	D232 FYM	L 253	D253 FYM
L 170	7 CLT	L 191	D191 FYM	L 212	D212 FYM	L 233	D233 FYM	L 254	D254 FYM
L 171	D171 FYM	L 192	D192 FYM	L 213	D213 FYM	L 234	D234 FYM	L 255	D255 FYM
L 172	WLT 372	L 193	D193 FYM	L 214	D214 FYM	L 235	D235 FYM	L 256	D256 FYM
L 173	VLT 173	L 194	D194 FYM	L 215	815 DYE	L 236	D236 FYM	L 257	D257 FYM
L 174	D174 FYM	L 195	D195 FYM	L 216	D216 FYM	L 237	D237 FYM	L 258	D258 FYM
L 175	D175 FYM	L 196	D196 FYM	L 217	217 CLT	L 238	D238 FYM	L 259	D259 FYM
L 176	D176 FYM	L 197	D197 FYM	L 218	D218 FYM	L 239	D239 FYM		
L 177	D177 FYM	L 198	D198 FYM	L 219	519 CLT	L 240	D240 FYM		

L 315–354   Leyland Olympian ON2R50C13Z4   Alexander RH   H43/25D   1992
Ex London Buses, 1994

L 315	J315 BSH	L 323	J323 BSH	L 331	J331 BSH	L 339	J339 BSH	L 347	J347 BSH
L 316	J316 BSH	L 324	J324 BSH	L 332	J332 BSH	L 340	J340 BSH	L 348	J348 BSH
L 317	J317 BSH	L 325	J325 BSH	L 333	J433 BSH	L 341	J341 BSH	L 349	J349 BSH
L 318	J318 BSH	L 326	J326 BSH	L 334	J334 BSH	L 342	J342 BSH	L 350	J350 BSH
L 319	J319 BSH	L 327	J327 BSH	L 335	J335 BSH	L 343	J343 BSH	L 351	J351 BSH
L 320	J320 BSH	L 328	J328 BSH	L 336	J336 BSH	L 344	J344 BSH	L 352	J352 BSH
L 321	J321 BSH	L 329	J329 BSH	L 337	J337 BSH	L 345	J345 BSH	L 353	J353 BSH
L 322	J322 BSH	L 330	J330 BSH	L 338	J338 BSH	L 346	J346 BSH	L 354	J354 BSH

L 514–556   *Leyland Olympian ON2R50C13Z   Northern Counties   H47/27D   1990
Ex Kentish Bus, 1997   *(L514/41/3/4/6–54/6 are ONCL10/1RZ)

L 514	G514 VBB	L 523	G523 VBB	L 532	G532 VBB	L 541	G541 VBB	L 550	G550 VBB
L 515	G515 VBB	L 524	G524 VBB	L 533	G533 VBB	L 542	G542 VBB	L 551	G551 VBB
L 516	G516 VBB	L 525	G525 VBB	L 534	G534 VBB	L 543	G543 VBB	L 552	G552 VBB
L 517	G517 VBB	L 526	G526 VBB	L 535	G535 VBB	L 544	G544 VBB	L 553	G553 VBB
L 518	G518 VBB	L 527	G527 VBB	L 536	G536 VBB	L 545	G545 VBB	L 554	G554 VBB
L 519	G519 VBB	L 528	G528 VBB	L 537	G537 VBB	L 546	G546 VBB	L 555	G555 VBB
L 520	G520 VBB	L 529	G529 VBB	L 538	G538 VBB	L 547	G547 VBB	L 556	G556 VBB
L 521	G521 VBB	L 530	G530 VBB	L 539	G539 VBB	L 548	G548 VBB		
L 522	G522 VBB	L 531	G531 VBB	L 540	G540 VBB	L 549	G549 VBB		

L 611   G611 BPH   Volvo Citybus B10M–50   East Lancs S-Type   H49/39F   1989
Ex Arriva Southern Counties, 1999

L 694–704   Volvo Olympian YN2RV16Z4   East Lancs E-Type   H44/30F   1994
Ex Arriva Southern Counties, 1999

L 694	M694 HPF	L 697	M697 HPF	L 700	M700 HPF	L 703	M703 HPF
L 695	M695 HPF	L 698	M698 HPF	L 701	M701 HPF	L 704	M704 HPF
L 696	M696 HPF	L 699	M699 HPF	L 702	M702 HPF		

LDR 2–21	Dennis Dart 9.8SDL3054		Plaxton Pointer 9.8m		B40F	1995

LDR 2	N672 GUM	LDR 7	N677 GUM	LDR 11	N681 GUM	LDR 15	N685 GUM	LDR 19	N689 GUM
LDR 3	N673 GUM	LDR 8	N678 GUM	LDR 12	N682 GUM	LDR 16	N686 GUM	LDR 20	N690 GUM
LDR 4	N674 GUM	LDR 9	N679 GUM	LDR 13	N683 GUM	LDR 17	N687 GUM	LDR 21	N691 GUM
LDR 5	N675 GUM	LDR 10	N680 GUM	LDR 14	N684 GUM	LDR 18	N688 GUM		

LDR 22–55	Dennis Dart SFD412BR5TGD1		Plaxton Pointer 9.8m		B40F	1996

LDR 22	P822 RWU	LDR 28	P828 RWU	LDR 34	P834 RWU	LDR 44	P844 PWW	LDR 50	P850 PWW
LDR 23	P823 RWU	LDR 29	P829 RWU	LDR 37	P837 RWU	LDR 45	P845 PWW	LDR 51	P851 PWW
LDR 24	P824 RWU	LDR 30	P830 RWU	LDR 38	P838 RWU	LDR 46	P846 PWW	LDR 52	P852 PWW
LDR 25	P825 RWU	LDR 31	P831 RWU	LDR 39	P839 RWU	LDR 47	P847 PWW	LDR 53	P853 PWW
LDR 26	P826 RWU	LDR 32	P832 RWU	LDR 41	P841 PWW	LDR 48	P848 PWW	LDR 54	P854 PWW
LDR 27	P827 RWU	LDR 33	P833 RWU	LDR 43	P843 PWW	LDR 49	P849 PWW	LDR 55	P855 PWW

M 441†	GYE 441W	MCW Metrobus DR101/12	MCW	H43/28D	1980
		Ex London Buses, 1994			
M 469t	GYE 469W	MCW Metrobus DR101/12	MCW	H43/28D	1980
		Ex London Buses, 1994			

M 535–798	MCW Metrobus DR101/14	MCW	H43/28D	1981/2

*Ex London Buses, 1994   *(M 537, 573 and 649 are ex Arriva London North East, 1998)

M 535	GYE 535W	M 649†	KYV 649X	M 704w	KYV 704X	M 733t	KYV 733X	M 773	KYV 773X
M 537†	GYE 537W	M 650	KYV 650X	M 712	KYV 712X	M 740	KYV 740X	M 775	KYV 775X
M 567	GYE 567W	M 651	KYV 651X	M 713	KYV 713X	M 744	KYV 744X	M 777†	KYV 777X
M 569t	GYE 569W	M 652t	KYV 652X	M 714	KYV 714X	M 747t	KYV 747X	M 778t	KYV 778X
M 573†	GYE 573W	M 665	KYV 665X	M 715	KYV 715X	M 750	KYV 750X	M 785	KYV 785X
M 575	GYE 575W	M 669	KYV 669X	M 716	KYV 716X	M 752t	KYV 752X	M 787at	KYV 787X
M 591	GYE 591W	M 675	KYV 675X	M 718	KYV 718X	M 757	KYV 757X	M 798t	KYV 798X
M 617	KYO 617X	M 688	KYV 688X	M 721t	KYV 721X	M 762t	KYV 762X		
M 619	KYO 619X	M 694	KYV 694X	M 723	KYV 723X	M 765t	KYV 765X		
M 636	KYV 636X	M 699	KYV 699X	M 724	KYV 724X	M 770t	KYV 770X		
M 637	KYV 637X	M 701	KYV 701X	M 732	KYV 732X	M 772	KYV 772X		

M 825–929	MCW Metrobus DR101/16	MCW	H43/28D	1983
	Ex London Buses, 1994			

M 825	OJD 825Y	M 903t	A903 SUL	M 919	A919 SUL	M 929†	A929 SUL

M 984	A984 SYF	MCW Metrobus DR101/17	MCW	H43/28D	1984
		Ex London Buses, 1984			
M 1000t	A700 THV	MCW Metrobus DR101/17	MCW	H43/28D	1984
		Ex London Buses, 1984			
M 1036	A736 THV	MCW Metrobus DR101/17	MCW	H43/28D	1984
		Ex London Buses, 1984			
M 1070	B70 WUL	MCW Metrobus DR101/17	MCW	H43/28D	1985
		Ex London Buses, 1994			
M 1074	B74 WUL	MCW Metrobus DR101/17	MCW	H43/28D	1985
		Ex London Buses, 1994			
M 1075†	B75 WUL	MCW Metrobus DR101/17	MCW	H43/28D	1985
		Ex London Buses, 1994			

M 1084–1105	MCW Metrobus DR134/1	MCW	H43/28D	1985
	Ex London Buses, 1994			

M 1084t B84 WUL	M 1094t B94 WUL	M 1097t B97 WUL	M 1100t B100 WUL	M 1104t B104 WUL
M 1092t B92 WUL	M 1095t B95 WUL	M 1098t B98 WUL	M 1101t B101 WUL	M 1105t B105 WUL
M 1093t B93 WUL	M 1096t B96 WUL	M 1099t B99 WUL	M 1103t B103 WUL	

M 1109–1437	MCW Metrobus DR101/17	MCW	H43/28D*	1985/6
	*Ex London Buses, 1994			

*(M 1248, 1367 & 1398 are DPH43/28D, 1379 is DPH43/28F, M1437 is DPH43/24F
and all five are ex Arriva London North East, 1998)

M 1109 B109 WUL	M 1170at B170 WUL	M 1253† B253 WUL	M 1314 C314 BUV	M 1362 C362 BUV
M 1121t B121 WUL	M 1173 B173 WUL	M 1254 B254 WUL	M 1317 C317 BUV	M 1367† C367 BUV
M 1123 B123 WUL	M 1175 B175 WUL	M 1265 B265 WUL	M 1318 C318 BUV	M 1379† VLT 88
M 1124 B124 WUL	M 1176 B176 WUL	M 1276 B276 WUL	M 1319 C319 BUV	M 1398† C398 BUV
M 1126† B126 WUL	M 1179t B179 WUL	M 1278 B278 WUL	M 1320† C320 BUV	M 1399 C399 BUV
M 1127 B127 WUL	M 1214 B214 WUL	M 1279 B279 WUL	M 1321 C321 BUV	M 1401 C401 BUV
M 1129t B129 WUL	M 1219 B219 WUL	M 1295 B295 WUL	M 1322 C322 BUV	M 1402 C402 BUV
M 1130 B130 WUL	M 1231† B231 WUL	M 1300 B300 WUL	M 1323 C323 BUV	M 1405 C405 BUV
M 1136 B136 WUL	M 1233 B233 WUL	M 1303 B303 WUL	M 1324 C324 BUV	M 1406 C406 BUV
M 1137 B137 WUL	M 1239 B239 WUL	M 1310 C310 BUV	M 1326† C326 BUV	M 1407 C407 BUV
M 1138 B138 WUL	M 1248† B248 WUL	M 1312 C312 BUV	M 1327 C327 BUV	M 1437† VLT 12
M 1140t B140 WUL	M 1252 B252 WUL	M 1313 C313 BUV	M 1332 C332 BUV	

MBT 713s L713 OVX	Iveco Turbo Daily 59.12	Marshall C31	B8FL	1994
	Ex Arriva EH & E, 1998			
MBT 714s L714 OVX	Iveco Turbo Daily 59.12	Marshall C31	B8FL	1994
	Ex Arriva EH & E, 1998			
MBT 715s L715 OVX	Iveco Turbo Daily 59.12	Marshall C31	B8FL	1994
	Ex Arriva EH & E, 1998			
MBT 716s L716 OVX	Iveco Turbo Daily 59.12	Marshall C31	B8FL	1994
	Ex Arriva EH & E, 1998			
MR 102u F102 YVP	MCW Metrorider MF150/115	MCW	B25F	1988
	Ex London Buses, 1994			
MR 104u F104 YVP	MCW Metrorider MF150/116	MCW	DP25F	1988
	Ex London Buses, 1994			
MRL 129u F129 YVP	MCW Metrorider MF158/16	MCW	B28F	1988
	Ex London Buses, 1994			

PDL 1–15	Dennis Dart SLF SFD612BR1XGW1	Plaxton Pointer 2 8.8m	B29F	2000

PDL 1 V421 DGT	PDL 4 V424 DGT	PDL 7 V427 DGT	PDL 10 V430 DGT	PDL 13 V433 DGT
PDL 2 V422 DGT	PDL 5 V425 DGT	PDL 8 V428 DGT	PDL 11 V431 DGT	PDL 14 V434 DGT
PDL 3 V423 DGT	PDL 6 V426 DGT	PDL 9 V429 DGT	PDL 12 V432 DGT	PDL 15 V435 DGT

PDL 16b W136 VGJ	Dennis Dart SLF SFD612BR1XGW1	Plaxton Pointer 2 8.8m	B21F	2000
PDL 17b W137 VGJ	Dennis Dart SLF SFD612BR1XGW1	Plaxton Pointer 2 8.8m	B21F	2000
PDL 18b W138 VGJ	Dennis Dart SLF SFD612BR1XGW1	Plaxton Pointer 2 8.8m	B21F	2000

PDL 19–38	Dennis Dart SLF SFD322BR1YGW1	Plaxton Pointer 2 10.7m	B31D	2000

PDL 19 X519 GGO	PDL 23 X523 GGO	PDL 27 X527 GGO	PDL 31 X531 GGO	PDL 35 X485 GGO
PDL 20 X471 GGO	PDL 24 X524 GGO	PDL 28 X478 GGO	PDL 32 X532 GGO	PDL 36 X536 GGO
PDL 21 X521 GGO	PDL 25 X475 GGO	PDL 29 X529 GGO	PDL 33 X533 GGO	PDL 37 X537 GGO
PDL 22 X522 GGO	PDL 26 X526 GGO	PDL 30 X481 GGO	PDL 34 X534 GGO	PDL 38 X538 GGO

PDL 39–49 Dennis Dart SLF SFD612BR1YGW1 Plaxton Pointer 2 8.8m B29F 2001

PDL 39 X239 PGT	**PDL 42** X242 PGT	**PDL 45** X546 GGO	**PDL 48** X248 PGT
PDL 40 X541 GGO	**PDL 43** X243 PGT	**PDL 46** X246 PGT	**PDL 49** X249 PGT
PDL 41 X241 PGT	**PDL 44** X244 PGT	**PDL 47** X247 PGT	

PDL 50–69 Dennis Dart SLF SFD612BR11GW1 Plaxton Pointer 2 8.8m B29F 2001

PDL 50 LJ51 DAA	**PDL 54** LJ51 DBU	**PDL 58** LJ51 DBZ	**PDL 62** LJ51 DCU	**PDL 66** LJ51 DCZ
PDL 51 LJ51 DAO	**PDL 55** LJ51 DBV	**PDL 59** LJ51 DCE	**PDL 63** LJ51 DCV	**PDL 67** LJ51 DDA
PDL 52 LJ51 DAU	**PDL 56** LJ51 DBX	**PDL 60** LJ51 DCF	**PDL 64** LJ51 DCX	**PDL 68** LJ51 DDE
PDL 53 LJ51 DBO	**PDL 57** LJ51 DBY	**PDL 61** LJ51 DCO	**PDL 65** LJ51 DCY	**PDL 69** LJ51 DDF

RM 5–2217 AEC Routemaster R2RH Park Royal H36/28R 1959–65
Ex London Buses, 1994 (RM 295, 385, 736, 1330 ex London Transport Buses, 1997. RM 313 ex Arriva TOLST, 1999)

RM 5 VLT 5	**RM 385** WLT 385	**RM 970** WLT 970	**RM 1398** KGJ 118A	**RM 1978** ALD 978B
RM 6 VLT 6	**RM 432** SVS 617	**RM 997** WLT 997	**RM 1593** 593 CLT	**RM 2179** CUV 179C
RM 25 VLT 25	**RM 467** XVS 651	**RM 1003** 3 CLT	**RM 1725** 725 DYE	**RM 2185** CUV 185C
RM 275 VLT 275	**RM 531** WLT 531	**RM 1124** VYJ 806	**RM 1734** 734 DYE	**RM 2217** CUV 217C
RM 295 VLT 295	**RM 664** WLT 664	**RM 1125** KGH 858A	**RM 1801** 801 DYE	
RM 311 KGJ 142A	**RM 676** WLT 676	**RM 1324** 324 CLT	**RM 1811** EGF 220B	
RM 313w WSJ 739	**RM 719** WLT 719	**RM 1330** KGH 975A	**RM 1822** 822 DYE	
RM 348 WLT 348	**RM 736** XYJ 418	**RM 1361** VYJ 808	**RM 1872** ALD 872B	

RMC 1453x 453 CLT AEC Routemaster R2RH Park Royal H32/25RD 1962
Ex Arriva EH & E, 1998

RMC 1464x 464 CLT AEC Routemaster R2RH Park Royal O32/25RD 1962
Ex Arriva EH & E, 1998

RML 882–901 AEC Routemaster R2RH Park Royal H40/32R 1961
Ex London Buses, 1994

RML 882 WLT 882	**RML 888** WLT 888	**RML 895** WLT 895	**RML 897** WLT 897
RML 884 WLT 884	**RML 892** WLT 892	**RML 896** WLT 896	**RML 901** WLT 901

RML 2261–2759 AEC Routemaster R2RH/1 Park Royal H40/32R 1965–68
*Ex London Buses, 1994
*(RML 2265, 2322, 2341, 2538, 2563, 2569, 2582, 2598, 2627, 2663, 2674, 2686, 2694 and
2756 ex Sovereign, 2001)

RML 2261 CUV 261C	**RML 2330** CUV 330C	**RML 2382** JJD 382D	**RML 2491** JJD 491D	**RML 2544** JJD 544D
RML 2264 CUV 264C	**RML 2333** CUV 333C	**RML 2383** JJD 383D	**RML 2492** JJD 492D	**RML 2545** JJD 545D
RML 2265 CUV 265C	**RML 2334** CUV 334C	**RML 2386** JJD 386D	**RML 2494** JJD 494D	**RML 2546** JJD 546D
RML 2266 CUV 266C	**RML 2340** CUV 340C	**RML 2387** JJD 387D	**RML 2503** JJD 503D	**RML 2548** JJD 548D
RML 2267 CUV 267C	**RML 2341** CUV 341C	**RML 2391** JJD 391D	**RML 2504** JJD 504D	**RML 2549** JJD 549D
RML 2277 CUV 277C	**RML 2343** CUV 343C	**RML 2394** JJD 394D	**RML 2505** JJD 505D	**RML 2552** JJD 552D
RML 2280 CUV 280C	**RML 2344** CUV 344C	**RML 2401** JJD 401D	**RML 2510** JJD 510D	**RML 2562** JJD 562D
RML 2287 CUV 287C	**RML 2346** CUV 346C	**RML 2406** JJD 406D	**RML 2412** JJD 512D	**RML 2563** JJD 563D
RML 2292 CUV 292C	**RML 2347** CUV 347C	**RML 2407** JJD 407D	**RML 2514** JJD 514D	**RML 2567** JJD 567D
RML 2294 CUV 294C	**RML 2350** CUV 350C	**RML 2408** JJD 408D	**RML 2518** JJD 518D	**RML 2569** JJD 569D
RML 2301 CUV 301C	**RML 2351** CUV 351C	**RML 2409** JJD 409D	**RML 2521** JJD 521D	**RML 2571** JJD 571D
RML 2304 CUV 304C	**RML 2354** CUV 354C	**RML 2410** JJD 410D	**RML 2523** JJD 523D	**RML 2572** JJD 572D
RML 2307 CUV 307C	**RML 2355** CUV 355C	**RML 2416** JJD 416D	**RML 2524** JJD 524D	**RML 2573** JJD 573D
RML 2315 CUV 315C	**RML 2356** CUV 356C	**RML 2418** JJD 418D	**RML 2525** JJD 525D	**RML 2574** JJD 574D
RML 2322 CUV 322C	**RML 2359** CUV 359C	**RML 2434** JJD 434D	**RML 2526** JJD 526D	**RML 2577** JJD 577D
RML 2323 CUV 323C	**RML 2366** JJD 366D	**RML 2452** JJD 452D	**RML 2528** JJD 528D	**RML 2582** JJD 582D
RML 2324 CUV 324C	**RML 2370** JJD 370D	**RML 2457** JJD 457D	**RML 2431** JJD 531D	**RML 2586** JJD 586D
RML 2325 CUV 325C	**RML 2372** JJD 372D	**RML 2460** JJD 460D	**RML 2533** JJD 533D	**RML 2588** JJD 588D
RML 2326 CUV 326C	**RML 2373** JJD 373D	**RML 2468** JJD 468D	**RML 2534** JJD 534D	**RML 2589** JJD 589D
RML 2328 CUV 328C	**RML 2375** JJD 375D	**RML 2477** JJD 477D	**RML 2536** JJD 536D	**RML 2591** JJD 591D
RML 2329 CUV 329C	**RML 2380** JJD 380D	**RML 2483** JJD 483D	**RML 2538** JJD 538D	**RML 2595** JJD 595D

RML 2597	JJD 597D	RML 2635	NML 635E	RML 2674	SMK 674F	RML 2708	SMK 708F	RML 2750	SMK 750F
RML 2598	JJD 598D	RML 2636	NML 636E	RML 2675	SMK 675F	RML 2715	SMK 715F	RML 2753	SMK 753F
RML 2608	NML 608E	RML 2638	NML 638E	RML 2678	SMK 678F	RML 2716	SMK 716F	RML 2754	SMK 754F
RML 2611	NML 611E	RML 2643	NML 643E	RML 2682	SMK 682F	RML 2718	SMK 718F	RML 2756	SMK 756F
RML 2617	NML 617E	RML 2653	NML 653E	RML 2684	SMK 684F	RML 2726	SMK 726F	RML 2758	SMK 758F
RML 2619	NML 619E	RML 2655	NML 655E	RML 2685	SMK 685F	RML 2730	SMK 730F	RML 2759	SMK 759F
RML 2625	NML 625E	RML 2658	SMK 658F	RML 2686	SMK 686F	RML 2741	SMK 741F		
RML 2627	NML 627E	RML 2660	SMK 660F	RML 2688	SMK 688F	RML 2742	SMK 742F		
RML 2628	NML 628E	RML 2663	SMK 663F	RML 2692	SMK 692F	RML 2746	SMK 746F		
RML 2632	NML 632E	RML 2666	SMK 666F	RML 2694	SMK 694F	RML 2747	SMK 747F		

RV 1x GJG 750D — AEC Regent V 2D3RA — Park Royal — H40/32F — 1966
Ex Arriva EH & E, 1998

S 159–183 — Scania N113DRB Northern Counties Palatine I — H42/25D — 1994–6
Ex Grey-Green 1998

S 159	L159 GYL	S 161	L161 GYL	S 179	M179 LYP	S 181	N181 OYH	S 183	N183 OYH
S 160	L160 GYL	S 178	M178 LYP	S 180	M180 LYP	S 182	N182 OYH		

TPL 1† 124 CLT — Leyland Tiger TRCTL11/3ARZM — Plaxton Paramount 3200 III — C53F — 1989
Ex Arriva EH & E, 1998

TPL 2† 361 CLT — Leyland Tiger TRCTL11/3ARZM — Plaxton Paramount 3200 III — C53F — 1989
Ex Arriva EH & E, 1998

TPL 8† 70 CLT — Leyland Tiger TRCL10/3ARZA — Plaxton Paramount 3200 III — C53F — 1991
Ex Arriva EH & E, 1998

TPL 518† 530 MUY — Leyland Tiger TRCTL11/3ARZ — Plaxton Paramount 3500 III — C51FT — 1988
Ex Arriva EH & E, 1998

VA 115–158 — Volvo Citybus B10M–50 — Alexander RV — H46/29D — 1988–90
Ex Grey-Green, 1998 (VA 136 is fitted with an East Lancs upper deck following accident damage)

VA 115	F115 PHM	VA 123	F123 FHM	VA 131	F131 PHM	VA 139	F139 PHM	VA 147	G147 TYT
VA 116	F116 PHM	VA 124	F124 PHM	VA 132	F132 PHM	VA 140	F140 PHM	VA 148	G148 TYT
VA 117	F117 PHM	VA 125	F125 PHM	VA 133	F133 PHM	VA 141	F141 PHM	VA 155	H155 XYU
VA 118	F118 PHM	VA 126	F126 PHM	VA 134	F134 PHM	VA 142	F142 PHM	VA 156	H156 XYU
VA 119	F119 PHM	VA 127	F127 PHM	VA 135	F135 PHM	VA 143	F143 PHM	VA 157	H157 XYU
VA 120	F120 PHM	VA 128	F128 PHM	VA 136	F136 PHM	VA 144	F144 PHM	VA 158	H158 XYU
VA 121	F121 PHM	VA 129	F129 PHM	VA 137	F137 PHM	VA 145	G145 TYT		
VA 122	F122 PHM	VA 130	F130 PHM	VA 138	F138 PHM	VA 146	G146 TYT		

VA 733 F113 TML — Volvo Citybus B10M–50 — Alexander RV — H47/29D — 1989
Ex Grey-Green 1998

VE 163–172 — Volvo B10M–61 — East Lancs E-type (re-bodied 1992) H44/30D — 1985
Ex Grey-Green 1998

VE 163	B863 XYR	VE 165	B865 XYR	VE 167	B867 XYR	VE 170	B870 XYR	VE 172	B872 XYR
VE 164	B864 XYR	VE 166	B866 XYR	VE 168	B868 XYR	VE 171	B871 XYR		

VLW 1–50	Volvo B7TL		Wright Eclipse Gemini 10.1m	H41/22D	2001

VLW 1	Y581 UGC	VLW 11	LJ51 DFU	VLW 21	LJ51 DGX	VLW 31	LJ51 DHL	VLW 41	
VLW 2	Y102 TGH	VLW 12	LJ51 DFV	VLW 22	LJ51 DGY	VLW 32	LJ51 DHN	VLW 42	
VLW 3	LJ51 DJF	VLW 13	LJ51 DFX	VLW 23	LJ51 DGZ	VLW 33	LJ51 DHO	VLW 43	
VLW 4	LJ51 DJK	VLW 14	LJ51 DFY	VLW 24	LJ51 DHA	VLW 34	LJ51 DHP	VLW 44	
VLW 5	LJ51 DJO	VLW 15	LJ51 DFZ	VLW 25	LJ51 DHC	VLW 35	LJ51 DHV	VLW 45	
VLW 6	LJ51 DFK	VLW 16	LJ51 DGE	VLW 26	LJ51 DHD	VLW 36	LJ51 DHX	VLW 46	
VLW 7	LJ51 DFL	VLW 17	LJ51 DGF	VLW 27	LJ51 DHE	VLW 37	LJ51 DHY	VLW 47	
VLW 8	LJ51 DFN	VLW 18	LJ51 DGO	VLW 28	LJ51 DHF	VLW 38	LJ51 DHZ	VLW 48	
VLW 9	LJ51 DFO	VLW 19	LJ51 DGU	VLW 29	LJ51 DHG	VLW 39	LJ51 DJD	VLW 49	
VLW 10	LJ51 DFP	VLW 20	LJ51 DGV	VLW 30	LJ51 DHK	VLW 40	LJ51 DJE	VLW 50	

VPL 3†	185 CLT	Volvo B10M–61	Plaxton Paramount 3200 II	C53F	1986
		Ex Arriva EH & E, 1998			
VPL 4†	205 CLT	Volvo B10M–61	Plaxton Paramount 3200 II	C53F	1986
		Ex Arriva EH & E, 1998			
VPL 503†	VLT 32	Volvo B10M–60	Plaxton Paramount 3500 III	C53F	1991
		Ex Arriva EH & E, 1998			

Previous registrations:

7 CLT	D170 FYM	815 DYE	D215 FYM	VLT 88	C379 BUV
70 CLT	H643 GRO	EGF 220B	811 DYE	VLT 173	D173 FYM
124 CLT	G661 WMD	J354 BSH	VLT 32, J354 BSH	VLT 244	D244 FYM
185 CLT	E892 KYW	KGH 858A	125 CLT	VYJ 806	124 CLT
205 CLT	E893 KYW	KGJ 118A	398 CLT	VYJ 808	361 CLT
217 CLT	D217 FYM	KGJ 142A	WLT 311	WLT 372	D172 FYM
319 CLT	D190 FYM	KGH 975A	330 CLT	WLT 554	D154 FYM
324 CLT	324 CLT, VYJ 807	SVS 617	WLT 432	WLT 751	D151 FYM
330 CLT	C32 CHM	T324 FGN	99 D 53451	WLT 807	C808 BYY
361 CLT	G662 WMD	T325 FGN	99 D 53440	WLT 916	C816 BYY
398 CLT	N552 LUA	VLT 12	C437 BUV	WSJ 739	WLT 313
480 CLT	D180 FYM	VLT 13	C813 BYY	XYJ 418	WLT 736
519 CLT	D219 FYM	VLT 27	C27 CHM	XVS 651	WLT 467
530 MUY	E118 KFV	VLT 32	H903 AHS		
656 DYE	D156 FYM	VLT 47	C47 CHM		

Special liveries:
† Leaside Travel (Maroon and blue)
a All over advertisement
x LT style red with cream relief
b Blue and green for special DHSS service

On order:
15 x DLP 10.2m for route 307
7 x DWL 10.8m for route 313

ARRIVA KENT THAMESIDE

Vehicles listed below are those most likely to be seen on LT supported services. Other vehicles of similar types may be seen on peripheral routes in west Kent.

1801–1808		Optare MetroRider MR17			Optare			B29F	1996
1801	N801 BKN	**1804**	N804 BKN	**1806**	N806 BKN	**1808**	N808 BKN		
1802	N802 BKN	**1805**	N805 BKN	**1807**	N807 BKN				

1852	N852 YKE	Optare MetroRider MR13	Optare	B25F	1995
		Ex Londonlinks, 1996			

3112–3158		Dennis Dart 9SDL3034			Northern Counties Paladin 9m			B35F	1994
3112	L112 YVK	**3134**	L134 YVK	**3142**	L142 YVK	**3148**	L148 YVK	**3155**	L155 YVK
3113	L113 YVK	**3135**	L135 YVK	**3143**	L143 YVK	**3150**	L150 YVK	**3156**	L156 YVK
3132	L132 YVK	**3138**	L138 YVK	**3144**	L144 YVK	**3153**	L153 YVK	**3158**	L158 BFT
3133	L133 YVK	**3139**	L139 YVK	**3145**	L145 YVK	**3154**	L154 YVK		

3179	P179 LKL	Dennis Dart SLF SFD322BR1TGW1	Plaxton Pointer 10.6m	B40F	1997
		Ex Maidstone & District, 1997			
3217	P217 MKL	Dennis Dart SLF SFD322BR1TGW1	Plaxton Pointer 10.6m	B40F	1997
		Ex Maidstone & District, 1997			
3218	P218 MKL	Dennis Dart SLF SFD322BR1TGW1	Plaxton Pointer 10.6m	B40F	1997
		Ex Maidstone & District, 1997			

3261–72		Dennis Dart SLF SFD322BR1VGW1			Plaxton Pointer 10.6m			B39F	1998
3261	R261 EKO	**3264**	R264 EKO	**3267**	R267 EKO	**3270**	R270 EKO		
3262	R262 EKO	**3265**	R265 EKO	**3268**	R268 EKO	**3271**	R271 EKO		
3263	R263 EKO	**3266**	R266 EKO	**3269**	R269 EKO	**3272**	R272 EKO		

3276–3289		Dennis Dart SLF SFD322AR1WGW1			Plaxton Pointer 2 10.7m			B39F	1999
3276	T276 JKM	**3279**	T279 JKM	**3282**	T282 JKM	**3285**	T285 JKM	**3288**	T288 JKM
3277	T277 JKM	**3280**	T280 JKM	**3283**	T283 JKM	**3286**	T286 JKM	**3289**	T289 JKM
3278	T278 JKM	**3281**	T281 JKM	**3284**	T284 JKM	**3287**	T287 JKM		

3291–3303		Dennis Dart SLF SFD322BR1YGW1			Plaxton Pointer 2 10.7m			B34D	2001
3291	Y291 TKJ	**3294**	Y294 TKJ	**3297**	Y297 TKJ	**3301**	Y301 TKJ		
3292	Y292 TKJ	**3295**	Y295 TKJ	**3298**	Y298 TKJ	**3302**	Y302 TKJ		
3293	Y293 TKJ	**3296**	Y296 TKJ	**3299**	Y299 TKJ	**3303**	Y303 TKJ		

5901–05		*Leyland Olympian ON2R50G13Z4			Northern Counties Palatine			H45/30F	1990
		*(5902/4 are ON2R50C13Z4)							
5901	G901 SKP	**5902**	G902 SKP	**5903**	G903 SKP	**5904**	G904 SKP	**5905**	G905 SKP

5906–09		Leyland Olympian ON2R50G13Z4			Northern Counties Palatine			H45/30F	1993
5906	K906 SKR	**5907**	K907 SKR	**5908**	K908 SKR	**5909**	K909 SKR		

7702–7709		Volvo Citybus B10M–50			East Lancs S-Type			H49/39F	1989–90
		Ex North Western, 1992							
7702	G641 CHF	**7706**	G648 EKA	**7708**	G659 DTJ				
7703	G642 CHF	**7707**	G649 EKA	**7709**	G660 DTJ				

Vehicles listed below are those most likely to appear on LT supported services.

2102	L600 BUS	Optare MetroRider MR11	Optare	B31F	1995
		Ex Lucketts, Watford, 1997			
2103	L700 BUS	Optare MetroRider MR11	Optare	B32F	1995
		Ex Lucketts, Watford, 1997			
2104	L800 BUS	Optare MetroRider MR11	Optare	B31F	1995
		Ex Lucketts, Watford, 1997			

2171–2175		Mercedes-Benz 814 Vario	Plaxton Beaver 2	B27F	1997

2171	R171 VBM	**2172**	R172 VBM	**2173**	R173 VBM	**2175**	R175 VBM

2196	R196 DNM	Mercedes-Benz Vario 814D	Plaxton Beaver 2	B31F	1998
2197	R197 DNM	Mercedes-Benz Vario 814D	Plaxton Beaver 2	B31F	1998
2198	R198 DNM	Mercedes-Benz Vario 814D	Plaxton Beaver 2	B31F	1998
3258	V258 HBH	Volvo B6BLE–55	Wright Crusader 2	B33D	1999
3259	V259 HBH	Volvo B6BLE–55	Wright Crusader 2	B33D	1999
3260	V260 HBH	Volvo B6BLE–55	Wright Crusader 2	B33D	1999
3387	P257 FPK	Dennis Dart SLF SFD322 BR1VGW1	Plaxton Pointer 10.6m	B39F	1997
3388	P258 FPK	Dennis Dart SLF SFD322 BR1VGW1	Plaxton Pointer 10.6m	B39F	1997
3389	P259 FPK	Dennis Dart SLF SFD322 BR1VGW1	Plaxton Pointer 10.6m	B39F	1997
3390	P260 FPK	Dennis Dart SLF SFD322 BR1VGW1	Plaxton Pointer 10.6m	B39F	1997

3404–3414		Dennis Dart SLF SFD212BR5TGD1	Plaxton Pointer 9m	B43F	1996

3404	P324 HVX	**3407**	P327 HVX	**3410**	P330 HVX	**3413**	P833 HVX
3405	P325 HVX	**3408**	P328 HVX	**3411**	P331 HVX	**3414**	P334 HVX
3406	P326 HVX	**3409**	P329 HVX	**3412**	P332 HVX		

3421–3431		Dennis Dart SLF SFD322BR1TGW1	Plaxton Pointer 10.7m	B43F	1996

3421	P421 HVX	**3424**	P424 HVX	**3426**	P426 HVX	**3428**	P428 HVX	**3431**	P431 HVX
3423	P423 HVX	**3425**	P425 HVX	**3427**	P427 HVX	**3429**	P429 HVX		

3461–3481		*Dennis Dart SLF SFD112BR1YGW1	Alexander ALX200 9.4m	B26D	2000
		*(3461 and 3462 are SFD112BR1XGW1)			

3461	W461 XKX	**3465**	W465 XKX	**3469**	W469 XKX	**3474**	W474 XKX	**3478**	W478 XKX
3462	W462 XKX	**3466**	W466 XKX	**3471**	W471 XKX	**3475**	W475 XKX	**3479**	W479 XKX
3463	W463 XKX	**3467**	W467 XKX	**3472**	W472 XKX	**3476**	W476 XKX	**3481**	W481 XKX
3464	W464 XKX	**3468**	W468 XKX	**3473**	W473 XKX	**3477**	W477 XKX		

3500	KE51 PSZ	Dennis Dart SLF SFD662	Plaxton Pointer 2 8.8m	B28F	2001
3501	KE51 PTO	Dennis Dart SLF SFD662	Plaxton Pointer 2 8.8m	B28F	2001
3502	KE51 PTU	Dennis Dart SLF SFD662	Plaxton Pointer 2 8.8m	B28F	2001

5111–25		Leyland Olympian ONCL10/1RZ	Leyland	H47/31F	1989/90
		Ex LCNW, 1990			

5111	G281 UMJ	**5115**	G285 UMJ	**5118**	G288 UMJ	**5121**	G291 UMJ	**5124**	G294 UMJ
5113	G283 UMJ	**5116**	G286 UMJ	**5119**	G289 UMJ	**5122**	G292 UMJ	**5125**	G295 UMJ
5114	G284 UMJ	**5117**	G287 UMJ	**5120**	G290 UMJ	**5123**	G293 UMJ		

5126–33		Leyland Olympian ON2R50C13Z4	Leyland	H47/29F	1991

5126	H196 GRO	**5128**	H198 GRO	**5130**	H200 GRO	**5133**	H203 GRO
5127	H197 GRO	**5129**	H199 GRO	**5132**	H202 GRO		

5250	BYX 240V	MCW Metrobus DR101/12	MCW	H43/30F	1980
		Ex Arriva London, 1999			
5251	KYV 681X	MCW Metrobus DR101/14	MCW	H43/30F	1981
		Ex Arriva London, 1999			
5252	KYO 612X	MCW Metrobus DR101/14	MCW	H43/30F	1981
		Ex Arriva London, 1999			
5253	B283 WUL	MCW Metrobus DR101/17	MCW	H43/30F	1985
		Ex Arriva London, 1999			
5255	B155 WUL	MCW Metrobus DR101/17	MCW	H43/30F	1985
		Ex Arriva London, 1999			
5257	KYV 771X	MCW Metrobus DR101/14	MCW	H43/30F	1982
		Ex Arriva London, 2000			
5260	BYX 290V	MCW Metrobus DR101/12	MCW	H43/30F	1980
		Ex Arriva London, 2000			
5263	BYX 230V	MCW Metrobus DR101/12	MCW	H43/30F	1980
		Ex Arriva London, 2000			
5269	B169 WUL	MCW Metrobus DR101/17	MCW	H43/30F	1985
		Ex Arriva London, 2000			
5348	KYV 786X	MCW Metrobus DR101/14	MCW	H43/30F	1982
		Ex Arriva London, 1999			
5367	GYE 508W	MCW Metrobus DR101/14	MCW	H43/30F	1981
		Ex Arriva London, 1999			
5370	A988 SYF	MCW Metrobus DR101/17	MCW	H43/30F	1984
		Ex Arriva London, 1999			

On order: 4 x Dennis Dart SFD/Plaxton Pointer 2 for routes 350 and W9.
11 x DAF SB120/Wright Cadet 10.2m for route 256.
3 x DAF SB120/Wright Cadet 9.4m for route 346.

BLUE TRIANGLE

DL 901–909		Dennis Trident 2 SFD113BR1XGX2		East Lancs Lolyne 10m		H45/21D	1999

DL 901	V901 FEC	DL 903	V903 FEC	DL 905	V905 FEC	DL 907	V907 FEC	DL 909	V909 FEC
DL 902	V902 FEC	DL 904	V904 FEC	DL 906	V906 FEC	DL 908	V908 FEC		

DL 910–923		Dennis Trident 2 SFD138		East Lancs Lolyne 10m		H46/20D	2001

DL 910	PO51 UMF	DL 913	PO51 UMJ	DL 916	PO51 UMM	DL 919	PO51 UMT	DL 922	PO51 UMX
DL 911	PO51 UMG	DL 914	PO51 UMK	DL 917	PO51 UMR	DL 920	PO51 UMV	DL 923	PO51 UMY
DL 912	PO51 UMH	DL 915	PO51 UML	DL 918	PO51 UMS	DL 921	PO51 UMW		

DN 181–188		Dennis Dart SLF SFD322BR1YGW1		Caetano Nimbus 11m		B36D	2001

DN 181*	Y181 RCR	DN 183*	Y183 RCR	DN 185	Y185 RCR	DN 187	Y187 RCR
DN 182*	Y182 RCR	DN 184	Y184 RCR	DN 186	Y186 RCR	DN 188	Y188 RCR

* 181 is named Eva, 182 is Debbie and 183 carries Kelly Ann.

MCW 19u	WYW 19T	MCW Metrobus DR101/9	MCW	H43/28D	1978
		Ex London United, 1998			
MCW 20u	UKA 20V	MCW Metrobus DR101/3	MCW	H43/30F	1980
		Ex Arriva TOLST, 1999			
MCW 21u	UKA 21V	MCW Metrobus DR103/2	MCW	H43/30F	1980
		Ex Arriva TOLST, 1999			
MCW 27	WYW 27T	MCW Metrobus DR101/9	MCW	H43/28D	1978
		Ex Metroline, 1999			
MCW 28	WYW 28T	MCW Metrobus DR101/9	MCW	H43/28D	1978
		Ex London United, 1998			
MCW 73u	ORJ 73W	MCW Metrobus DR102/21	MCW	H43/30F	1981
		Ex Greater Manchester South, 1997			
MCW 95u	ORJ 95W	MCW Metrobus DR102/21	MCW	H43/30F	1981
		Ex Greater Manchester South, 1997			
MCW 146u	BYW 146V	MCW Metrobus DR101/9	MCW	H43/28D	1979
		Ex London United, 1998			
MCW 160	BYW 160V	MCW Metrobus DR101/9	MCW	H43/28D	1979
		Ex Metroline, 1999			
MCW 179u	BYW 179V	MCW Metrobus DR101/9	MCW	H43/28D	1979
		Ex London United, 1998			
MCW 195	BYW 195V	MCW Metrobus DR101/9	MCW	H43/28D	1979
		Ex London United, 1998			
MCW 270u	BYW 270V	MCW Metrobus DR101/12	MCW	H43/28D	1980
		Ex London General, 1999			
MCW 271	BYW 271V	MCW Metrobus DR101/12	MCW	H43/28D	1980
		Ex London General, 1999			
MCW 462u	GYE 462W	MCW Metrobus DR101/12	MCW	H43/28D	1980
		Ex London United, 1998			
MCW 463	GYE 463W	MCW Metrobus DR101/12	MCW	H43/28D	1980
		Ex London General, 1999			
MCW 497	MNC 497W	MCW Metrobus DR102/10	MCW	H43/30F	1980
		Ex Arriva TOLST, 1999			
MCW 503	GBU 3V	MCW Metrobus DR102/10	MCW	H43/30F	1980
		Ex Merseyside, 1997			
MCW 514	DAE 514W	MCW Metrobus DR103/4	MCW	CH43/30F	1980
		Ex Merseyside, 1996			
MCW 555	C955 LWJ	MCW Metrobus DR102/53	MCW	CH42/28D	1986
		Ex Mainline			
MCW 639w	KYV 639X	MCW Metrobus DR101/14	MCW	H43/28D	1981
		Ex Metroline, 1989			

MCW 932	A932 SUL	MCW Metrobus DR101/16 Ex London United, 1999	MCW	H43/28D	1983
MCW 981	A981 SYF	MCW Metrobus DR101/17 Ex London United, 1999	MCW	H43/28D	1984
MCW 1012	A712 THV	MCW Metrobus DR101/18 Ex London United, 1998	MCW	H43/28D	1984
MCW 1033	A733 THV	MCW Metrobus DR101/17 Ex Metroline, 1999	MCW	H43/28D	1984
T 2	THX 402S	Leyland Titan TNTL112RRsp Ex Stagecoach London, 2001	Park Royal	H44/24D	1978
T 4	WYV 4T	Leyland Titan TNTL112RRsp Ex Stagecoach London, 2001	Park Royal	H44/24D	1978
T 8	WYV 8T	Leyland Titan TNTL112RRsp Ex Stagecoach London, 2001	Park Royal	H44/24D	1979
T 9	WYV 9T	Leyland Titan TNTL112RRsp Ex Stagecoach London, 2001	Park Royal	H44/24D	1979
T 11	WYV 11T	Leyland Titan TNTL112RRsp Ex Stagecoach London, 2001	Park Royal	H44/24D	1979
T 12	WYV 12T	Leyland Titan TNTL112RRsp Ex Stagecoach London, 2001	Park Royal	H44/24D	1979
T 25	WYV 25T	Leyland Titan TNTL112RRsp Ex Stagecoach London, 2001	Park Royal	H44/24D	1979
T 28	WYV 28T	Leyland Titan TNTL112RRsp Ex Stagecoach London, 2001	Park Royal	H44/24D	1979
T 33	WYV 33T	Leyland Titan TNTL112RRsp Ex Stagecoach London, 2001	Park Royal	H44/24D	1979
T 349	KYV 349X	Leyland Titan TNLXB2RR Ex South London, 1995	Leyland	H44/24D	1981
T 908	A908 SYE	Leyland Titan TNLXB2RR Ex London Central, 1999	Leyland	H44/26D	1983
T 1041	A641 THV	Leyland Titan TNLXB2RR Ex London Central, 1999	Leyland	H44/26D	1984
T 1055	A655 THV	Leyland Titan TNLXB2RR Ex London Central, 1999	Leyland	H44/26D	1984
T 1094	B94 WUV	Leyland Titan TNLXB2RR Ex Avon, Prenton, 2001	Leyland	H44/26D	1984
T 1095	B95 WUV	Leyland Titan TNLXB2RR Ex Avon, Prenton, 2001	Leyland	H44/26D	1984
T 1101	B101 WUV	Leyland Titan TNLXB2RR Ex Avon, Prenton, 2001	Leyland	H44/26D	1984
T 1120	B120 WUV	Leyland Titan TNLXB2RR Ex Avon, Prenton, 2001	Leyland	H44/26D	1984

Other miscellaneous vehicles are owned by the Company and are usually allocated to private hire duties.

CONNEX

DA 1–18 · *Dennis Dart SLF SFD612BR1YGW1 · Alexander ALX200 8.9m · B28F · 2000–1
*(DA 15–18 are SFD612BR11GW1)

DA 1	W601 MWJ	**DA 5**	W605 MWJ	**DA 9**	W609 MWJ	**DA 13**	W613 MWJ	**DA 17**	Y117 HWB
DA 2	W602 MWJ	**DA 6**	W606 MWJ	**DA 10**	C8 NEX	**DA 14**	W614 MWJ	**DA 18**	Y118 HWB
DA 3	W603 MWJ	**DA 7**	W607 MWJ	**DA 11**	W611 MWJ	**DA 15**	Y215 HWF		
DA 4	W604 MWJ	**DA 8**	W608 MWJ	**DA 12**	W612 MWJ	**DA 16**	Y116 HWB		

DCL 401–419 · *Dennis Dart SLF SFD322BR1WGW1 · Caetano Compass 10.7m · *B30D · 1999
Ex Limebourne, 2001 · *(DCL 409–411, 413–419 are SFD322BR1XGW1. DCL 401–4 and 406–408 are B31D)

DCL 401	T401 LGP	**DCL 406**	T406 LGP	**DCL 410**	T410 LGP	**DCL 415**	T415 LGP	**DCL 419**	T419 LGP
DCL 402	T402 LGP	**DCL 407**	T407 LGP	**DCL 411**	T411 LGP	**DCL 416**	T416 LGP		
DCL 403	T403 LGP	**DCL 408**	T408 LGP	**DCL 413**	T413 LGP	**DCL 417**	T417 LGP		
DCL 404	T404 LGP	**DCL 409**	T409 LGP	**DCL 414**	T414 LGP	**DCL 418**	T418 LGP		

DCL 421–437 · Dennis Dart SLF SFD322BR1XGW1 · Caetano Compass 10.7m · B30D · 1999
Ex Limebourne, 2001

DCL 421	T421 LGP	**DCL 425**	T425 LGP	**DCL 429**	T429 LGP	**DCL 433**	T433 LGP	**DCL 437**	V537 KGF
DCL 422	T422 LGP	**DCL 426**	T426 LGP	**DCL 430**	T430 LGP	**DCL 434**	V534 KGF		
DCL 423	T423 LGP	**DCL 427**	T427 LGP	**DCL 431**	T431 LGP	**DCL 435**	V535 KGF		
DCL 424	T424 LGP	**DCL 428**	T428 LGP	**DCL 432**	T432 LGP	**DCL 436**	V536 KGF		

DPL 11–14 · Dennis Dart SLF SFD · Plaxton Pointer 2 10.7m · B37F · 2001

DPL 11	Y211 HWJ	**DPL 12**	Y212 HWJ	**DPL 13**	Y213 HWJ	**DPL 14**	Y214 HWJ

DT125–157 · Dennis Dart 8.5SDL3003 · Carlyle Dartline 8.5m · B28F · 1990–1
Ex Limebourne, 2001

DT 125	H125 MOB	**DT 126**	H126 MOB	**DT 134**	H134 MOB	**DT 136**	H136 MOB	**DT 157**	H157 NON

L 1	A101 SYE	Leyland Olympian ONTL11/1R	ECW	H47/28D	1984
		Ex Arriva London, 2000			
L 2	A102 SYE	Leyland Olympian ONLXB/1R	ECW	H47/28D	1984
		Ex Arriva London, 2000			
L 3	A103 SYE	Leyland Olympian ONLXB/1R	ECW	H47/28D	1984
		Ex Arriva London, 2000			
M 54	WYW 54T	MCW Metrobus DR101/8	MCW	H43/28D	1979
		Ex Rigarlsford, Rainham, 2000			
M 565	GYE 565W	MCW Metrobus DR101/14	MCW	H43/28D	1981
		Ex Rigarlsford, Rainham, 2000			

S 231–240 · Optare Solo M850 · Optare · B26F · 1999
Ex Limebourne, 2001

S 231	S231 EWU	**S 233**	S233 EWU	**S 235**	S235 EWU	**S 237**	S237 EWU	**S 239**	S239 EWU
S 232	S232 EWU	**S 234**	S234 EWU	**S 236**	S236 EWU	**S 238**	S238 EWU	**S 240**	S240 EWU

TA 1–30 · Dennis Trident 2 SFD123BR1XGX1 · Alexander ALX400 9.9m · H45/20D · 2000

TA 1	V301 KGW	**TA 7**	V307 KGW	**TA 13**	V313 KGW	**TA 19**	V319 KGW	**TA 26**	V326 KGW
TA 2	V302 KGW	**TA 8**	V308 KGW	**TA 14**	V314 KGW	**TA 20**	V320 KGW	**TA 27**	V327 KGW
TA 3	V303 KGW	**TA 9**	V309 KGW	**TA 15**	V315 KGW	**TA 22**	V322 KGW	**TA 28**	V328 KGW
TA 4	V304 KGW	**TA 10**	V310 KGW	**TA 16**	V316 KGW	**TA 23**	V323 KGW	**TA 29**	V329 KGW
TA 5	V305 KGW	**TA 11**	V311 KGW	**TA 17**	V317 KGW	**TA 24**	V324 KGW	**TA 30**	V330 KGW
TA 6	V306 KGW	**TA 12**	V312 KGW	**TA 18**	V318 KGW	**TA 25**	V325 KGW		

TA 31–38		Dennis Trident 2 SFD123BR21GX2		Alexander ALX400 9.9m				H43/20D	2001
TA 31	Y131 HWB	**TA 33**	Y133 HWB	**TA 35**	Y235 HWF	**TA 37**	Y37 HWB		
TA 32	Y32 HWB	**TA 34**	Y134 HWB	**TA 36**	Y36 HWB	**TA 38**	Y38 HWB		

TA 39–72		Dennis Trident 2 SFD		Alexander ALX400 9.9m				H43/19D	2001
TA 39	YN51 KUU	**TA 46**	YN51 KVC	**TA 53**	YN51 KVK	**TA 60**		**TA 67**	
TA 40	YN51 KUV	**TA 47**	YN51 KVD	**TA 54**	YN51 KVL	**TA 61**		**TA 68**	
TA 41	YN51 KUW	**TA 48**	YN51 KVE	**TA 55**	YN51 KVM	**TA 62**		**TA 69**	
TA 42	YN51 KUX	**TA 49**	YN51 KVF	**TA 56**		**TA 63**		**TA 70**	
TA 43	YN51 KUY	**TA 50**	YN51 KVG	**TA 57**		**TA 64**		**TA 71**	
TA 44	YN51 KVA	**TA 51**	YN51 KVH	**TA 58**		**TA 65**		**TA 72**	
TA 45	YN51 KVB	**TA 52**	YN51 KVJ	**TA 59**		**TA 66**			

XL 401–422		Optare Excel L960 Ex Limebourne, 2001		Optare				B26D	1998
XL 401	R401 HWU	**XL 407**	R407 HWU	**XL 412**	R412 HWU	**XL 417**	R417 HWU	**XL 422**	R422 HWU
XL 402	R402 HWU	**XL 408**	R408 HWU	**XL 413**	R413 HWU	**XL 418**	R418 HWU		
XL 403	R403 HWU	**XL 409**	R409 HWU	**XL 414**	R414 HWU	**XL 419**	R419 HWU		
XL 404	R404 HWU	**XL 410**	R410 HWU	**XL 415**	R415 HWU	**XL 420**	R420 HWU		
XL 405	R405 HWU	**XL 411**	R411 HWU	**XL 416**	R416 HWU	**XL 421**	R421 HWU		

Following the takeover of Limebourne during 2001, many of the former Limebourne buses retain their red and green skirt livery.

CRYSTALS

(LBSL fleet only)

H427 KPA	Mercedes-Benz 811D Ex Tillingbourne, 2001	Dormobile Routemaker	B29F	1991
K286 ESF	Mercedes-Benz 709D Ex Dennis, Duckinfield, 1998	Dormobile Routemaker	B27F	1993
L67 DPE	Mercedes-Benz 709D	Crystals	B19FL	1994
L76 DPE	Mercedes-Benz 709D	Crystals	B18FL	1994
L168 EKR	Mercedes-Benz 711D Ex Crystals demonstrator, 1994	Crystals	B18FL	1994
M569 TJL	Mercedes-Benz 709D	Crystals	B19FL	1995
N601 JGP	Mercedes-Benz 709D	Crystals	B25F	1995
N602 JGP	Mercedes-Benz 709D	Crystals	B25F	1995
N603 JGP	Mercedes-Benz 709D	Crystals	B25F	1995
N604 JGP	Mercedes-Benz 811D	Crystals	B29F	1995
N605 JGP	Mercedes-Benz 811D	Crystals	B29F	1995
N606 JGP	Mercedes-Benz 811D	Crystals	B29F	1995
P347 HKU	Mercedes-Benz 711D	Crystals	B20FL	1997
P348 HKU	Mercedes-Benz 711D	Crystals	B20FL	1997
S107 HGX	Mercedes-Benz Vario 814D	Plaxton Beaver 2	B27F	1999
S108 HGX	Mercedes-Benz Vario 814D	Plaxton Beaver 2	B27F	1999
W427 CWX	Optare Solo M850 Ex demonstrator, 2001	Optare	B30F	2000
W441 CWX	Optare Solo M850	Optare	B17FL	2000
W442 CWX	Optare Solo M850	Optare	B17FL	2000
Y291 PDN	Optare Solo M850	Optare	B27F	2001
Y293 PDN	Optare Solo M850	Optare	B27F	2001
Y294 PDN	Optare Solo M850	Optare	B27F	2001
Y295 PDN	Optare Solo M850	Optare	B27F	2001
Y296 PDN	Optare Solo M850	Optare	B27F	2001

Special Liveries: K286 ESF, N601–606JGP and S107/8 HGX are blue for use in the Orpington area.

The mobility buses are red with yellow relief. Others listed are red. A significant private hire and contract vehicle fleet is also operated, these being in white livery.

EAST THAMES BUSES

317t	OJD 831Y	MCW Metrobus DR101/16 Ex London United, 2001	MCW	H43/28D	1983
318t	OJD 832Y	MCW Metrobus DR101/16 Ex London United, 2001	MCW	H43/28D	1983
319	M649 RCP	DAF DB250RS505 Ex Harris Bus, Grays, 2000	Northern Counties Palatine II	H47/30F	1995

320–334		Optare Excel L1070 Ex Harris Bus, Grays, 2000	Optare	B35F	1996–7

320	P320 KAR	**323**	P323 KAR	**326**	P326 NHJ	**329**	P329 NHJ	**332**	P332 NHJ
321	P321 KAR	**324**	P324 NHJ	**327**	P327 NHJ	**330**	P330 NHJ	**333**	P333 HBC
322	P322 KAR	**325**	P325 NHJ	**328**	P328 NHJ	**331**	P331 NHJ	**334**	P334 NHJ

335	P335 ROO	DAF DE02RSDB250 Ex Harris Bus, Grays, 2000	Northern Counties Palatine II	H43/25D	1997
336	P336 ROO	DAF DE02RSDB250 Ex Harris Bus, Grays, 2000	Northern Counties Palatine II	H43/25D	1997
337	P337 ROO	DAF DE02RSDB250 Ex Harris Bus, Grays, 2000	Northern Counties Palatine II	H43/25D	1997

338–372		Volvo Olympian OLY–56 Ex Harris Bus, Grays, 2000	East Lancs Pyoneer *(351–359 are H51/35F)	*H51/28D	1997/8

338	P338 ROO	**345**	P345 ROO	**352**	P352 ROO	**359**	R359 XVX	**366**	R366 DJN
339	P339 ROO	**346**	P346 ROO	**353**	P353 ROO	**360**	R360 DJN	**367**	R367 DJN
340	P340 ROO	**347**	P347 ROO	**354**	R354 XVX	**361**	R361 DJN	**368**	R368 DJN
341	P341 ROO	**348**	P348 ROO	**355**	R355 XVX	**362**	R362 DJN	**369**	R369 DJN
342	P342 ROO	**349**	P349 ROO	**356**	R356 XVX	**363**	R363 DJN	**370**	R370 DJN
343	P343 ROO	**350**	P350 ROO	**357**	R357 XVX	**364**	R364 DJN	**371**	R371 DJN
344	P344 ROO	**351**	P351 ROO	**358**	R358 XVX	**365**	R365 DJN	**372**	R372 DJN

373–380		Optare Excel L1070 Ex Harris Bus, Grays, 2000	Optare	B35F	1998

373	R373 DJN	**375**	R375 DJN	**377**	R377 DJN	**379**	R379 DJN		
374	R374 DJN	**376**	R376 DJN	**378**	R378 DJN	**380**	R380 DJN		

381	R381 GTW	DAF DE02RSDB250 Ex Harris Bus, Grays, 2000	Northern Counties Palatine II	H43/25D	1998
382	R382 GTW	DAF DE02RSDB250 Ex Harris Bus, Grays, 2000	Northern Counties Palatine II	H43/25D	1998

Buses on loan:

S721 KNV	Dennis Dart SLF SFD322	Marshall Capital	B41F	
T553 HNH	Dennis Dart SLF SFD322BR1XGW1 Ex Tellings-Golden Miller, 2000	Plaxton Pointer 2 10.7m	B41F	1999
V388 SVV	Dennis Dart SLF SFD322	Plaxton Pointer 2 10.7m	B37F	

On order:
New buses for routes 180 and 393. Details not known at time of going to press.

Reg	Chassis	Body	Seating	Year
D600 RGJ	Bedford YMT	Plaxton Derwent	B60F	1987
E204 YGC	Mercedes-Benz 709D	Reeve Burgess Beaver	DP25F	1988
E205 YGC	Mercedes-Benz 709D	Reeve Burgess Beaver	DP25F	1988
F207 DGT	Mercedes-Benz 709D	Reeve Burgess Beaver	DP25F	1988
F208 GGH	Mercedes-Benz 709D	Robin Hood	B26F	1988
G47 TGW	Dennis Dart 8.5SDL3003 Ex London United, 2000	Carlyle Dartline 8.5m	DP28F	1990
K593 BEG	Mercedes-Benz 709D	Marshall C19	B27F	1992
K892 CSX	Dennis Dart 9.8SDL3017	Alexander Dash 9.8m	B40F	1992
K321 GEW	Dennis Dart 9.8SDL3017	Marshall C27 9.8m	B40F	1993
K112 NGK	Dennis Dart 9.8SDL3012	Plaxton Pointer 9.8m	B40F	1993
K113 NGK	Dennis Dart 9.8SDL3012	Plaxton Pointer 9.8m	B40F	1993
L894 NAV	Mercedes-Benz 709D	Marshall C19	B27F	1993
M960 CGF	Dennis Dart 9.8SDL3040	Plaxton Pointer 9.8m	B40F	1994
N401 SPA	Dennis Dart 9.8SDL3054	Plaxton Pointer 9.8m	B40F	1995
N402 SPA	Dennis Dart 9.8SDL3054	Plaxton Pointer 9.8m	B40F	1995
P570 APJ	Mercedes-Benz 709D	Plaxton Beaver	B27F	1997
R211 MGT	Mercedes-Benz 814 Vario	U.V.G.Citistar	B27F	1997
R212 MGT	Mercedes-Benz 814 Vario	U.V.G.Citistar	B27F	1997
R213 MGT	Mercedes-Benz 814 Vario	U.V.G.Citistar	B27F	1997
S451 LGN	Mercedes-Benz 814 Vario	Plaxton Beaver 2	B27F	1998
S452 LGN	Mercedes-Benz 814 Vario	Plaxton Beaver 2	B27F	1998
S453 LGN	Mercedes-Benz 814 Vario	Plaxton Beaver 2	B27F	1998
S454 LGN	Mercedes-Benz 814 Vario	Plaxton Beaver 2	B27F	1998
S455 LGN	Mercedes-Benz 814 Vario	Plaxton Beaver 2	B27F	1998
S456–466 LGN	Dennis Dart SLF SFD612BR1WGW1	Plaxton Pointer 2 8.8m	B29F	1998–9

S456 LGN	S459 LGN	S462 LGN	S465 LGN
S457 LGN	S460 LGN	S463 LGN	S466 LGN
S458 LGN	S461 LGN	S464 LGN	

Reg	Chassis	Body	Seating	Year
T467 EGT	Dennis Dart SLF SFD212BR1WGW1	Plaxton Pointer 2 10.1m	B33F	1999
T468 EGT	Dennis Dart SLF SFD212BR1WGW1	Plaxton Pointer 2 10.1m	B33F	1999
W937 JNF	Dennis Dart SLF SFD612BR1XGW1	Alexander ALX200 8.9m	B29F	2000
W871–6 VGT	Dennis Dart SLF SFD612BR1XGW1	Alexander ALX200 8.9m	B29F	2000

W871 VGT	W873 VGT	W875 VGT
W872 VGT	W874 VGT	W876 VGT

Currently on hire:

Reg	Chassis	Body	Seating	Year
T51 JBA	Dennis Dart SLF SFD322BR1XGW1	Plaxton Pointer 2 10.7m	B36F	1999
V943 DNB	Dennis Dart SLF SFD612	Plaxton Pointer 2 8.8m	B26F	1999

Special liveries:
K321 GEW is all blue.
K892 CSX carries an allover advert for Milner Carpets
N402 SPA carries an allover advert for Brinton's carpets.
At the time of going to press, numerous vehicles were gaining red livery.

FIRST CAPITAL
(Part of the First London Group)

D 605	N605 XJM	Dennis Dart 9.8SDL3054 Ex First CentreWest, 2001	Plaxton Pointer 9.8m	B37F	1996

DM 681–748		Dennis Dart SLF SFD112AR1YGW1	Marshall Capital 9.3m	B24D	2000

DM 681 W681 ULL	**DM 685** W685 ULL	**DM 689** X689 HLF	**DM 699** X699 HLF	**DM 748** X748 JLO
DM 682 W682 ULL	**DM 686** W686 ULL	**DM 690** X501 JLO	**DM 700** X502 JLO	
DM 683 W683 ULL	**DM 687** W687 ULL	**DM 697** X697 HLF	**DM 746** X746 JLO	
DM 684 W684 ULL	**DM 688** X688 HLF	**DM 698** X698 HLF	**DM 747** X747 JLO	

DM 773–788	Dennis Dart SLF SFD112AR1YGW1	Marshall Capital 9.3m	B27F	2001

DM 773 X773 HLR	**DM 777** X512 HLR	**DM 781** X781 HLR	**DM 785** X785 HLR
DM 774 X774 HLR	**DM 778** X778 HLR	**DM 782** X782 HLR	**DM 786** X514 HLR
DM 775 X511 HLR	**DM 779** X779 HLR	**DM 783** X783 HLR	**DM 787** X787 HLR
DM 776 X776 HLR	**DM 780** X513 HLR	**DM 784** X784 HLR	**DM 788** X788 HLR

DM 790–795	Dennis Dart SLF	Marshall Capital 9.3m	B	2002

DM 790	**DM 792**	**DM 794**
DM 791	**DM 793**	**DM 795**

DML 307–329	Dennis Dart SLF SFD212BR1XGW1	Marshall Capital 10.2m	B28D	1999

DML 307 V307 GBY	**DML 312** V312 GBY	**DML 317** V317 GBY	**DML 322** V322 GBY	**DML 327** V327 GBY
DML 308 V308 GBY	**DML 313** V313 GBY	**DML 318** V318 GBY	**DML 323** V323 GBY	**DML 328** V328 GBY
DML 309 V309 GBY	**DML 314** V314 GBY	**DML 319** V319 GBY	**DML 324** V324 GBY	**DML 329** V329 GBY
DML 310 V310 GBY	**DML 315** V315 GBY	**DML 320** V320 GBY	**DML 325** V325 GBY	
DML 311 V311 GBY	**DML 316** V316 GBY	**DML 321** V421 GBY	**DML 326** V326 GBY	

DML 718–772	Dennis Dart SLF SFD212AR1YGW1	Marshall Capital 10.2m	B28D	2000–01

DML 718 W718 ULL	**DML 728** W728 VLO	**DML 738** X738 HLF	**DML 754** X754 HLR	**DML 764** X764 HLR
DML 719 W719 ULL	**DML 729** X729 HLF	**DML 740** X504 JLO	**DML 755** X506 HLR	**DML 765** X508 HLR
DML 720 W133 VLO	**DML 730** X503 JLO	**DML 741** X741 HLF	**DML 756** X756 HLR	**DML 766** X766 HLR
DML 721 W721 ULL	**DML 731** X731 HLF	**DML 742** X742 HLF	**DML 757** X757 HLR	**DML 767** X767 HLR
DML 722 W722 ULL	**DML 732** X732 HLF	**DML 743** X743 HLF	**DML 758** X758 HLR	**DML 768** X768 HLR
DML 723 W723 ULL	**DML 733** X733 HLF	**DML 744** X744 HLF	**DML 759** X759 HLR	**DML 769** X769 HLR
DML 724 W724 ULL	**DML 734** X734 HLF	**DML 745** X745 HLF	**DML 760** X507 HLR	**DML 770** X509 HLR
DML 725 W425 VLO	**DML 735** X735 HLF	**DML 751** X751 JLO	**DML 761** X761 HLR	**DML 771** X771 HLR
DML 726 W726 ULL	**DML 736** X736 HLF	**DML 752** X752 HLR	**DML 762** X762 HLR	**DML 772** X772 HLR
DML 727 W727 ULL	**DML 737** X737 HLF	**DML 753** X753 HLR	**DML 763** X763 HLR	

DMS 330–335	Dennis Dart SLF SFD612AR1XGW1	Marshall Capital 8.9m	B25F	1999

DMS 330 V330 GBY	**DMS 332** V332 GBY	**DMS 334** V334 GBY
DMS 331 V331 GBY	**DMS 333** V433 HBY	**DMS 335** V335 GBY

DMS 349 V349 DLH	Dennis Dart SLF SFD612BR1XGW1 Ex First CentreWest, 2001	Marshall Capital 8.9m	B25F	1999

EC 2001–2011	Mercedes-Benz Citaro	B.. Due 2001/2

EC 2001	**EC 2004**	**EC 2007**	**EC 2010**
EC 2002	**EC 2005**	**EC 2008**	**EC 2011**
EC 2003	**EC 2006**	**EC 2009**	

ES 797–799		Mercedes-Benz Sprinter		Koch		B
ES 797		**ES 798**		**ES 799**		

M 369	GYE 369W	MCW Metrobus DR101/12	MCW		H43/28D	1980
		Ex First CentreWest, 2001				
M 882	OJD 882Y	MCW Metrobus DR101/16	MCW		H43/28D	1983
		Ex First CentreWest, 2001				
M 883	OJD 883Y	MCW Metrobus DR101/16	MCW		H43/28D	1983
		Ex First CentreWest, 2001				
M 884	OJD 884Y	MCW Metrobus DR101/16	MCW		H43/28D	1983
		Ex First CentreWest, 2001				
M 892	A892 SUL	MCW Metrobus DR101/16	MCW		H43/28D	1983
		Ex First CentreWest, 2001				
M 979	A979 SYF	MCW Metrobus DR101/17	MCW		H43/28D	1984
		Ex First CentreWest, 2001				
RM 120	SSL 809	AEC Routemaster R2RH	Park Royal		O36/28R	1959

TAL 931–952 Dennis Trident 2 SFD313BR1XGX2 Alexander ALX400 10.5m H45/24D 2000

TAL 931	W931 ULL	**TAL 936**	W936 ULL	**TAL 941**	W941 ULL	**TAL 946**	W946 ULL
TAL 932	W932 ULL	**TAL 937**	W937 ULL	**TAL 942**	W942 ULL	**TAL 947**	W947 ULL
TAL 933	W933 ULL	**TAL 938**	W938 ULL	**TAL 943**	W943 ULL	**TAL 948**	W948 ULL
TAL 934	W934 ULL	**TAL 939**	W939 ULL	**TAL 944**	W944 ULL	**TAL 949**	W949 ULL
TAL 935	W935 ULL	**TAL 940**	W840 VLO	**TAL 945**	W945 ULL	**TAL 950**	W132 VLO

TAL 951	W951 ULL	
TAL 952	W952 ULL	

TN 801–822 Dennis Trident 2 SFD113BR1XGX2 Plaxton President 9.9m H39/20D 1999

TN 801	T801 LLC	**TN 806**	T806 LLC	**TN 811**	T811 LLC	**TN 816**	T816 LLC	**TN 821**	T821 LLC
TN 802	T802 LLC	**TN 807**	T807 LLC	**TN 812**	T812 LLC	**TN 817**	T817 LLC	**TN 822**	T822 LLC
TN 803	T803 LLC	**TN 808**	T808 LLC	**TN 813**	T813 LLC	**TN 818**	T818 LLC		
TN 804	T804 LLC	**TN 809**	T809 LLC	**TN 814**	T814 LLC	**TN 819**	T819 LLC		
TN 805	T805 LLC	**TN 810**	T810 LLC	**TN 815**	T815 LLC	**TN 820**	T820 LLC		

TN 854–887 Dennis Trident 2 SFD113BR1XGX2 Plaxton President 9.9m H39/20D 1999

TN 854	T854 KLF	**TN 861**	V861 HBY	**TN 868**	T868 KLF	**TN 875**	T875 KLF	**TN 882**	V882 HBY
TN 855	V855 HBY	**TN 862**	V862 HBY	**TN 869**	V869 HBY	**TN 876**	T876 KLF	**TN 883**	T883 KLF
TN 856	V856 HBY	**TN 863**	V863 HBY	**TN 870**	T870 KLF	**TN 877**	V877 HBY	**TN 884**	T884 KLF
TN 857	V857 HBY	**TN 864**	T864 KLF	**TN 871**	T871 KLF	**TN 878**	T878 KLF	**TN 885**	T885 KLF
TN 858	V858 HBY	**TN 865**	T865 KLF	**TN 872**	V872 HBY	**TN 879**	T879 KLF	**TN 886**	V886 HBY
TN 859	V859 HBY	**TN 866**	T866 KLF	**TN 873**	T873 KLF	**TN 880**	T880 KLF	**TN 887**	V887 HBY
TN 860	T860 KLF	**TN 867**	V867 HBY	**TN 874**	V874 HBY	**TN 881**	T881 KLF		

TN 1048–1071 Dennis Trident 2 Plaxton President 9.9m H 2002

TN 1048	**TN 1053**	**TN 1058**	**TN 1063**	**TN 1068**
TN 1049	**TN 1054**	**TN 1059**	**TN 1064**	**TN 1069**
TN 1050	**TN 1055**	**TN 1060**	**TN 1065**	**TN 1070**
TN 1051	**TN 1056**	**TN 1061**	**TN 1066**	**TN 1071**
TN 1052	**TN 1057**	**TN 1062**	**TN 1067**	

TNL 1001–1036 Dennis Trident 2 SFD339BR21GX2 Plaxton President 10.5m H42/23D 2001

TNL 1001	LK51 UZO	**TNL 1009**	LK51 UZG	**TNL 1017**	LK51 UYU	**TNL 1025**	LK51 UYF	**TNL 1033**	LK51 UYP
TNL 1002	LK51 UZP	**TNL 1010**	LK51 UZH	**TNL 1018**	LK51 UYV	**TNL 1026**	LK51 UYG	**TNL 1034**	LK51 UYR
TNL 1003	LK51 UZS	**TNL 1011**	LK51 UZJ	**TNL 1019**	LK51 UYW	**TNL 1027**	LK51 UYH	**TNL 1035**	LK51 UYD
TNL 1004	LK51 UZT	**TNL 1012**	LK51 UZL	**TNL 1020**	LK51 UYX	**TNL 1028**	LK51 UYJ	**TNL 1036**	LK51 UYE
TNL 1005	LK51 UZC	**TNL 1013**	LK51 UZM	**TNL 1021**	LK51 UYY	**TNL 1029**	LK51 UYL		
TNL 1006	LK51 UZD	**TNL 1014**	LK51 UZN	**TNL 1022**	LK51 UYZ	**TNL 1030**	LK51 UYM		
TNL 1007	LK51 UZE	**TNL 1015**	LK51 UYS	**TNL 1023**	LK51 UZA	**TNL 1031**	LK51 UYN		
TNL 1008	LK51 UZF	**TNL 1016**	LK51 UYT	**TNL 1024**	LK51 UZB	**TNL 1032**	LK51 UYO		

Special Note:
The following vehicles still carry their former Capital Citybus fleet numbers, although First London now officially refer to these vehicles with class prefixes. Until these new class prefixes are carried, rather than causing confusion to readers, the old numbers are listed.

107	G107 FJW	MCW Metrobus DR102/70 Ex Capital Citybus, 1998		MCW				H43/30F	1989

121–128		Leyland Olympian ON2R50C13Z4 Ex First CentreWest, 1999		Northern Counties				H47/30F	1990
121	H141 FLX	**123**	H130 FLX	**125**	H135 FLX	**127**	H137 FLX		
122	H142 FLX	**124**	H144 FLX	**126**	H136 FLX	**128**	H145 FLX		

129–132		Leyland Olympian ON2R50C13Z4 Ex Capital Citybus, 1998		Northern Counties				H47/30F	1991
129	J129 YRM	**130**	J130 YRM	**131**	J131 YRM	**132**	J132 YRM		

133	H132 FLX	Leyland Olympian ON2R50C13Z4 Ex First CentreWest, 1999		Northern Counties				H47/30F	1990
134	J134 YRM	Leyland Olympian ON2R50C13Z4 Ex Capital Citybus, 1998		Northern Counties				H47/29F	1991
135	J135 YRM	Leyland Olympian ON2R50C13Z4 Ex Capital Citybus, 1998		Northern Counties				H47/29F	1991

136–158		Leyland Olympian ON2R50C13Z4 Ex Capital Citybus, 1998 *(141–158 are H45/30F)		Leyland				*H47/29F	1991
136	J136 YRM	**142**	J142 YRM	**147**	J247 YRM	**152**	J152 YRM	**157**	J157 YRM
138	J138 YRM	**143**	J143 YRM	**148**	J148 YRM	**153**	J153 YRM	**158**	J158 YRM
139	J139 YRM	**144**	J144 YRM	**149**	J149 YRM	**154**	J154 YRM		
140	J140 YRM	**145**	J145 YRM	**150**	J150 YRM	**155**	J155 YRM		
141	J141 YRM	**146**	J146 YRM	**151**	J151 YRM	**156**	J156 YRM		

167	L888 YTT	Volvo Olympian YN2RV18Z4 Ex Capital Citybus, 1998		Northern Counties Palatine II				H47/29F	1993
168	L888 TTT	Volvo Olympian YN2RV18Z4 Ex Capital Citybus, 1998		Northern Counties Palatine II				H47/29F	1993
170	E470 SON	MCW Metrobus DR102/63 Ex Capital Citybus, 1998		MCW				H45/30F	1988
171	E461 SON	MCW Metrobus DR102/63 Ex Capital Citybus, 1998		MCW				H45/30F	1988
172	E472 SON	MCW Metrobus DR102/63 Ex Capital Citybus, 1998		MCW				H45/30F	1988
173	H129 FLX	Leyland Olympian ON2R50C13Z4 Ex First CentreWest, 1999		Northern Counties				H47/30F	1990
178	E478 SON	MCW Metrobus DR102/63 Ex Capital Citybus, 1998		MCW				H45/30F	1988
179	H139 FLX	Leyland Olympian ON2R50C13Z4 Ex First CentreWest, 1999		Northern Counties				H47/30F	1990
180	H140 FLX	Leyland Olympian ON2R50C13Z4 Ex First CentreWest, 1999		Northern Counties				H47/30F	1990
181	J181 HME	Dennis Dominator DDA2004 Ex Capital Citybus, 1998		Northern Counties				H45/29F	1991
182	J182 HME	Dennis Dominator DDA2002 Ex Capital Citybus, 1998		Northern Counties				H45/29F	1991

206–222		Volvo Olympian OLY–4953		Northern Counties Palatine 1			H47/27D	1998
206	S206 LLO	210	S210 LLO	214	S214 LLO	218	S218 LLO	222	S422 LLO
207	S207 LLO	211	S211 LLO	215	S215 LLO	219	S219 LLO
208	S208 LLO	212	S212 LLO	216	S216 LLO	220	S220 LLO
209	S209 LLO	213	S213 LLO	217	S217 LLO	221	S221 LLO

223–238		Volvo Olympian OLY–50 Ex Capital Citybus, 1998		Alexander RH (Belfast)			H47/25D	1997
223	P223 MPU	226	P226 MPU	229	P229 MPU	232	P232 MPU	236	P236 MPU
224	P224 MPU	227	P227 MPU	230	P230 MPU	233	P233 MPU	237	P237 MPU
225	P225 MPU	228	P228 MPU	231	P231 MPU	234	P234 MPU	238	P238 MPU

239–249		Volvo Olympian YN2RV18Z4 Ex Capital Citybus, 1998		Northern Counties Palatine I			H47/27D	1996
239	P239 HMD	242	P242 HMD	245	P245 HMD	248	P248 HMD
240	P240 HMD	243	P243 HMD	246	P246 HMD	249	P249 HMD
241	N241 CMP	244	N244 CMP	247	N247 CMP

250	J135 PVC	Leyland Olympian ON2R50C13Z4 Ex Volvo, Warwick, 1991	Leyland		H47/25D	1991

251–274		Dennis Dominator DDA1001 Ex Capital Citybus, 1998		Northern Counties			H47/29D	1990
251	H251 KVX	258	H258 KVX	263	H263 KVX	268	H268 KVX	273	H273 KVX
252	H252 KVX	259	H259 KVX	264	H264 KVX	269	H269 KVX	274	H274 KVX
253	H253 KVX	260	H460 KVX	265	H265 KVX	270	H270 KVX
255	H255 KVX	261	H261 KVX	266	H266 KVX	271	H271 KVX
257	H257 KVX	262	H262 KVX	267	H267 KVX	272	H272 KVX

279–294		MCW Metrobus DR102/71 Ex Capital Citybus, 1998		MCW			H46/31F	1988
279	F279 NHJ	282	F282 NHJ	285	F285 NHJ	288	F288 NHJ	291	F291 NHJ
280	F280 NHJ	283	F283 NHJ	286	F286 NHJ	289	F289 NHJ	293	F293 NHJ
281	F281 NHJ	284	F284 NHJ	287	F287 NHJ	290	F290 NHJ	294	F294 NHJ

302t	GYE 479W	MCW Metrobus DR101/12 Ex London General, 1998	MCW	H43/10D	1980
303t	GYE 546W	MCW Metrobus DR101/14 Ex London General, 1998	MCW	H43/10D	1981
306	KYO 606X	MCW Metrobus DR101/14 Ex London General, 1998	MCW	H43/28D	1981
309t	BYX 249V	MCW Metrobus DR101/12 Ex London General, 1998	MCW	H43/10D	1980
316	GYE 416W	MCW Metrobus DR101/12 Ex London General, 1998	MCW	H43/28D	1980
317t	GYE 457W	MCW Metrobus DR101/12 Ex London General, 1998	MCW	H43/10D	1980
323	OJD 843Y	MCW Metrobus DR101/16 Ex First CentreWest, 1998	MCW	H43/28D	1983
324	GYE 348W	MCW Metrobus DR101/12 Ex London General, 1999	MCW	H43/28D	1980
325	GYE 465W	MCW Metrobus DR101/12 Ex First CentreWest, 2000	MCW	H43/28D	1980
327	OJD 872Y	MCW Metrobus DR101/16 Ex First CentreWest, 2000	MCW	H43/28D	1983

329	A898 SUL	MCW Metrobus DR101/16	MCW		H43/28D	1983
		Ex First CentreWest, 2000				
331	A941 SUL	MCW Metrobus DR101/16	MCW		H43/28D	1983
		Ex First CentreWest, 2000				
351	A751 THV	MCW Metrobus DR101/19	MCW		H43/28D	1984
		Ex First CentreWest, 2000				
352	A952 SUL	MCW Metrobus DR101/16	MCW		H43/28D	1983
		Ex First CentreWest, 2000				
354	OJD 874Y	MCW Metrobus DR101/16	MCW		H43/28D	1983
		Ex First CentreWest, 2000				
361	OJD 861Y	MCW Metrobus DR101/16	MCW		H43/28D	1983
		Ex First CentreWest, 2000				

401–412 Dennis Arrow SFD121BR2TGL6 Northern Counties Palatine II H47/33F 1996
Ex Capital Citybus, 1998

401	P401 PLE	404	P404 PLE	407	P407 PLE	410	P410 PLE
402	P402 PLE	405	P405 PLE	408	P408 PLE	411	P411 PLE
403	P403 PLE	406	P406 PLE	409	P409 PLE	412	P412 PLE

413–416 Dennis Arrow SFD121BR2SGL6 Northern Counties Palatine II H47/35F 1996
Ex Capital Citybus, 1998

| 413 | P413 MTW | 414 | P414 MTW | 415 | P415 MTW | 416 | P416 MTW |

417–426 *Dennis Arrow SFD121BR3TGL6 East Lancs Pyoneer *H49/28D 1997
Ex Capital Citybus, 1998 *(426 is SFD121BR3VGL6. 418 and 426 are H49/27D)

| 417 | P417 PVW | 419 | P419 PVW | 421 | P421 PVW | 423 | P423 PVW | 425 | P425 PVW |
| 418 | P418 PVW | 420 | P420 PVW | 422 | P422 PVW | 424 | P424 PVW | 426 | R426 SOY |

427–454 *Dennis Arrow SFD121BR4WGL6 East Lancs Pyoneer H49/27D 1998
427–450 ex Capital Citybus, 1998 *(427 is SFD121BR4VGL6)

427	R427 ULE	433	R433 ULE	439	R439 ULE	445	R445 ULE	451	S451 SLL
428	R428 ULE	434	R434 ULE	440	R440 ULE	446	R446 ULE	452	S452 SLL
429	R429 ULE	435	R435 ULE	441	R441 ULE	447	R447 ULE	453	S453 SLL
430	R430 ULE	436	R436 ULE	442	R442 ULE	448	R448 ULE	454	S454 SLL
431	R431 ULE	437	R437 ULE	443	R443 ULE	449	R449 ULE		
432	R432 ULE	438	R438 ULE	444	R844 YLC	450	R450 ULE		

571–579 Mercedes-Benz 814 Vario Marshall Master B28F 1997
Ex First Thamesway, 1998

| 571 | R411 VPU | 573 | R413 VPU | 575 | R415 VPU | 577 | R417 VPU | 579 | R419 VPU |
| 572 | R412 VPU | 574 | R414 VPU | 576 | R416 VPU | 578 | R418 VPU | | |

622	J622 HMH	Optare MetroRider	Optare		B28F	1992
		Ex Capital Citybus, 1998				
625	J625 HMH	Optare MetroRider	Optare		B28F	1992
		Ex Capital Citybus, 1998				
628	J628 HMH	Optare MetroRider	Optare		B28F	1992
		Ex Capital Citybus, 1998				
630	J630 HMH	Optare MetroRider	Optare		B28F	1992
		Ex Capital Citybus, 1998				

639–645 Dennis Dart 8.5SDL3003 Wright Handybus 8.5m B26F 1991
Ex First CentreWest, 1998

| 639 | JDZ 2339 | 641 | JDZ 2341 | 643 | JDZ 2343 | 645 | JDZ 2373 |
| 640 | JDZ 2340 | 642 | JDZ 2342 | 644 | JDZ 2372 | | |

669	J459 JOW	Dennis Dart 9SDL3011	Wadham Stringer Portsdown 9m	B37F	1991
		Ex Wealden PSV, Five Oaks Green, 1995			
670	L670 SMC	Dennis Dart 9SDL3034	Northern Counties Paladin 9m	B31F	1994
		Ex Capital Citybus, 1998			

| 691–696 | | Dennis Dart 9SDL3016 | Plaxton Pointer 9m | B35F | 1992 |
| | | Ex First Thamesway, 1998 | | | |

| 691 | K901 CVW | 693 | K903 CVW | 695 | K905 CVW |
| 692 | K902 CVW | 694 | K904 CVW | 696 | K906 CVW |

| 701–704 | | Optare Excel L1000 | Optare | B33F | 1996 |
| | | Ex Capital Citybus, 1998 | | | |

| 701 | P701 HMT | 702 | P702 HMT | 703 | P703 HMT | 704 | P704 HMT |

| 705–717 | | Dennis Dart SLF SFD212BR1VGW1 | East Lancs Spryte 10.2m | B37F | 1998 |

705	R705 VLA	708	R708 VLA	711	R711 VLA	714	R714 VLA	717	R717 VLA
706	R706 VLA	709	R709 VLA	712	R712 VLA	715	R715 VLA		
707	R707 VLA	710	R710 VLA	713	R713 VLA	716	R716 VLA		

739w	KRS 539V	Leyland National 2 NL106L11/1R		B44F	1980
		Ex Bluebird Northern, 1993			
749w	B359 LOY	Leyland National 2 NL116L11/3R		B49F	1985
		Ex British Airways, 1993			

| 774–786 | | Dennis Dart SFD412BR5TGD1 | Plaxton Pointer 9.8m | B40F | 1996 |
| | | Ex First Thamesway, 1998 | | | |

| 774 | N974 EHJ | 778 | N978 EHJ | 780 | N980 EHJ | 782 | N982 EHJ | 784 | N984 EHJ |
| 777 | N977 EHJ | 779 | N979 EHJ | 781 | N981 EHJ | 783 | N983 EHJ | 785 | N985 EHJ |

789	T789 KNW	Optare Solo M920	Optare	B30F	1999
		Owned by London Borough of Waltham Forest			
796	M796 MPM	Dennis Lance 11SDA3108	Alexander PS	B46F	1991
		Ex Dennis Development Vehicle, 1998			

Liveries:
The majority of the fleet is now predominantly red with yellow relief. However, a significant number retain the former Capital Citybus livery of yellow.
Additionally, ex-Thamesway vehicles 571/2/5–579, 777/8, 781,784–6 carry their former Thamesway livery.

Special liveries:
317 carries training livery of red and yellow. 789 is all-white.

Previous Registrations:

GYE 479W	GYE 479W, VLT 179	P404 PLE	P904 HMH	P409 PLE	P909 HMH
KRS 539V	GSO 5V	P405 PLE	P905 HMH	P410 PLE	P910 HMH
P401 PLE	P901 HMH	P406 PLE	P906 HMH	P411 PLE	P911 HMH
P402 PLE	P902 HMH	P407 PLE	P907 HMH	P412 PLE	P912 HMH
P403 PLE	P903 HMH	P408 PLE	P908 HMH	SSL 809	VLT 120

D 33–41		Dennis Dart SFD412BR5TGD1		Plaxton Pointer 9.8m			B37F	1996
D 33	N633 ACF	**D 35**	N635 ACF	**D 37**	N637 ACF	**D 39**	P409 MLA	**D 41** P411 MLA
D 34	N634 ACF	**D 36**	N636 ACF	**D 38**	P408 MLA	**D 40**	P410 MLA	

DM 117–164		Dennis Dart SLF SFD112BR1VGW1		Marshall Capital 9.3m			B31F	1997/8
		(DM158–162, 164 are SFD112BR1WGW1)						
DM 117 P117 NLW		**DM 127** P127 NLW		**DM 137** P137 NLW		**DM 147** P247 OEW		**DM 157** P157 NLW
DM 118 P118 NLW		**DM 128** P128 NLW		**DM 138** P138 NLW		**DM 148** P148 NLW		**DM 158** R158 TLM
DM 119 P119 NLW		**DM 129** P129 NLW		**DM 139** P139 NLW		**DM 149** P149 NLW		**DM 159** R159 TLM
DM 120 P120 NLW		**DM 130** P130 NLW		**DM 140** P140 NLW		**DM 150** P150 NLW		**DM 160** R160 TLM
DM 121 P121 NLW		**DM 131** P131 NLW		**DM 141** P141 NLW		**DM 151** P151 NLW		**DM 161** R161 TLM
DM 122 P122 NLW		**DM 132** P132 NLW		**DM 142** P142 NLW		**DM 152** P152 NLW		**DM 162** R162 TLM
DM 123 P123 NLW		**DM 133** P133 NLW		**DM 143** P143 NLW		**DM 153** P153 NLW		**DM 163** R163 TLM
DM 124 P124 NLW		**DM 134** P134 NLW		**DM 144** P144 NLW		**DM 154** P154 NLW		**DM 164** R164 TLM
DM 125 P125 NLW		**DM 135** P135 NLW		**DM 145** P145 NLW		**DM 155** P255 RFL		
DM 126 P126 NLW		**DM 136** P136 NLW		**DM 146** P146 NLW		**DM 156** P156 NLW		

DM 201–234		Dennis Dart SLF SFD112BR1WGW1		Marshall Capital 9.3m			B22D	1998
DM 201 R201 TLM		**DM 208** R208 TLM		**DM 215** R215 TLM		**DM 222** R322 TLM		**DM 229** R229 TLM
DM 202 R202 TLM		**DM 209** R209 TLM		**DM 216** R216 TLM		**DM 223** R223 TLM		**DM 230** R230 TLM
DM 203 R203 TLM		**DM 210** R210 TLM		**DM 217** R217 TLM		**DM 224** R224 TLM		**DM 231** R231 TLM
DM 204 R204 TLM		**DM 211** R211 TLM		**DM 218** R218 TLM		**DM 225** R225 TLM		**DM 232** R232 TLM
DM 205 R205 TLM		**DM 212** R212 TLM		**DM 219** R219 TLM		**DM 226** R226 TLM		**DM 233** R233 TLM
DM 206 R206 TLM		**DM 213** R213 TLM		**DM 220** R220 TLM		**DM 227** R227 TLM		**DM 234** R234 TLM
DM 207 R207 TLM		**DM 214** R214 TLM		**DM 221** R221 TLM		**DM 228** R228 TLM		

DM 264–306		Dennis Dart SLF SFD112BR1XGW1		Marshall Capital 9.3m			B22D	1999
DM 264 T264 JLD		**DM 273** T273 JLD		**DM 282** T282 JLD		**DM 291** T291 JLD		**DM 300** T430 JLD
DM 265 T265 JLD		**DM 274** T274 JLD		**DM 283** T283 JLD		**DM 292** T292 JLD		**DM 301** T301 JLD
DM 266 T266 JLD		**DM 275** T275 JLD		**DM 284** T284 JLD		**DM 293** T293 JLD		**DM 302** T302 JLD
DM 267 T267 JLD		**DM 276** T276 JLD		**DM 285** T285 JLD		**DM 294** T294 JLD		**DM 303** T303 JLD
DM 268 T268 JLD		**DM 277** T277 JLD		**DM 286** T286 JLD		**DM 295** T295 JLD		**DM 304** T304 JLD
DM 269 T269 JLD		**DM 278** T278 JLD		**DM 287** T287 JLD		**DM 296** T296 JLD		**DM 305** T305 JLD
DM 270 T270 JLD		**DM 279** T279 JLD		**DM 288** T288 JLD		**DM 297** T297 JLD		**DM 306** T306 JLD
DM 271 T271 JLD		**DM 280** T280 JLD		**DM 289** T289 JLD		**DM 298** T298 JLD		
DM 272 T272 JLD		**DM 281** T281 JLD		**DM 290** T290 JLD		**DM 299** T299 JLD		

DM 432–438		Dennis Dart SLF SFD		Marshall Capital 9.3m	B	Due for 2001 delivery
DM 432		**DM 434**		**DM 436**	**DM 438**	
DM 433		**DM 435**		**DM 437**		

DM 461–472		Dennis Dart SLF SFD		Marshall Capital 9.3m	B	Due for 2001 delivery
DM 461		**DM 464**		**DM 467**	**DM 470**	
DM 462		**DM 465**		**DM 468**	**DM 471**	
DM 463		**DM 466**		**DM 469**	**DM 472**	

DML 165–200 *Dennis Dart SLF SFD212BR1VGW1   Marshall Capital 10.2m   B33F   1997
*(DML 179–200 are SFD212BR1WGW1)

DML 165 R165 TLM	**DML 173** R173 TLM	**DML 181** R181 TLM	**DML 189** R189 TLM	**DML 197** S197 KLM
DML 166 R166 TLM	**DML 174** R174 TLM	**DML 182** R182 TLM	**DML 190** R190 TLM	**DML 198** S198 KLM
DML 167 R167 TLM	**DML 175** R175 TLM	**DML 183** R183 TLM	**DML 191** R191 VLD	**DML 199** S199 KLM
DML 168 R168 TLM	**DML 176** R176 TLM	**DML 184** R184 TLM	**DML 192** R192 VLD	**DML 200** S220 KLM
DML 169 R169 TLM	**DML 177** R177 TLM	**DML 185** R185 TLM	**DML 193** R193 VLD	
DML 170 R170 TLM	**DML 178** R178 TLM	**DML 186** R186 TLM	**DML 194** R194 VLD	
DML 171 R171 TLM	**DML 179** R179 TLM	**DML 187** R187 TLM	**DML 195** R195 VLD	
DML 172 R172 TLM	**DML 180** R180 TLM	**DML 188** R188 TLM	**DML 196** R196 VLD	

DML 235–256 Dennis Dart SLF SFD212BR1WGW1   Marshall Capital 10.2m   29D   1998

DML 235 S235 KLM	**DML 239** S239 KLM	**DML 243** S243 KLM	**DML 247** S247 KLM	**DML 255** S255 JLP
DML 236 S236 KLM	**DML 240** S240 KLM	**DML 244** S244 KLM	**DML 248** S248 KLM	**DML 256** S256 JLP
DML 237 S237 KLM	**DML 241** S241 KLM	**DML 245** S245 KLM	**DML 253** S253 JLP	
DML 238 S238 KLM	**DML 242** S242 KLM	**DML 246** S246 KLM	**DML 254** S254 JLP	

DML 336 T336 ALR   Dennis Dart SLF SFD212BR1XGW1   Marshall Capital 10.2m   B33F   1999

DML 362–380 Dennis Dart SLF SFD212BR1XGW1   Marshall Capital 10.2m   B28D   2000

DML 362 W362 VLN	**DML 366** W366 VLN	**DML 370** W358 VLN	**DML 374** W374 VLN	**DML 378** W378 VLN
DML 363 W363 VLN	**DML 367** W367 VLN	**DML 371** W371 VLN	**DML 375** W359 VLN	**DML 379** W379 VLN
DML 364 W364 VLN	**DML 368** W368 VLN	**DML 372** W372 VLN	**DML 376** W376 VLN	**DML 380** W361 VLN
DML 365 W365 VLN	**DML 369** W369 VLN	**DML 373** W373 VLN	**DML 377** W377 VLN	

DML 381–402 Dennis Dart SLF SFD212AR1YGW1   Marshall Capital 10.2m   B28D   2000

DML 381 X381 HLR	**DML 386** X386 HLR	**DML 391** X391 HLR	**DML 396** X396 HLR	**DML 401** X401 HLR
DML 382 X382 HLR	**DML 387** X387 HLR	**DML 392** X392 HLR	**DML 397** X397 HLR	**DML 402** X402 HLR
DML 383 X383 HLR	**DML 388** X388 HLR	**DML 393** X393 HLR	**DML 398** X398 HLR	
DML 384 X384 HLR	**DML 389** X389 HLR	**DML 394** X394 HLR	**DML 399** X399 HLR	
DML 385 X385 HLR	**DML 390** X78 HLR	**DML 395** X395 HLR	**DML 400** X79 HLR	

DML 403–431 Dennis Dart SLF SFD2B2CR31GW1   Marshall Capital 10.2m   B28D   2001

DML 403 133 CLT	**DML 409** 810 DYE	**DML 415** LN51 DWY	**DML 421** LN51 DXE	**DML 427**
DML 404 292 CLT	**DML 410** 811 DYE	**DML 416** LN51 DWZ	**DML 422** LN51 DXF	**DML 428**
DML 405 503 CLT	**DML 411** LK51 JYJ	**DML 417** LN51 DXA	**DML 423**	**DML 429**
DML 406 WLT 659	**DML 412** LK51 JYL	**DML 418** LN51 DXB	**DML 424**	**DML 430**
DML 407 676 DYE	**DML 413** LK51 JYN	**DML 419** LN51 DXC	**DML 425**	**DML 431**
DML 408 809 DYE	**DML 414** LK51 JYO	**DML 420** LN51 DXD	**DML 426**	

DML 633–653 Dennis Dart SLF SFD212BR1VGW1   Marshall Capital 10.2m   *B37F   1997/8
*(DML 633–641 currently being converted to B33F)

DML 633 R633 VLX	**DML 637** R637 VLX	**DML 641** R641 VLX	**DML 645** R645 TLM	**DML 650** R650 TLM
DML 634 R634 VLX	**DML 638** R638 VLX	**DML 642** R642 TLM	**DML 646** R646 TLM	**DML 651** R651 TLM
DML 635 R835 VLX	**DML 639** R639 VLX	**DML 643** R643 TLM	**DML 647** R647 TLM	**DML 652** R652 TLM
DML 636 R636 VLX	**DML 640** R640 VLX	**DML 644** R644 TLM	**DML 649** R649 TLM	**DML 653** R653 TLM

DMS 257–263 Dennis Dart SLF SFD612BR1WGW1   Marshall Capital 8.9m   B25F   1999

DMS 257 T257 JLD	**DMS 259** T259 JLD	**DMS 261** T261 JLD	**DMS 263** T263 JLD
DMS 258 T258 JLD	**DMS 260** T260 JLD	**DMS 262** T262 JLD	

DMS 337–361 Dennis Dart SLF SFD612BR1XGW1   Marshall Capital 8.9m   B25F   1999

DMS 337 T337 ALR	**DMS 339** T339 ALR	**DMS 341** T341 ALR	**DMS 343** T343 ALR	**DMS 345** V345 DLH
DMS 338 T338 ALR	**DMS 340** T340 ALR	**DMS 342** T342 ALR	**DMS 344** T344 ALR	**DMS 346** V346 DLH

DMS 347 V347 DLH	DMS 351 V351 DLH	DMS 354 V354 DLH	DMS 357 V357 DLH	DMS 360 V360 DLH
DMS 348 V348 DLH	DMS 352 V352 DLH	DMS 355 V355 DLH	DMS 358 V358 DLH	DMS 361 V361 DLH
DMS 350 V350 DLH	DMS 353 V353 DLH	DMS 356 V356 DLH	DMS 359 V359 DLH	

DMS 439–461 Dennis Dart SLF SFD… Marshall Capital 8.9m B Due for 2001 delivery

DMS 439	DMS 444	DMS 449	DMS 454	DMS 459
DMS 440	DMS 445	DMS 450	DMS 455	DMS 460
DMS 441	DMS 446	DMS 451	DMS 456	DMS 461
DMS 442	DMS 447	DMS 452	DMS 457	
DMS 443	DMS 448	DMS 453	DMS 458	

DP 1–17 Dennis Dart 9SDL3053 Plaxton Pointer 9m B32F 1995

DP 1	N801 FLW	DP 5	N805 FLW	DP 9	N809 FLW	DP 13	N813 FLW	DP 17	N817 FLW
DP 2	N802 FLW	DP 6	N806 FLW	DP 10	N810 FLW	DP 14	N814 FLW		
DP 3	N803 FLW	DP 7	N807 FLW	DP 11	N811 FLW	DP 15	N815 FLW		
DP 4	N804 FLW	DP 8	N808 FLW	DP 12	N812 FLW	DP 16	N816 FLW		

DW 1–75 Dennis Dart 8.5SDL3003 Wright Handybus 8.5m *B26F 1990
Ex London Buses, 1994 *(DW1–14 are B30F)

DW 1	JDZ 2301	DW 6	JDZ 2306	DW 11	JDZ 2311	DW 16	JDZ 2316	DW 75	JDZ 2375
DW 2	JDZ 2302	DW 7	JDZ 2307	DW 12	JDZ 2312	DW 17	JDZ 2317		
DW 3	JDZ 2303	DW 8	JDZ 2308	DW 13	JDZ 2313	DW 22	JDZ 2322		
DW 4	JDZ 2304	DW 9	JDZ 2309	DW 14	JDZ 2314	DW 23	JDZ 2323		
DW 5	JDZ 2305	DW 10	JDZ 2310	DW 15	JDZ 2315	DW 24	JDZ 2324		

DW 124 LDZ 9124 Dennis Dart 8.5SDL3015 Wright Handybus 8.5m B26F 1992
Ex London Buses, 1994

DW 125 LDZ 9125 Dennis Dart 8.5SDL3015 Wright Handybus 8.5m B26F 1992
Ex London Buses, 1994

DW 162–170 Dennis Dart 8.5SDL3015 Wright Handybus 8.5m *B29F 1993
Ex London Buses, 1994 *(DW 169 and 170 are B26F)

DW 162	NDZ 3162	DW 164	NDZ 3164	DW 166	NDZ 3166	DW 168	NDZ 3168	DW 170	NDZ 3170
DW 163	NDZ 3163	DW 165	NDZ 3165	DW 167	NDZ 3167	DW 169	NDZ 3169		

L 1–7 Dennis Dart SLF SFD212BR1TGW1 Plaxton Pointer 10m B34F 1996
L 7 ex First Beeline, 2000

L 1	P401 MLA	L 3	P403 MLA	L 5	P405 MLA	L 7	P407 MLA
L 2	P402 MLA	L 4	P404 MLA	L 6	P406 MLA		

LA 24–28 Leyland Olympian ON2R50C13Z4 Alexander RH H45/29F 1993
Ex London Buslines, 1997

LA 24	L24 GAN	LA 25	L25 GAN	LA 26	L26 GAN	LA 27	L27 GAN	LA 28	L28 GAN

LC 1–3 LDV 400 Crystals DP10FL 1995

LC 1	N921 LUF	LC 2	N922 LUF	LC 3	N923 LUF

LLW 31 M221 EAF Dennis Lance SLF 11SDA3201 Wright Pathfinder 320 B40F 1995
Ex Leeds Citylink, 1998

LN 31–43 Leyland Olympian ON2R50C13Z4 Northern Counties H47/30F 1990
Ex London Buslines, 1996/7

LN 31	H131 FLX	LN 33	H133 FLX	LN 34	H134 FLX	LN 38	H138 FLX	LN 43	H143 FLX

M 859	OJD 859Y	MCW Metrobus DR101/16		MCW			H43/28D	1983
		Ex London Buses, 1994						

M 1199–1438 MCW Metrobus DR101/17 MCW H43/28D 1985/6
Ex London Buses, 1994

M 1199	B199 WUL	**M 1259**	B259 WUL	**M 1340**t	C340 BUV	**M 1382**	C382 BUV	**M 1418**t	C418 BUV
M 1245	B245 WUL	**M 1260**t	B260 WUL	**M 1376**	C376 BUV	**M 1384**t	C384 BUV	**M 1419**t	C419 BUV
M 1246	B246 WUL	**M 1328**t	C328 BUV	**M 1377**	C377 BUV	**M 1400**	C400 BUV	**M 1420**t	C420 BUV
M 1256	B256 WUL	**M 1335**t	C335 BUV	**M 1378**	C378 BUV	**M 1412**t	C412 BUV	**M 1422**t	C422 BUV
M 1258	B258 WUL	**M 1338**t	C338 BUV	**M 1380**t	C380 BUV	**M 1415**	C415 BUV	**M 1438**	C438 BUV

MA 1u	F601 XMS	Mercedes-Benz 811D		Alexander AM		B26F	1988
		Ex London Buses, 1994					
MB 592t	H392 MAR	Mercedes-Benz 709D		Reeve Burgess Beaver		B23F	1991
		Ex First Capital, 2001					
RB 551	K651 DBL	Renault-Dodge S75		Plaxton Beaver		B18FL	1992
		Ex First London Buslines, 2000					
RB 552	K652 DBL	Renault-Dodge S75		Plaxton Beaver		B18FL	1992
		Ex First London Buslines, 2000					
RB 553	K653 DBL	Renault-Dodge S75		Plaxton Beaver		B18FL	1992
		Ex First London Buslines, 2000					
RF 326sp	MLL 963	AEC Regal IV 9821LT		Metro-Cammell		B39F	1952
		Ex preservation, 1996					
RM 871	WLT 871	AEC Routemaster R2RH		Park Royal		H36/28R	1962
		Ex Reading Mainline, 2000					
RM 1650	650 DYE	AEC Routemaster R2RH		Park Royal		H36/28R	1963
		Ex Reading Mainline, 2000					
RM 1941	ALD 941B	AEC Routemaster R2RH		Park Royal		H36/28R	1964
		Ex Stagecoach Cumberland, 2000					
RMC 1510	510 CLT	AEC Routemaster R2RH		Park Royal		O32/25RD	1962
		Ex London Buses, 1994					
RML 885	WLT 885	AEC Routemaster R2RH		Park Royal		H40/32R	1961
		Ex London Buses, 1994					

RML 2268–2740 AEC Routemaster R2RH/1 Park Royal H40/32R 1965–7
Ex London Buses, 1994

RML 2268	CUV 268C	**RML 2374**	JJD 374D	**RML 2476**	JJD 476D	**RML 2553**	JJD 553D	**RML 2672**	SMK 672F
RML 2278	CUV 278C	**RML 2378**	JJD 378D	**RML 2480**	JJD 480D	**RML 2555**	JJD 555D	**RML 2677**	SMK 677F
RML 2281	CUV 281C	**RML 2379**	JJD 379D	**RML 2486**	JJD 486D	**RML 2559**	JJD 559D	**RML 2687**	SMK 687F
RML 2291	CUV 291C	**RML 2388**	JJD 388D	**RML 2490**	JJD 490D	**RML 2602**	NML 602E	**RML 2717**	SMK 717F
RML 2309	CUV 309C	**RML 2390**	JJD 390D	**RML 2498**	JJD 498D	**RML 2609**	NML 609E	**RML 2724**	SMK 724F
RML 2313	CUV 313C	**RML 2405**	JJD 405D	**RML 2501**	JJD 501D	**RML 2623**	NML 623E	**RML 2735**	SMK 735F
RML 2352	CUV 352C	**RML 2428**	JJD 428D	**RML 2506**	JJD 506D	**RML 2647**	NML 647E	**RML 2740**	SMK 740F
RML 2357	CUV 357C	**RML 2442**	JJD 442D	**RML 2522**	JJD 522D	**RML 2656**	NML 656E		
RML 2365	JJD 365D	**RML 2467**	JJD 467D	**RML 2530**	JJD 530D	**RML 2664**	SMK 664F		
RML 2369	JJD 369D	**RML 2473**	JJD 473D	**RML 2542**	JJD 542D	**RML 2667**	SMK 667F		

TN 823–853 Dennis Trident 2 SFD113BR1XGX2 Plaxton President 9.9m H39/20D 1999

TN 823	T823 LLC	**TN 830**	T830 LLC	**TN 837**	T837 LLC	**TN 844**	T844 LLC	**TN 851**	T851 LLC
TN 824	T824 LLC	**TN 831**	T831 LLC	**TN 838**	T838 LLC	**TN 845**	T845 LLC	**TN 852**	T852 LLC
TN 825	T825 LLC	**TN 832**	T832 LLC	**TN 839**	T839 LLC	**TN 846**	T846 LLC	**TN 853**	T853 LLC
TN 826	T826 LLC	**TN 833**	T833 LLC	**TN 840**	T840 LLC	**TN 847**	T847 LLC		
TN 827	T827 LLC	**TN 834**	T834 LLC	**TN 841**	T841 LLC	**TN 848**	T848 LLC		
TN 828	T828 LLC	**TN 835**	T835 LLC	**TN 842**	T842 LLC	**TN 849**	T849 LLC		
TN 829	T829 LLC	**TN 836**	T836 LLC	**TN 843**	T843 LLC	**TN 850**	T850 LLC		

TN 954–1000 *Dennis Trident 2 SFD113BR1YGX2   Plaxton President 9.9m   H39/23D   2001
*(TN 984–1000 are SFD113BR21GX2)

TN 954	X954 HLT	TN 964	X964 HLT	TN 974	X974 HLT	TN 984	Y984 NLP	TN 994	Y994 NLP
TN 955	X611 HLT	TN 965	X965 HLT	TN 975	X975 HLT	TN 985	Y985 NLP	TN 995	Y995 NLP
TN 956	X956 HLT	TN 966	X966 HLT	TN 976	Y223 NLF	TN 986	Y986 NLP	TN 996	Y996 NLP
TN 957	X957 HLT	TN 967	X967 HLT	TN 977	X977 HLT	TN 987	Y987 NLP	TN 997	Y997 NLP
TN 958	X958 HLT	TN 968	X968 HLT	TN 978	X978 HLT	TN 988	Y988 NLP	TN 998	Y998 NLP
TN 959	X959 HLT	TN 969	X969 HLT	TN 979	Y224 NLF	TN 989	Y989 NLP	TN 999	Y933 NLP
TN 960	X612 HLT	TN 970	X613 HLT	TN 980	X614 HLT	TN 990	Y932 NLP	TN 1000	Y934 NLP
TN 961	X961 HLT	TN 971	X971 HLT	TN 981	X981 HLT	TN 991	Y991 NLP		
TN 962	X962 HLT	TN 972	X972 HLT	TN 982	Y346 NLF	TN 992	Y992 NLP		
TN 963	X963 HLT	TN 973	X973 HLT	TN 983	Y344 NLF	TN 993	Y993 NLP		

TN 1037–1047 Dennis Trident 2 SFD   Plaxton President 9.9m   H   Due for 2001 delivery

TN 1037	TN 1040	TN 1043	TN 1046
TN 1038	TN 1041	TN 1044	TN 1047
TN 1039	TN 1042	TN 1045	

TNL 888–930 Dennis Trident 2 SFD313BR1XGX3   Plaxton President 10.5m   H43/24D   2000

TNL 888	V988 HLH	TNL 897	V897 HLH	TNL 906	W906 VLN	TNL 915	W915 VLN	TNL 924	W924 VLN
TNL 889	V889 HLH	TNL 898	V898 HLH	TNL 907	W907 VLN	TNL 916	W916 VLN	TNL 925	W898 VLN
TNL 890	V890 HLH	TNL 899	V899 HLH	TNL 908	W908 VLN	TNL 917	W917 VLN	TNL 926	W926 VLN
TNL 891	V891 HLH	TNL 900	V990 HLH	TNL 909	W909 VLN	TNL 918	W918 VLN	TNL 927	W927 VLN
TNL 892	V892 HLH	TNL 901	W901 VLN	TNL 910	W895 VLN	TNL 919	W919 VLN	TNL 928	W928 VLN
TNL 893	V893 HLH	TNL 902	W902 VLN	TNL 911	W896 VLN	TNL 920	W897 VLN	TNL 929	W929 VLN
TNL 894	V894 HLH	TNL 903	W903 VLN	TNL 912	W912 VLN	TNL 921	W921 VLN	TNL 930	W899 VLN
TNL 895	V895 HLH	TNL 904	W904 VLN	TNL 913	W913 VLN	TNL 922	W922 VLN		
TNL 896	V896 HLH	TNL 905	W905 VLN	TNL 914	W914 VLN	TNL 923	W923 VLN		

V 1–12 Volvo Olympian YN2RV18Z4   Northern Counties Palatine 11   H43/29F   1995

V 1	N301 JBV	V 4	N304 JBV	V 7	N307 JBV	V 10	N310 JBV
V 2	N302 JBV	V 5	N305 JBV	V 8	N308 JBV	V 11	N311 JBV
V 3	N303 JBV	V 6	N306 JBV	V 9	N309 JBV	V 12	N312 JBV

V 41–55 Volvo Olympian OLY–50   Northern Counties Palatine 11   H43/27F   1996

V 41	P241 UCW	V 44	P244 UCW	V 47	P247 UCW	V 50	P250 UCW	V 53	P253 UCW
V 42	P242 UCW	V 45	P245 UCW	V 48	P248 UCW	V 51	P251 UCW	V 54	P254 UCW
V 43	P243 UCW	V 46	P246 UCW	V 49	P249 UCW	V 52	P252 UCW	V 55	P255 UCW

VE 953 X578 RJW Volvo B7TL   East Lancs Vyking 10.2m   H41/22D   2000
Demonstrator on loan from Volvo UK

VN 88–107 Volvo Olympian OLY–50   Northern Counties Palatine 1   H47/27D   1999

VN 88	T988 KLF	VN 92	T892 KLF	VN 96	T896 KLF	VN 100	T990 KLF	VN 104	T904 KLF
VN 89	T889 KLF	VN 93	T893 KLF	VN 97	T897 KLF	VN 101	T901 KLF	VN 105	T905 KLF
VN 90	T890 KLF	VN 94	T894 KLF	VN 98	T898 KLF	VN 102	T902 KLF	VN 106	T906 KLF
VN 91	T891 KLF	VN 95	T895 KLF	VN 99	T899 KLF	VN 103	T903 KLF	VN 107	T907 KLF

On loan for trials:

AV 1t	Y151 ROT	Volvo B7LA	Wright Eclipse Fusion	AB56D	2001
		On loan from First Hampshire, 2001			
AV 2t	Y152 ROT	Volvo B7LA	Wright Eclipse Fusion	AB56D	2001
		On loan from First Hampshire, 2001			
AV 6	V606 GGB	Volvo B10LA	Wright Fusion	AB55D	1999
		On loan from First Glasgow, 2001			

AV 7	V607 GGB	Volvo B10LA		Wright Fusion	AB55D	1999
		On loan from First Glasgow, 2001				
AV 8	V608 GGB	Volvo B10LA		Wright Fusion	AB55D	1999
		On loan from First Glasgow, 2001				
AV 10t	V610 GGB	Volvo B10LA		Wright Fusion	AB55D	1999
		On loan from First Glasgow, 2001				

Special liveries:
The training buses are predominantly yellow.
DML 362–380 carry special Tramlink livery.
L 1–6 are in Heathrow Fast blue livery.
LC 1–3 are all white for dedicated L.B. of Richmond contract.
V 41–55 carry a special red and white livery dedicated for express route 607.
Many of the former London Buslines buses acquired during 2001 carry their former owner's livery.

Previous registration:

N633 ACF   133 CLT, N633 ACF

On order: 17 x Dennis Trident/Plaxton President for route 91.
13 x Volvo B7TL/Plaxton President for route 61.

FIRST THAMESWAY   (LT fleet only)   (Part of the First Group)

401–410			Mercedes-Benz 711D		Plaxton Beaver			B23F	1996
401	P401 HPU	**403**	P403 HPU	**405**	P405 HPU	**407**	P407 HPU	**409**	P409 HPU
402	P402 HPU	**404**	P404 HPU	**406**	P406 HPU	**408**	P408 HPU	**410**	P410 HPU

852–854			Dennis Dart 9SDL3053		Marshall C36 9m	B17FL	1995
852	N852 CPU	**853**	N853 CPU	**854**	N854 CPU		

855	S979 JLM	Dennis Dart SLF SFD612AR1WGW1	Marshall Capital 8.9m	B27FL	1998
		Ex First Eastern Counties, 2000			

On order: 12 x Optare Solo's for route 193.

HACKNEY COMMUNITY TRANSPORT   (LBSL fleet)

HDC 1–11			Dennis Dart SLF SFD212BR1YGW1		Caetano Nimbus 10.5m		B26D	2001
HDC 1	X584 ORV	**HDC 4**	X587 ORV	**HDC 7**	X591 ORV	**HDC 10**	X594 ORV	
HDC 2	X585 ORV	**HDC 5**	X588 ORV	**HDC 8**	X592 ORV	**HDC 11**	X595 ORV	
HDC 3	X586 ORV	**HDC 6**	X589 ORV	**HDC 9**	X593 ORV			

		Fiat-Ducato 3 axle		Rohill		B14FL	1999
	T157 HGT		T159 HGT	T247 FLJ		T248 FLJ	

	Y207 OEE	Renault Mascott		Rohill	B18FL	2001
	Y208 OEE	Renault Mascott		Rohill	B18FL	2001

LONDON CENTRAL & LONDON GENERAL

(Part of the Go Ahead Group)

AV 1–9		Volvo Olympian YN2RC16Z4			Alexander Royale			H45/29F	1995
AV 1	M81 MYM	AV 3	M83 MYM	AV 5	M85 MYM	AV 7	M87 MYM	AV 9	WLT 789
AV 2	M82 MYM	AV 4	M84 MYM	AV 6	M86 MYM	AV 8	M91 MYM		

AVL 1–46		Volvo B7TL			Alexander ALX400 10.1m			H43/20D	1999/2000
AVL 1	V101 LGC	AVL 11	V211 LGC	AVL 21	V221 LGC	AVL 31	V131 LGC	AVL 41	V141 LGC
AVL 2	V102 LGC	AVL 12	V112 LGC	AVL 22	V122 LGC	AVL 32	V132 LGC	AVL 42	V142 LGC
AVL 3	V103 LGC	AVL 13	V113 LGC	AVL 23	V223 LGC	AVL 33	V133 LGC	AVL 43	V143 LGC
AVL 4	V104 LGC	AVL 14	V114 LGC	AVL 24	V124 LGC	AVL 34	V134 LGC	AVL 44	V144 LGC
AVL 5	V105 LGC	AVL 15	V115 LGC	AVL 25	V125 LGC	AVL 35	V135 LGC	AVL 45	V145 LGC
AVL 6	V106 LGC	AVL 16	V116 LGC	AVL 26	V126 LGC	AVL 36	V136 LGC	AVL 46	46 CLT
AVL 7	V107 LGC	AVL 17	V117 LGC	AVL 27	V127 LGC	AVL 37	V137 LGC		
AVL 8	V108 LGC	AVL 18	V118 LGC	AVL 28	V128 LGC	AVL 38	V138 LGC		
AVL 9	V109 LGC	AVL 19	V119 LGC	AVL 29	V129 LGC	AVL 39	V139 LGC		
AVL 10	V110 LGC	AVL 20	V120 LGC	AVL 30	V130 LGC	AVL 40	V140 LGC		

DML 1–29		Dennis Dart SLF SFD112BR1XGW1			Marshall Capital 9.3m			B30F	1999
DML 1	T401 AGP	DML 7	T407 AGP	DML 13	T413 AGP	DML 19	T499 AGP	DML 25	T425 AGP
DML 2	T402 AGP	DML 8	T408 AGP	DML 14	T414 AGP	DML 20	T392 AGP	DML 26	T426 AGP
DML 3	T403 AGP	DML 9	T409 AGP	DML 15	T415 AGP	DML 21	T421 AGP	DML 27	T427 AGP
DML 4	T404 AGP	DML 10	T410 AGP	DML 16	T416 AGP	DML 22	T422 AGP	DML 28	T428 AGP
DML 5	T405 AGP	DML 11	T411 AGP	DML 17	T417 AGP	DML 23	T423 AGP	DML 29	T429 AGP
DML 6	T406 AGP	DML 12	T512 AGP	DML 18	T418 AGP	DML 24	T424 AGP		

DMS 1–15		Dennis Dart SLF SFD612BR1WGW1			Marshall Capital 8.9m			B28F	1999
DMS 1	T101 KGP	DMS 4	T104 KGP	DMS 7	T107 KGP	DMS 10	T110 KGP	DMS 13	T113 KGP
DMS 2	T102 KGP	DMS 5	T105 KGP	DMS 8	T108 KGP	DMS 11	101 CLT	DMS 14	T114 KGP
DMS 3	T103 KGP	DMS 6	T106 KGP	DMS 9	T109 KGP	DMS 12	T112 KGP	DMS 15	T115 KGP

DPL 1–16		Dennis Dart 9SDL3053			Plaxton Pointer 9m			B35F	1995
DPL 1	M201 EGF	DPL 5	M205 EGF	DPL 9	M209 EGF	DPL 13	M213 EGF		
DPL 2	M202 EGF	DPL 6	M206 EGF	DPL 10	M210 EGF	DPL 14	M214 EGF		
DPL 3	M203 EGF	DPL 7	M207 EGF	DPL 11	M211 EGF	DPL 15	M215 EGF		
DPL 4	M204 EGF	DPL 8	M208 EGF	DPL 12	M212 EGF	DPL 16	M216 EGF		

DR 38–52		Dennis Dart 8.5SDL3003 Ex London Buses, 1994			Plaxton Pointer 8.5 m			B28F	1991
DR 38w	H538 XGK	DR 43w	H543 XGK	DR 46w	H546 XGK	DR 49w	H549 XGK		
DR 39w	H539 XGK	DR 44w	H544 XGK	DR 47w	H547 XGK	DR 51w	H551 XGK		
DR 41w	H541 XGK	DR 45w	H545 XGK	DR 48w	H548 XGK	DR 52w	H552 XGK		

DR 149–153		Dennis Dart 8.5SDL3015 Ex London Buses, 1994			Plaxton Pointer 8.5 m			B28F	1992
DR 149w	K149 LGO	DR 150w	K150 LGO	DR 151	K151 LGO	DR 152	K152 LGO	DR 153	K153 LGO

DRL 53–73		Dennis Dart 9SDL3016 Ex London Buses, 1994			Plaxton Pointer 9m			B34F	1992
DRL 53	K853 LGN	DRL 57	K857 LGN	DRL 61	K861 LGN	DRL 65	K865 LGN	DRL 69w	K869 LGN
DRL 54	K854 LGN	DRL 58	K858 LGN	DRL 62	K862 LGN	DRL 66	K866 LGN	DRL 70	K870 LGN
DRL 55w	K855 LGN	DRL 59	K859 LGN	DRL 63	K863 LGN	DRL 67	K867 LGN	DRL 72	K872 LGN
DRL 56	K856 LGN	DRL 60	K860 LGN	DRL 64	K864 LGN	DRL 68	K868 LGN	DRL 73	K873 LGN

DRL 74–95   Dennis Dart 9SDL3024   Plaxton Pointer 9m   B32F   1993
Ex London Buses, 1994

DRL 74	K574 MGT	**DRL 78**	K578 MGT	**DRL 82**	K582 MGT	**DRL 87**	K587 MGT	**DRL 93**	K593 MGT
DRL 75	K575 MGT	**DRL 79**	K579 MGT	**DRL 83**	K583 MGT	**DRL 90u**	K590 MGT	**DRL 94**	K767 OGK
DRL 76	K576 MGT	**DRL 80**	K580 MGT	**DRL 84**	K584 MGT	**DRL 91**	K591 MGT	**DRL 95**	WLT 395
DRL 77	K577 MGT	**DRL 81**	K581 MGT	**DRL 85**	K585 MGT	**DRL 92**	K592 MGT		

DW 44–58   Dennis Dart 8.5SDL3003   Wright Handybus 8.5m   B30F   1990/1
Ex London Buses, 1994

DW 44w	JDZ 2344	**DW 48w**	G551 SGT	**DW 55w**	JDZ 2355	**DW 56w**	JDZ 2356	**DW 58w** JDZ 2358

DW 128–132   Dennis Dart 8.5SDL3015   Wright Handybus 8.5m   B30F   1992/3
Ex London Buses, 1994

DW 128w	K128 LGO	**DW 131w**	K131 LGO	**DW 132w**	K132 LGO

GLS 438–506   Leyland National 2 NL106AL11/2R   East Lancs Greenway (1992–4)   *B24D   1981
Ex London Buses, 1994   *(GLS 448, 483–87/96 are B38D, 459 & 473 are B36D)

GLS 438	GUW 438W	**GLS 450**	GUW 450W	**GLS 471**	GUW 471W	**GLS 481**	GUW 481W	**GLS 498** WLT 598
GLS 439	GUW 439W	**GLS 452**	GUW 452W	**GLS 473**	GUW 473W	**GLS 483**	83 CLT	**GLS 499** GUW 499W
GLS 440	GUW 440W	**GLS 455**	GUW 455W	**GLS 474**	GUW 474W	**GLS 487**	WLT 487	**GLS 500** GUW 500W
GLS 442	GUW 442W	**GLS 459**	GUW 459W	**GLS 476**	GUW 476W	**GLS 490**	GUW 490W	**GLS 501w** GUW 501W
GLS 443	WLT 843	**GLS 460**	GUW 460W	**GLS 477**	GUW 477W	**GLS 491**	GUW 491W	**GLS 502** GUW 502W
GLS 446	GUW 446W	**GLS 467**	WLT 467	**GLS 478**	GUW 478W	**GLS 492**	GUW 492W	**GLS 505** GUW 505W
GLS 448	WLT 648	**GLS 468**	GUW 468W	**GLS 479**	GUW 479W	**GLS 493**	GUW 493W	**GLS 506** GUW 506W
GLS 449	GUW 449W	**GLS 469**	GUW 469W	**GLS 480w**	VLT 180	**GLS 496**	WLT 696		

LDP 1–17   Dennis Dart SLF SFD112BR1TGW1   Plaxton Pointer 9.2m   B32F   1996

LDP 1	P501 RYM	**LDP 5**	P505 RYM	**LDP 9**	WLT 379	**LDP 13**	P513 RYM	**LDP 17** P517 RYM
LDP 2	P502 RYM	**LDP 6**	P506 RYM	**LDP 10**	P510 RYM	**LDP 14**	P514 RYM	
LDP 3	P503 RYM	**LDP 7**	P507 RYM	**LDP 11**	P511 RYM	**LDP 15**	P515 RYM	
LDP 4	P504 RYM	**LDP 8**	188 CLT	**LDP 12**	P512 RYM	**LDP 16**	P516 RYM	

LDP 18–44   Dennis Dart SLF SFD212BR1TGW1   Plaxton Pointer 10m   B36F   1996

LDP 18	P718 RYL	**LDP 24**	P724 RYL	**LDP 30**	P730 RYL	**LDP 36**	P736 RYL	**LDP 42** P742 RYL
LDP 19	P719 RYL	**LDP 25**	P725 RYL	**LDP 31**	P731 RYL	**LDP 37**	P737 RYL	**LDP 43** P743 RYL
LDP 20	P720 RYL	**LDP 26**	P726 RYL	**LDP 32**	P732 RYL	**LDP 38**	P738 RYL	**LDP 44** P744 RYL
LDP 21	P721 RYL	**LDP 27**	P727 RYL	**LDP 33**	P733 RYL	**LDP 39**	P739 RYL	
LDP 22	P722 RYL	**LDP 28**	P728 RYL	**LDP 34**	P734 RYL	**LDP 40**	P740 RYL	
LDP 23	P723 RYL	**LDP 29**	P729 RYL	**LDP 35**	P735 RYL	**LDP 41**	P741 RYL	

LDP 45–89   Dennis Dart SLF SFD212BR1VGW1   Plaxton Pointer 10m   B35F   1997

LDP 45	R445 LGH	**LDP 55**	R455 LGH	**LDP 64**	R464 LGH	**LDP 73**	R473 LGH	**LDP 83** R483 LGH
LDP 46	R446 LGH	**LDP 56**	R456 LGH	**LDP 65**	R465 LGH	**LDP 74**	174 CLT	**LDP 84** R484 LGH
LDP 47	R447 LGH	**LDP 57**	R457 LGH	**LDP 66**	R466 LGH	**LDP 75**	R475 LGH	**LDP 85** R485 LGH
LDP 48	R448 LGH	**LDP 58**	R458 LGH	**LDP 67**	R467 LGH	**LDP 76**	176 CLT	**LDP 86** R486 LGH
LDP 49	R449 LGH	**LDP 59**	R459 LGH	**LDP 68**	R468 LGH	**LDP 77**	R477 LGH	**LDP 87** R487 LGH
LDP 51	R451 LGH	**LDP 60**	R460 LGH	**LDP 69**	R469 LGH	**LDP 78**	R478 LGH	**LDP 88** R488 LGH
LDP 52	R452 LGH	**LDP 61**	R461 LGH	**LDP 70**	R470 LGH	**LDP 79**	R479 LGH	**LDP 89** R489 LGH
LDP 53	R453 LGH	**LDP 62**	R462 LGH	**LDP 71**	R471 LGH	**LDP 81**	R481 LGH	
LDP 54	R454 LGH	**LDP 63**	R463 LGH	**LDP 72**	WLT 872	**LDP 82**	R482 LGH	

LDP 90–117   Dennis Dart SLF SFD212AR1WGW1   Plaxton Pointer 2 10.1m   B29D   1998/9

LDP 90 S638 JGP	**LDP 96** S96 EGK	**LDP 103** S103 EGK	**LDP 109** S109 EGK	**LDP 115** S115 EGK
LDP 91 S91 EGK	**LDP 97** S97 EGK	**LDP 104** S104 EGK	**LDP 110** S110 EGK	**LDP 116** S116 EGK
LDP 92 S92 EGK	**LDP 98** S98 EGK	**LDP 105** S105 EGK	**LDP 111** WLT 311	**LDP 117** S117 EGK
LDP 93 S93 EGK	**LDP 99** WLT 599	**LDP 106** S106 EGK	**LDP 112** S112 EGK	
LDP 94 S94 EGK	**LDP 101** S101 EGK	**LDP 107** S107 EGK	**LDP 113** S113 EGK	
LDP 95 S95 EGK	**LDP 102** S102 EGK	**LDP 108** S108 EGK	**LDP 114** S114 EGK	

LDP 118–128   Dennis Dart SLF SFD212AR1WGW1   Plaxton Pointer 2 10.1m   B31D   1999

LDP 118 T118 KGP	**LDP 121** T121 KGP	**LDP 124** T124 KGP	**LDP 127** T127 KGP
LDP 119 T119 KGP	**LDP 122** T122 KGP	**LDP 125** T125 KGP	**LDP 128** T128 KGP
LDP 120 T110 KGP	**LDP 123** T123 KGP	**LDP 126** T126 KGP	

LDP 129–133   Dennis Dart SLF SFD612BR1YGW1   Plaxton Pointer 2 8.8m   B29F   2001

LDP 129 Y829 TGH	**LDP 130** Y803 TGH	**LDP 131** Y831 TGH	**LDP 132** Y832 TGH	**LDP 133** Y833 TGH

LDP 134–141   Dennis Dart SLF SFD322BR1YGW1   Plaxton Pointer 2 10.7m   B31D   2001

LDP 134 Y834 LGH	**LDP 136** Y836 LGH	**LDP 138** Y838 LGH	**LDP 140** Y840 LGH
LDP 135 Y835 LGH	**LDP 137** Y837 LGH	**LDP 139** Y839 LGH	**LDP 141** Y841 LGH

LDP 142–148   Dennis Dart SLF SFD612AR1YGW1   Plaxton Pointer 2 8.8m   B29F   2001

LDP 142 Y842 TGH	**LDP 144** Y844 TGH	**LDP 146** Y846 TGH	**LDP 148** Y848 TGH
LDP 143 Y843 TGH	**LDP 145** Y845 TGH	**LDP 147** Y847 TGH	

LDP 149–152   Dennis Dart SLF SFD612AR11GW1   Plaxton Pointer 2 8.8m   B29F   Due for 2001 delivery

LDP 149	**LDP 150**	**LDP 151**	**LDP 152**

LDP 153–190   Dennis Dart SLF SFD112AR11GW1   Plaxton Pointer 2 9.3m   B29F   2001

LDP 153 Y853 TGH	**LDP 161** Y861 TGH	**LDP 169** Y969 TGH	**LDP 177** Y977 TGH	**LDP 185** Y985 TGH
LDP 154 Y854 TGH	**LDP 162** Y862 TGH	**LDP 170** Y907 TGH	**LDP 178** Y978 TGH	**LDP 186** Y986 TGH
LDP 155 Y705 TGH	**LDP 163** Y863 TGH	**LDP 171** Y971 TGH	**LDP 179** Y979 TGH	**LDP 187** Y987 TGH
LDP 156 Y856 TGH	**LDP 164** Y864 TGH	**LDP 172** Y972 TGH	**LDP 180** Y908 TGH	**LDP 188** Y988 TGH
LDP 157 Y857 TGH	**LDP 165** Y865 TGH	**LDP 173** Y973 TGH	**LDP 181** Y981 TGH	**LDP 189** Y989 TGH
LDP 158 Y858 TGH	**LDP 166** Y866 TGH	**LDP 174** Y974 TGH	**LDP 182** Y982 TGH	**LDP 190** Y909 TGH
LDP 159 Y859 TGH	**LDP 167** Y967 TGH	**LDP 175** Y975 TGH	**LDP 183** Y983 TGH	
LDP 160 Y806 TGH	**LDP 168** Y968 TGH	**LDP 176** Y976 TGH	**LDP 184** Y984 TGH	

OM 171 VLT 71	MCW Metrobus DR101/9	MCW		O43/27D	1979
	Ex London Buses, 1994				
M 196 BYX 196V	MCW Metrobus DR101/9	MCW		H43/28D	1979
	Ex London Buses, 1994				
M 198t SGK 374V	MCW Metrobus DR101/9	MCW		H43/28D	1979
	Ex London Buses, 1994				
M 202t BYX 202V	MCW Metrobus DR101/9	MCW		H43/28D	1979
	Ex London Buses, 1994				
OM 241 BYX 241V	MCW Metrobus DR101/12	MCW		O43/27F	1980
	Ex London Buses, 1994				
OM 420 GYE 420W	MCW Metrobus DR101/12	MCW		O43/28D	1980
	Ex London Buses, 1994				
M 472 GYE 472W	MCW Metrobus DR101/12	MCW		H43/28D	1980
	Ex London Buses, 1994				
M 475 GYE 475W	MCW Metrobus DR101/12	MCW		H43/28D	1980
	Ex London Buses, 1994				
M 490t GYE 490W	MCW Metrobus DR101/12	MCW		H43/28D	1980
	Ex London Buses, 1994				

| M 808–953 | | MCW Metrobus DR101/16 | | MCW | | | | H43/28D | 1983 |
| | | Ex London Buses, 1994 | | | | | | | |

| M 808 | OJD 808Y | M 880 | OJD 880Y | M 905w | A905 SUL | M 922w | A922 SUL | M 944 | A944 SUL |
| M 818 | OJD 818Y | M 904 | A904 SUL | M 908 | A908 SUL | M 923t | A923 SUL | M 953 | A953 SUL |

| M 975–1440 | | MCW Metrobus DR101/17 | | MCW | | | | *H43/28D | 1984–6 |
| | | Ex London Buses, 1994 | | *(1435/40 are DPH43/28D) | | | | | |

M 975	A975 SYF	M 1196	B196 WUL	M 1235	B235 WUL	M 1315	C109 NGH	M 1388	C388 BUV
M 976t	A976 SYF	M 1203	B203 WUL	M 1237	B237 WUL	M 1337	C337 BUV	M 1389t	89 CLT
M 977	A977 SYF	M 1211	B211 WUL	M 1264w	B264 WUL	M 1347	C347 BUV	M 1391	C391 BUV
M 978t	A978 SYF	M 1215	B215 WUL	M 1301	B301 WUL	M 1357	C357 BUV	M 1410t	C410 BUV
M 1046	A746 THV	M 1220t	B220 WUL	M 1302	B302 WUL	M 1370	C370 BUV	M 1411t	C411 BUV
M 1055t	A755 THV	M 1224	B224 WUL	M 1304	304 CLT	M 1371t	C371 BUV	M 1434t	WLT 434
M 1107	B107 WUL	M 1225	B225 WUL	M 1305	B305 WUL	M 1372t	772 DYE	M 1435	435 CLT
M 1177	B177 WUL	M 1226	B226 WUL	M 1306	C306 BUV	M 1373t	C373 BUV	M 1436t	VLT 136
M 1180	B180 WUL	M 1230	B230 WUL	M 1311	C311 BUV	M 1387	C387 BUV	M 1440	C440 BUV

| MD 1–17 | | *DAF DE02GSSB220 | | East Lancs Myllennium 12m | | | | B33D | 1999 |
| | | *(MD 8–10 are DE02GGSB220) | | | | | | | |

MD 1	V1 GMT	MD 5	V5 GMT	MD 9	V9 GMT	MD 13	V13 GMT	MD 17	V17 GMT
MD 2	V2 GMT	MD 6	V6 GMT	MD 10	V10 GMT	MD 14	V14 GMT		
MD 3	V3 GMT	MD 7	V7 GMT	MD 11	V11 GMT	MD 15	V15 GMT		
MD 4	V4 GMT	MD 8	V8 GMT	MD 12	V12 GMT	MD 16	V16 GMT		

| NV 1–27 | | Volvo Olympian YN2RV18Z4 | | Northern Counties Palatine I | | | | H47/30F | 1995 |

NV 1	M401 RVU	NV 6	M406 RVU	NV 14	N414 JBV	NV 19	N419 JBV	NV 24	N424 JBV
NV 2	M402 RVU	NV 7	M407 RVU	NV 15	WLT 815	NV 20	N420 JBV	NV 25	N425 JBV
NV 3	M403 RVU	NV 11	N411 JBV	NV 16	N416 JBV	NV 21	N421 JBV	NV 26	N426 JBV
NV 4	M404 RVU	NV 12	N412 JBV	NV 17	N417 JBV	NV 22	N422 JBV	NV 27	WLT 527
NV 5	M405 RVU	NV 13	N413 JBV	NV 18	N418 JBV	NV 23	N423 JBV		

| NV 29–48 | | Volvo Olympian YN2RV18Z4 | | Northern Counties Palatine I | | | | H48/27D | 1996 |

| NV 29 | VLT 29 | NV 36 | N536 LHG | NV 44 | N544 LHG | NV 46 | N546 LHG | NV 48 | N548 LHG |
| NV 34 | N534 LHG | NV 43 | N543 LHG | NV 45 | N545 LHG | NV 47 | N547 LHG | | |

| NV 49–99 | | Volvo Olympian OLY–4953 | | Northern Counties Palatine I | | | | *H47/27D | 1997/8 |
| | | *(NV 58 & 60 are DPH47/27D) | | | | | | | |

NV 49	P549 WGT	NV 59	R259 LGH	NV 69	R269 LGH	NV 79	R279 LGH	NV 90	R390 LGH
NV 50	P550 WGT	NV 60	260 CLT	NV 70	R270 LGH	NV 81	R281 LGH	NV 91	R391 LGH
NV 51	R251 LGH	NV 61	R261 LGH	NV 71	R271 LGH	NV 82	R282 LGH	NV 92	R392 LGH
NV 52	R252 LGH	NV 62	R262 LGH	NV 72	R272 LGH	NV 83	R283 LGH	NV 93	R393 LGH
NV 53	R253 LGH	NV 63	R263 LGH	NV 73	R273 LGH	NV 84	R284 LGH	NV 94	R394 LGH
NV 54	R254 LGH	NV 64	R264 LGH	NV 74	R274 LGH	NV 85	R285 LGH	NV 95	R395 LGH
NV 55	R255 LGH	NV 65	R265 LGH	NV 75	R275 LGH	NV 86	R286 LGH	NV 96	R396 LGH
NV 56	R256 LGH	NV 66	R266 LGH	NV 76	R276 LGH	NV 87	R287 LGH	NV 97	R397 LGH
NV 57	R257 LGH	NV 67	R267 LGH	NV 77	R277 LGH	NV 88	R288 LGH	NV 98	R398 LGH
NV 58	R258 LGH	NV 68	WLT 868	NV 78	R278 LGH	NV 89	R389 LGH	NV 99	R399 LGH

NV 101–159 *Volvo Olympian YN2RV18Z4 Northern Counties Palatine I *H47/27D 1997/8
*(NV 131–159 are Volvo Olympian OLY–4953. NV 146 is DP47/27D)

NV 101 P901 RYO	**NV 113** P913 RYO	**NV 125** P925 RYO	**NV 137** R337 LGH	**NV 150** R550 LGH
NV 102 P902 RYO	**NV 114** P914 RYO	**NV 126** P926 RYO	**NV 138** R338 LGH	**NV 151** R551 LGH
NV 103 P903 RYO	**NV 115** P915 RYO	**NV 127** P927 RYO	**NV 139** R339 LGH	**NV 152** 352 CLT
NV 104 P904 RYO	**NV 116** P916 RYO	**NV 128** P928 RYO	**NV 141** R341 LGH	**NV 153** R553 LGH
NV 105 P905 RYO	**NV 117** P917 RYO	**NV 129** P929 RYO	**NV 142** R342 LGH	**NV 154** R554 LGH
NV 106 P906 RYO	**NV 118** P918 RYO	**NV 130** P930 RYO	**NV 143** R343 LGH	**NV 155** R355 LGH
NV 107 P907 RYO	**NV 119** 19 CLT	**NV 131** R331 LGH	**NV 144** R344 LGH	**NV 156** R556 LGH
NV 108 698 DYE	**NV 120** P920 RYO	**NV 132** R332 LGH	**NV 145** 545 CLT	**NV 157** R557 LGH
NV 109 P909 RYO	**NV 121** P921 RYO	**NV 133** R433 LGH	**NV 146** WLT 346	**NV 158** R558 LGH
NV 110 P910 RYO	**NV 122** P922 RYO	**NV 134** R334 LGH	**NV 147** R347 LGH	**NV 159** R559 LGH
NV 111 P911 RYO	**NV 123** P923 RYO	**NV 135** R335 LGH	**NV 148** WLT 548	
NV 112 P912 RYO	**NV 124** P924 RYO	**NV 136** R336 LGH	**NV 149** R549 LGH	

NV 161–187 Volvo Olympian OLY–4953 Northern Counties Palatine II DPH47/26D 1997/8

NV 161 R361 LGH	**NV 167** R367 LGH	**NV 173** R373 LGH	**NV 179** VLT 179	**NV 185** R385 LGH
NV 162 R362 LGH	**NV 168** R368 LGH	**NV 174** R374 LGH	**NV 180** R380 LGH	**NV 186** R386 LGH
NV 163 R363 LGH	**NV 169** R369 LGH	**NV 175** R375 LGH	**NV 181** R381 LGH	**NV 187** 197 CLT
NV 164 R364 LGH	**NV 170** WLT 470	**NV 176** R376 LGH	**NV 182** R382 LGH	
NV 165 R365 LGH	**NV 171** R371 LGH	**NV 177** VLT 277	**NV 183** R383 LGH	
NV 166 166 CLT	**NV 172** R372 LGH	**NV 178** 78 CLT	**NV 184** VLT 284	

PDL 1–13 Dennis Trident 2 SFD111BR1YGX2 Plaxton President 9.9m H41/23D 2000

PDL 1 X601 EGK	**PDL 4** X604 EGK	**PDL 7** X607 EGK	**PDL 10** X701 EGK	**PDL 13** X613 EGK
PDL 2 X602 EGK	**PDL 5** X605 EGK	**PDL 8** X608 EGK	**PDL 11** X611 EGK	
PDL 3 X603 EGK	**PDL 6** X606 EGK	**PDL 9** X609 EGK	**PDL 12** X612 EGK	

PVL 1–143 Volvo B7TL Plaxton President 10m H41/21D 2000

PVL 1 V301 LGC	**PVL 30** V330 LGC	**PVL 59** W459 WGH	**PVL 88** W488 WGH	**PVL 117** W517 WGH
PVL 2 V302 LGC	**PVL 31** V331 LGC	**PVL 60** W996 WGH	**PVL 89** W489 WGH	**PVL 118** W518 WGH
PVL 3 V303 LGC	**PVL 32** WLT 532	**PVL 61** W461 WGH	**PVL 90** W409 WGH	**PVL 119** W519 WGH
PVL 4 V304 LGC	**PVL 33** V233 LGC	**PVL 62** W462 WGH	**PVL 91** W491 WGH	**PVL 120** W402 WGH
PVL 5 V305 LGC	**PVL 34** V334 LGC	**PVL 63** W463 WGH	**PVL 92** W492 WGH	**PVL 121** W521 WGH
PVL 6 V306 LGC	**PVL 35** V335 LGC	**PVL 64** W464 WGH	**PVL 93** W493 WGH	**PVL 122** W522 WGH
PVL 7 V307 LGC	**PVL 36** V336 LGC	**PVL 65** W465 WGH	**PVL 94** W494 WGH	**PVL 123** W523 WGH
PVL 8 V308 LGC	**PVL 37** V337 LGC	**PVL 66** W466 WGH	**PVL 95** W495 WGH	**PVL 124** W524 WGH
PVL 9 V209 LGC	**PVL 38** V338 LGC	**PVL 67** W467 WGH	**PVL 96** W496 WGH	**PVL 125** W425 WGH
PVL 10 V310 LGC	**PVL 39** W439 WGH	**PVL 68** W468 WGH	**PVL 97** W497 WGH	**PVL 126** W526 WGH
PVL 11 V311 LGC	**PVL 40** W440 WGH	**PVL 69** W469 WGH	**PVL 98** W498 WGH	**PVL 127** W527 WGH
PVL 12 V312 LGC	**PVL 41** W441WGH	**PVL 70** 170 CLT	**PVL 99** W399 WGH	**PVL 128** W428 WGH
PVL 13 V313 LGC	**PVL 42** W442 WGH	**PVL 71** W471 WGH	**PVL 100** W997 WGH	**PVL 129** W529 WGH
PVL 14 V314 LGC	**PVL 43** W443 WGH	**PVL 72** W472 WGH	**PVL 101** W501 WGH	**PVL 130** W403 WGH
PVL 15 V315 LGC	**PVL 44** W544 WGH	**PVL 73** W473 WGH	**PVL 102** W502 WGH	**PVL 131** W531 WGH
PVL 16 V816 KGF	**PVL 45** W445 WGH	**PVL 74** W474 WGH	**PVL 103** W503 WGH	**PVL 132** W532 WGH
PVL 17 V317 LGC	**PVL 46** W446 WGH	**PVL 75** W475 WGH	**PVL 104** W504 WGH	**PVL 133** W533 WGH
PVL 18 V218 LGC	**PVL 47** W447 WGH	**PVL 76** W476 WGH	**PVL 105** W905 WGH	**PVL 134** W534 WGH
PVL 19 V319 LGC	**PVL 48** W448 WGH	**PVL 77** W477 WGH	**PVL 106** W506 WGH	**PVL 135** W435 WGH
PVL 20 V220 LGC	**PVL 49** W449 WGH	**PVL 78** W478 WGH	**PVL 107** W507 WGH	**PVL 136** W536 WGH
PVL 21 V921 KGF	**PVL 50** W499 WGH	**PVL 79** W479 WGH	**PVL 108** W508 WGH	**PVL 137** W537 WGH
PVL 22 V322 LGC	**PVL 51** W451 WGH	**PVL 80** W408 WGH	**PVL 109** W509 WGH	**PVL 138** W538 WGH
PVL 23 V923 KGF	**PVL 52** W452 WGH	**PVL 81** W481 WGH	**PVL 110** W401 WGH	**PVL 139** W539 WGH
PVL 24 V324 LGC	**PVL 53** W453 WGH	**PVL 82** W482 WGH	**PVL 111** W511 WGH	**PVL 140** W404 WGH
PVL 25 V325 LGC	**PVL 54** W454 WGH	**PVL 83** W483 WGH	**PVL 112** W512 WGH	**PVL 141** W541 WGH
PVL 26 V226 LGC	**PVL 55** W998 WGH	**PVL 84** W484 WGH	**PVL 113** W513 WGH	**PVL 142** W542 WGH
PVL 27 V327 LGC	**PVL 56** W956 WGH	**PVL 85** W485 WGH	**PVL 114** W514 WGH	**PVL 143** W543 WGH
PVL 28 V228 LGC	**PVL 57** W457 WGH	**PVL 86** W486 WGH	**PVL 115** W415 WGH	
PVL 29 V329 LGC	**PVL 58** W458 WGH	**PVL 87** W487 WGH	**PVL 116** W516 WGH	

PVL 144–249 — Volvo B7TL — Plaxton President 10m — H41/23D — 2000–1

PVL 144 X544 EGK	PVL 166 X566 EGK	PVL 188 X588 EGK	PVL 210 Y801 TGH	PVL 232 Y732 TGH
PVL 145 X745 EGK	PVL 167 X567 EGK	PVL 189 X589 EGK	PVL 211 Y811 TGH	PVL 233 Y733 TGH
PVL 146 X546 EGK	PVL 168 X568 EGK	PVL 190 X509 EGK	PVL 212 Y812 TGH	PVL 234 Y734 TGH
PVL 147 X547 EGK	PVL 169 X569 EGK	PVL 191 X591 EGK	PVL 213 Y813 TGH	PVL 235 Y735 TGH
PVL 148 X548 EGK	PVL 170 X707 EGK	PVL 192 X592 EGK	PVL 214 Y814 TGH	PVL 236 Y736 TGH
PVL 149 X549 EGK	PVL 171 X571 EGK	PVL 193 X593 EGK	PVL 215 Y815 TGH	PVL 237 Y737 TGH
PVL 150 X599 EGK	PVL 172 X572 EGK	PVL 194 X594 EGK	PVL 216 Y816 TGH	PVL 238 Y738 TGH
PVL 151 X551 EGK	PVL 173 X573 EGK	PVL 195 X595 EGK	PVL 217 Y817 TGH	PVL 239 Y739 TGH
PVL 152 X552 EGK	PVL 174 X574 EGK	PVL 196 X596 EGK	PVL 218 Y818 TGH	PVL 240 Y704 TGH
PVL 153 X553 EGK	PVL 175 X676 EGK	PVL 197 X597 EGK	PVL 219 Y819 TGH	PVL 241 Y741 TGH
PVL 154 X554 EGK	PVL 176 X576 EGK	PVL 198 X598 EGK	PVL 220 Y802 TGH	PVL 242 Y742 TGH
PVL 155 X615 EGK	PVL 177 X577 EGK	PVL 199 X699 EGK	PVL 221 Y821 TGH	PVL 243 Y743 TGH
PVL 156 X556 EGK	PVL 178 X578 EGK	PVL 200 X502 EGK	PVL 222 Y822 TGH	PVL 244 Y744 TGH
PVL 157 X557 EGK	PVL 179 X579 EGK	PVL 201 X501 EGK	PVL 223 Y823 TGH	PVL 245 Y745 TGH
PVL 158 X558 EGK	PVL 180 X508 EGK	PVL 202 X702 EGK	PVL 224 Y824 TGH	PVL 246 Y746 TGH
PVL 159 X559 EGK	PVL 181 X581 EGK	PVL 203 X503 EGK	PVL 225 Y825 TGH	PVL 247 Y747 TGH
PVL 160 X616 EGK	PVL 182 X582 EGK	PVL 204 X504 EGK	PVL 226 Y826 TGH	PVL 248 Y748 TGH
PVL 161 X561 EGK	PVL 183 X583 EGK	PVL 205 X705 EGK	PVL 227 Y827 TGH	PVL 249 Y749 TGH
PVL 162 X562 EGK	PVL 184 X584 EGK	PVL 206 X506 EGK	PVL 228 Y828 TGH	
PVL 163 X563 EGK	PVL 185 X585 EGK	PVL 207 X507 EGK	PVL 229 Y729 TGH	
PVL 164 X564 EGK	PVL 186 X586 EGK	PVL 208 Y808 TGH	PVL 230 Y703 TGH	
PVL 165 X656 EGK	PVL 187 X587 EGK	PVL 209 Y809 TGH	PVL 231 Y731 TGH	

RM 9–2151 — AEC Routemaster R2RH — Park Royal — H36/28R — 1959–65

*Ex London Buses, 1994
*(RM 838, 1640 ex Reading Mainline, 2000. RM 875 ex Stagecoach Cumberland, 2000. RM 1280, 1312 ex preservation, 2000)

RM 9 VLT 9	RM 838 XYJ 440	RM 1082 82 CLT	RM 1312 MFF 509	RM 1977 ALD 977B
RM 202 VLT 202	RM 875 OVS 940	RM 1097 97 CLT	RM 1380 380 CLT	RM 1980 ALD 980B
RM 436 WLT 436	RM 928 WLT 928	RM 1104 104 CLT	RM 1400 KGJ 339A	RM 2022 ALM 22B
RM 478 WLT 478	RM 967 WLT 967	RM 1119 119 CLT	RM 1621 KGJ 187A	RM 2051 ALM 51B
RM 541 WLT 51	RM 994 WLT 994	RM 1168 168 CLT	RM 1640 640 DYE	RM 2106 CUV 106C
RM 687 WLT 687	RM 1002 OYM 368A	RM 1174 JSJ 797	RM 1666 KGJ 341A	RM 2109 CUV 109C
RM 758 WLT 758	RM 1033 33 CLT	RM 1260 JSJ 743	RM 1797 797 DYE	RM 2128 CUV 128C
RM 782 WLT 782	RM 1058 58 CLT	RM 1280 280 CLT	RM 1955 ALD 955B	RM 2151 CUV 151C
RM 787 WLT 787	RM 1062 62 CLT	RM 1305 305 CLT	RM 1962 ALD 962B	

RML 883–899 — AEC Routemaster R2RH — Park Royal — H40/32R — 1961

Ex London Buses, 1994

RML 883 WLT 883	RML 887 WLT 887	RML 889 WLT 889	RML 894 WLT 894	RML 899 WLT 899

RML 2262–2752 — AEC Routemaster R2RH/1 — Park Royal — *H40/32R — 1965–68

Ex London Buses, 1994   *(RML 2516 is H40/32RD and carries fleet number DRM 2516)

RML 2262 CUV 262C	RML 2316 CUV 316C	RML 2361 CUV 361C	RML 2411 JJD 411D	RML 2482 JJD 482D
RML 2263 CUV 263C	RML 2317 CUV 317C	RML 2362 CUV 362C	RML 2412 JJD 412D	RML 2484 JJD 484D
RML 2270 CUV 270C	RML 2318 CUV 318C	RML 2363 CUV 363C	RML 2422 JJD 422D	RML 2499 JJD 499D
RML 2271 CUV 271C	RML 2321 CUV 321C	RML 2364 JJD 364D	RML 2440 JJD 440D	RML 2502 JJD 502D
RML 2273 CUV 273C	RML 2327 CUV 327C	RML 2371 JJD 371D	RML 2441 JJD 441D	RML 2507 JJD 507D
RML 2275 CUV 275C	RML 2332 CUV 332C	RML 2376 JJD 376D	RML 2453 JJD 453D	RML 2513 JJD 513D
RML 2276 CUV 276C	RML 2335 CUV 335C	RML 2381 JJD 381D	RML 2454 JJD 454D	RML 2515 JJD 515D
RML 2279 CUV 279C	RML 2336 CUV 336C	RML 2385 JJD 385D	RML 2461 JJD 461D	DRM 2516 WLT 516
RML 2283 CUV 283C	RML 2338 CUV 338C	RML 2389 JJD 389D	RML 2465 JJD 465D	RML 2517 JJD 517D
RML 2290 CUV 290C	RML 2339 CUV 339C	RML 2396 JJD 396D	RML 2466 JJD 466D	RML 2520 JJD 520D
RML 2297 CUV 297C	RML 2342 CUV 342C	RML 2397 JJD 397D	RML 2469 JJD 469D	RML 2529 JJD 529D
RML 2302 CUV 302C	RML 2345 CUV 345C	RML 2398 JJD 398D	RML 2472 JJD 472D	RML 2535 JJD 535D
RML 2305 CUV 305C	RML 2358 CUV 358C	RML 2400 JJD 400D	RML 2474 JJD 474D	RML 2539 JJD 539D
RML 2314 CUV 314C	RML 2360 CUV 360C	RML 2403 JJD 403D	RML 2475 JJD 475D	RML 2540 JJD 540D

RML 2543 JJD 543D	**RML 2580** JJD 580D	**RML 2612** NML 612E	**RML 2644** NML 644E	**RML 2714** SMK 714F
RML 2551 JJD 551D	**RML 2583** JJD 583D	**RML 2613** NML 613E	**RML 2648** NML 648E	**RML 2725** SMK 725F
RML 2554 JJD 554D	**RML 2584** JJD 584D	**RML 2614** NML 614E	**RML 2654** NML 654E	**RML 2732** SMK 732F
RML 2556 JJD 556D	**RML 2587** JJD 587D	**RML 2615** NML 615E	**RML 2669** SMK 669F	**RML 2733** SMK 733F
RML 2560 JJD 560D	**RML 2590** JJD 590D	**RML 2618** NML 618E	**RML 2673** SMK 673F	**RML 2736** SMK 736F
RML 2564 JJD 564D	**RML 2593** JJD 593D	**RML 2626** NML 626E	**RML 2676** SMK 676F	**RML 2745** SMK 745F
RML 2568 JJD 568D	**RML 2596** JJD 596D	**RML 2629** NML 629E	**RML 2680** SMK 680F	**RML 2752** SMK 752F
RML 2570 JJD 570D	**RML 2601** NML 601E	**RML 2630** NML 630E	**RML 2683** SMK 683F	
RML 2575 JJD 575D	**RML 2604** NML 604E	**RML 2631** NML 631E	**RML 2693** SMK 693F	
RML 2576 JJD 576D	**RML 2605** NML 605E	**RML 2637** NML 637E	**RML 2711** SMK 711F	
RML 2578 JJD 578D	**RML 2606** NML 606E	**RML 2640** NML 640E	**RML 2712** SMK 712F	

T 172	CUL 172V	Leyland Titan TNLXB2RRsp Ex London Buses, 1994	Park Royal	H44/26D	1979

T 677–1102		Leyland Titan TNLXB2RR Ex London Buses, 1994	Leyland	*H44/24D	1980–4

*(T 793 is H44/23D. T 831–1102 are H44/26D. OT 803 is O44/26D. T 1060 is H44/24F. T 875 and T 1064 not known)
(T875 is used as a mobile rest room for night bus drivers at Victoria Station. Tables and refreshment machines are fitted)
(T 1064 is converted for use as an anti-vandalism exhibition unit for London Central and Thameslink Trains, both part of the Go-Ahead Group)

T 677t	OHV 677Y	**T 870**t	A870 SUL	**T 980**	A980 SYE	**T 1040**t	A640 THV	**T 1073**t	A73 THX
T 774t	OHV 774Y	**T 875**sp	A875 SUL	**T 991**	A991 SYE	**T 1044**t	A644 THV	**T 1086**	B86 WUV
T 793t	OHV 793Y	**T 919**t	A919 SYE	**T 1000**	ALM 1B	**T 1051**	A651 THV	**T 1090**	B90 WUV
OT 803sp	OHV 803Y	**T 928**t	A928 SYE	**T 1001**w	A601 THV	**T 1057**	257 CLT	**T 1102**	B102 WUV
T 831t	A831 SUL	**T 931**t	A931 SYE	**T 1005**	A605 THV	**T 1060**t	A60 THX	**T 1104**w	B104 WUV
T 835t	A835 SUL	**T 946**	A946 SYE	**T 1014**	A614 THV	**T 1062**	A62 THX		
T 839t	A839 SUL	**T 954**	A954 SYE	**T 1018**	A618 THV	**T 1064**sp	A64 THX		
T 844t	A844 SUL	**T 956**t	A956 SYE	**T 1033**	A633 THV	**T 1071**	A71 THX		
T 851t	A851 SUL	**T 963**	A963 SYE	**T 1037**	A637 THV	**T 1072**t	A72 THX		

T 1129	WDA 4T	Leyland Titan TNLXB1RF Ex London Buses, 1994	Park Royal	DPH43/29F	1979
TPL 10	C377 PCD	Leyland Tiger TRCTL11/3RH (On long term loan to Northdown Motor Services)	Plaxton Paramount 3500 II	C49F	1986
VC 1	G101 NGN	Volvo Citybus B10M–50 Ex London Buses, 1994	Northern Counties	DPH45/35D	1989
VC 2	G102 NGN	Volvo Citybus B10M–50 Ex London Buses, 1994	Northern Counties	DPH45/35D	1989
VC 3	WLT 803	Volvo Citybus B10M–50 Ex London Buses, 1994	Northern Counties	DPH45/35D	1989
VC 4	WLT 474	Volvo Citybus B10M–50 Ex London Buses, 1994	Northern Counties	H45/35D	1989
VC 5	G105 NGN	Volvo Citybus B10M–50 Ex London Buses, 1994	Northern Counties	H45/35D	1989
VC 6	VLT 60	Volvo Citybus B10M–50 Ex London Buses, 1994	Northern Counties	H45/35D	1989

VC 10–39		Volvo Citybus B10M–50 Ex London Buses, 1994	Northern Counties	H47/35D	1989–91

VC 10	G110 NGN	**VC 16**	G116 NGN	**VC 22**	G122 NGN	**VC 28**	528 CLT	**VC 34**	G134 PGK
VC 11	G647 SGT	**VC 17**	G117 NGN	**VC 23**	G123 NGN	**VC 29**	229 CLT	**VC 35**	G135 PGK
VC 12	312 CLT	**VC 18**	WLT 818	**VC 24**	G124 NGN	**VC 30**	G130 PGK	**VC 36**	836 DYE
VC 13	G113 NGN	**VC 19**	619 DYE	**VC 25**	125 CLT	**VC 31**	G131 PGK	**VC 37**	WLT 837
VC 14	614 DYE	**VC 20**	WLT 920	**VC 26**	G126 NGN	**VC 32**	G132 PGK	**VC 38**	G138 PGK
VC 15	G115 NGN	**VC 21**	621 DYE	**VC 27**	G127 NGN	**VC 33**	G133 PGK	**VC 39**	839 DYE

Special Liveries:
OMs 171, 241, 420, M 1440 and Ts 172 and 803 are red with white or cream relief in differing styles.
Most of the training fleet carry a red and blue livery.

On Order:
31 x Mercedes-Benz Citara G 18m articulated buses for the Red Arrow network. Due for delivery during 2002.
36 x Volvo B7TL/East Lancs Vykings for routes 93 and 154.
20 x Dennis Dart SLF/Plaxton Pointer 2 10.1m for routes 151 and 163.
19 x PVLs for route 51.

Previous registrations:

A746 THV	VLT 46, A746 THV	**839 DYE**	J139 DGF	**WLT 31**	From new
ALM 1B	A600 THV	**G101 NGN**	101 CLT, G101 NGN	**WLT 346**	R346 LGH
C109 NGH	VLT 15, C315 BUV	**G551 SGT**	WLT 548, JDZ 2348	**WLT 379**	P509 RYM
C377 PCD	PCN 762,VLT 71,	**G123 NGN**	23 CLT, G123 NGN	**WLT 395**	K595 MGT
	C377 PCD	**G647 SGT**	WLT 311, G111 NGN	**WLT 432**	(Retained)
2 CLT	(Retained)	**GUW 499W**	WLT 599, GUW 499W	**WLT 434**	C434 BUV
19 CLT	P919 RYO	**H546 XGK**	46 CLT, H546 XGK	**WLT 463**	(Retained)
23 CLT	(Retained)	**JSJ 743**	260 CLT	**WLT 467**	GUW 467W
46 CLT	V146 LGC	**JSJ 797**	174 CLT	**WLT 470**	R370 LGH
78 CLT	R378 LGH	**KGJ 187A**	621 DYE	**WLT 474**	G104 NGN
83 CLT	GUW 483W	**KGJ 339A**	400 CLT	**WLT 487**	GUW 487W
89 CLT	C389 BUV	**M402 RVU**	2 CLT, M402 RVU	**WLT 516**	JJD 516D
101 CLT	G101 NGN	**M410 RVU**	WLT 990, M410 RVU	**WLT 527**	N427 JBV
125 CLT	G125 NGN	**MFF 509**	312 CLT	**WLT 532**	V332 LGC
166 CLT	R366 LGH	**N416 JBV**	N421 JBV	**WLT 548**	R348 LGH
170 CLT	From new	**N420 JBV**	N422 JBV	**WLT 598**	GUW 498W
174 CLT	R474 LGH	**N421 JBV**	N424 JBV	**WLT 599**	From new
176 CLT	R476 LGH	**N422 JBV**	N416 JBV	**WLT 625**	W425 WGH
186 CLT	(Retained)	**N423 JBV**	N425 JBV	**WLT 648**	GUW 448W
188 CLT	P508 RYM	**N424 JBV**	N426 JBV	**WLT 696**	GUW 496W
197 CLT	R387 LGH	**N425 JBV**	N427 JBV	**WLT 735**	(Retained)
229 CLT	G129 NGN	**N426 JBV**	N420 JBV	**WLT 736**	(Retained)
257 CLT	A57 THX	**N427 JBV**	N423 JBV	**WLT 789**	M89 MYM
260 CLT	R260 LGH	**OVS 940**	WLT 875	**WLT 803**	G103 NGN
304 CLT	B304 WUL	**OYM 368A**	2 CLT	**WLT 815**	N415 JBV
312 CLT	G112 NGN	**S638 JGP**	WLT 990	**WLT 818**	G118 NGN
352 CLT	R552 LGH	**SGC 671Y**	VLT 53, OJD 853Y	**WLT 825**	(Retained)
435 CLT	C435 BUV	**V209 LGC**	V309 LGC	**WLT 837**	G137 NGN
528 CLT	G128 NGN	**VLT 9**	OYM 374A, VLT 9	**WLT 838**	M408 RVU
542 CLT	(Retained)	**VLT 29**	N529 LHG	**WLT 843**	GUW 443W
545 CLT	R345 LGH	**VLT 60**	G106 NGN	**WLT 868**	R268 LGH
614 DYE	G114 NGN	**VLT 71**	BYX 171V	**WLT 872**	R472 LGH
619 DYE	G119 NGN	**VLT 136**	C436 BUV	**WLT 920**	G120 NGN
621 DYE	G121 NGN	**VLT 179**	R379 LGH	**WLT 990**	(Retained)
698 DYE	P908 RYO	**VLT 180**	GUW 480W	**WLT 994**	VLT 89, WLT 994
772 DYE	C372 BUV	**VLT 277**	R377 LGH	**XYJ 440**	WLT 838
836 DYE	G136 NGN	**VLT 284**	R384 LGH		

LONDON EASYLINK

M 478t	GYE 478W	MCW Metrobus DR101/12 Ex Arriva London, 2000	MCW	H43/28D	1980

VP 149–173		Volvo B7TL	Plaxton President 10m		H41/23D	2001

VP 149	X149 FBB	**VP 154**	X154 FBB	**VP 161**	X161 FBB	**VP 165**	X165 FBB	**VP 169**	X169 FBB
VP 151	X151 FBB	**VP 157**	X157 FBB	**VP 162**	X162 FBB	**VP 166**	X166 FBB	**VP 171**	X171 FBB
VP 152	X152 FBB	**VP 158**	X158 FBB	**VP 163**	X163 FBB	**VP 167**	X167 FBB	**VP 172**	X172 FBB
VP 153	X153 FBB	**VP 159**	X159 FBB	**VP 164**	X164 FBB	**VP 168**	X168 FBB	**VP 173**	X173 FBB

LONDON UNITED

CD 1–8		Dennis Dart SLF SFD212BR1TGW1	Wright Crusader 10.2m	B32F	1996

CD 1	VDZ 8001	**CD 3**	VDZ 8003	**CD 5**	VDZ 8005	**CD 7**	VDZ 8007
CD 2	VDZ 8002	**CD 4**	VDZ 8004	**CD 6**	VDZ 8006	**CD 8**	VDZ 8008

DN 1–12		DAF DE23RSDB250	Northern Counties Palatine II	H43/24D	1998

Ex Arriva Croydon & North Surrey, 1999

DN 1	R201 CKO	**DN 4**	R204 CKO	**DN 7**	R207 CKO	**DN 10**	R210 CKO
DN 2	R202 CKO	**DN 5**	R205 CKO	**DN 8**	R208 CKO	**DN 11**	R211 CKO
DN 3	R203 CKO	**DN 6**	R206 CKO	**DN 9**	R209 CKO	**DN 12**	R212 CKO

DP 1–11		Dennis Dart SLF SFD322BR1WGW1	Plaxton Pointer 2 10.7m	B36F	1998

DP 1	S301 MKH	**DP 4**	S304 MKH	**DP 7**	S307 MKH	**DP 10**	S310 MKH
DP 2	S302 MKH	**DP 5**	S305 MKH	**DP 8**	S308 MKH	**DP 11**	S311 MKH
DP 3	S303 MKH	**DP 6**	S306 MKH	**DP 9**	S309 MKH		

DP 12–17		Dennis Dart SLF SFD322AR1WGW1	Plaxton Pointer 2 10.7m	B31D	1999

DP 12	T412 KAG	**DP 14**	T414 KAG	**DP 16**	T416 KAG
DP 13	T413 KAG	**DP 15**	T415 KAG	**DP 17**	T417 KAG

DP 18–22		Dennis Dart SLF SFD322AR1WGW1	Plaxton Pointer 2 10.7m	B27D	1999

DP 18	T418 KAG	**DP 19**	T419 KAG	**DP 20**	T420 KAG	**DP 21**	T421 KAG	**DP 22**	T422 KAG

DP 23–33		Dennis Dart SLF SFD322AR1WGW1	Plaxton Pointer 2 10.7m	B34D	1999

DP 23	T423 KAG	**DP 26**	T426 KAG	**DP 29**	T429 KAG	**DP 32**	T432 KAG
DP 24	T424 KAG	**DP 27**	T427 KAG	**DP 30**	T430 KAG	**DP 33**	T433 KAG
DP 25	T425 KAG	**DP 28**	T428 KAG	**DP 31**	T431 KAG		

DP 34–99		Dennis Dart SLF SFD322BR1XGW1	Plaxton Pointer 2 10.7m	B31D	1999

DP 34	T334 PRH	**DP 44**	T344 PRH	**DP 54**	T354 PRH	**DP 64**	T364 PRH	**DP 74**	T374 PRH
DP 35	T335 PRH	**DP 45**	T345 PRH	**DP 55**	T455 PRH	**DP 65**	T365 PRH	**DP 75**	T375 PRH
DP 36	T336 PRH	**DP 46**	T346 PRH	**DP 56**	T356 PRH	**DP 66**	T366 PRH	**DP 76**	T976 SRH
DP 37	T337 PRH	**DP 47**	T347 PRH	**DP 57**	T357 PRH	**DP 67**	T367 PRH	**DP 77**	T977 SRH
DP 38	T338 PRH	**DP 48**	T348 PRH	**DP 58**	T358 PRH	**DP 68**	T368 PRH	**DP 78**	T978 SRH
DP 39	T339 PRH	**DP 49**	T349 PRH	**DP 59**	T359 PRH	**DP 69**	T369 PRH	**DP 79**	T979 SRH
DP 40	T340 PRH	**DP 50**	T350 PRH	**DP 60**	T360 PRH	**DP 70**	T370 PRH	**DP 80**	T980 SRH
DP 41	T341 PRH	**DP 51**	T351 PRH	**DP 61**	T361 PRH	**DP 71**	T371 PRH	**DP 81**	V781 FKH
DP 42	T342 PRH	**DP 52**	T352 PRH	**DP 62**	T362 PRH	**DP 72**	T372 PRH	**DP 82**	V782 FKH
DP 43	T343 PRH	**DP 53**	T353 PRH	**DP 63**	T363 PRH	**DP 73**	T373 PRH	**DP 83**	V783 FKH

DP 84	V784 FKH	DP 88	V788 FKH	DP 92	V792 FKH	DP 96	V796 FKH
DP 85	V785 FKH	DP 89	V789 FKH	DP 93	V793 FKH	DP 97	V797 FKH
DP 86	V886 FKH	DP 90	V790 FKH	DP 94	V794 FKH	DP 98	V798 FKH
DP 87	V787 FKH	DP 91	V791 FKH	DP 95	V795 FKH	DP 99	V799 FKH

DP 500–509 Dennis Dart SLF SFD322BR1YGW2 Plaxton Pointer 2 10.7m B31D 2000

DP 500	X611 OKH	DP 502	X602 OKH	DP 504	X604 OKH	DP 506	X606 OKH	DP 508	X608 OKH
DP 501	X601 OKH	DP 503	X603 OKH	DP 505	X605 OKH	DP 507	X607 OKH	DP 509	X609 OKH

DPK Dennis Dart SLF SFD Plaxton Pointer 2 8.8m B 2001

DPK		DPK		DPK		DPK		DPK
DPK		DPK		DPK		DPK		
DPK		DPK		DPK		DPK		

DPS 1–16 Dennis Dart SLF SFD212AR1XGW2 Plaxton Pointer 2 10.1m B27D 1999

DPS 1	V801 KAG	DPS 5	V805 KAG	DPS 9	V809 KAG	DPS 13	V813 KAG
DPS 2	V802 KAG	DPS 6	V806 KAG	DPS 10	V810 KAG	DPS 14	V814 KAG
DPS 3	V803 KAG	DPS 7	V807 KAG	DPS 11	V811 KAG	DPS 15	V815 KAG
DPS 4	V904 KAG	DPS 8	V808 KAG	DPS 12	V812 KAG	DPS 16	V816 KAG

DPS 511–533 Dennis Dart SLF SFD212AR1YGW1 Plaxton Pointer 2 10.1m B27D 2000

DPS 511 X511 UAT	DPS 516 X516 UAT	DPS 521 X521 UAT	DPS 526 X526 UAT	DPS 532 X532 UAT
DPS 512 X512 UAT	DPS 517 X517 UAT	DPS 522 X522 UAT	DPS 527 X527 UAT	DPS 533 X533 UAT
DPS 513 X513 UAT	DPS 518 X518 UAT	DPS 523 X523 UAT	DPS 529 X529 UAT	
DPS 514 X514 UAT	DPS 519 X519 UAT	DPS 524 X524 UAT	DPS 531 X531 UAT	

DPS 534–557 Dennis Dart SLF SFD212AR11GW2 Plaxton Pointer 2 10.1m B30D 2001

DPS 534 Y534 XAG	DPS 539 Y539 XAG	DPS 544 Y544 XAG	DPS 549 Y549 XAG	DPS 554 Y554 XAG
DPS 536 Y536 XAG	DPS 541 Y541 XAG	DPS 546 Y546 XAG	DPS 551 Y551 XAG	DPS 556 Y556 XAG
DPS 537 Y537 XAG	DPS 542 Y542 XAG	DPS 547 Y547 XAG	DPS 552 Y552 XAG	DPS 557 Y557 XAG
DPS 538 Y538 XAG	DPS 543 Y543 XAG	DPS 548 Y548 XAG	DPS 553 Y553 XAG	

DR 1	H101 THE	Dennis Dart 8.5SDL3003	Reeve Burgess Pointer 8.5m	B28F	1991
		Ex London Buses, 1994			
DR 4	H104 THE	Dennis Dart 8.5SDL3003	Reeve Burgess Pointer 8.5m	B28F	1991
		Ex London Buses, 1994			
DR 12	H112 THE	Dennis Dart 8.5SDL3003	Reeve Burgess Pointer 8.5m	B28F	1991
		Ex London Buses, 1994			
DR 53	J653 XHL	Dennis Dart 8.5SDL3010	Plaxton Pointer 8.5m	B28F	1991
		Ex London Buses, 1994			
DR 54	J654 XHL	Dennis Dart 8.5SDL3010	Plaxton Pointer 8.5m	B28F	1991
		Ex London Buses, 1994			
DR 55	J655 XHL	Dennis Dart 8.5SDL3010	Plaxton Pointer 8.5m	B28F	1991
		Ex London Buses, 1994			
DR 57	J157 GAT	Dennis Dart 8.5SDL3010	Plaxton Pointer 8.5m	B28F	1991
		Ex London Buses, 1994			

DR 59–141

Dennis Dart 8.5SDL3010 — Plaxton Pointer 8.5m — B24F — 1991/2
Ex London Buses, 1994

DR 59	J159 GAT	DR 72	J372 GKH	DR 103	J103 DUV	DR 116	J116 DUV	DR 129	J129 DUV
DR 60	J160 GAT	DR 73	J373 GKH	DR 104	J104 DUV	DR 117	J117 DUV	DR 130	J130 DUV
DR 61	J161 GAT	DR 74	J374 GKH	DR 105	J105 DUV	DR 118	J118 DUV	DR 131	J131 DUV
DR 62	J362 GKH	DR 75	J375 GKH	DR 106	J106 DUV	DR 119	J119 DUV	DR 132	J132 DUV
DR 63	J363 GKH	DR 76	J376 GKH	DR 107	J107 DUV	DR 120	J120 DUV	DR 133	J133 DUV
DR 64	J364 GKH	DR 77	J377 GKH	DR 108	J108 DUV	DR 121	J121 DUV	DR 134	J134 DUV
DR 65	J365 GKH	DR 78	J378 GKH	DR 109	J109 DUV	DR 122	J122 DUV	DR 135	J135 DUV
DR 66	J366 GKH	DR 79	J379 GKH	DR 110	J110 DUV	DR 123	J123 DUV	DR 136	J136 DUV
DR 67	J367 GKH	DR 80	J380 GKH	DR 111	WLT 946	DR 124	J124 DUV	DR 137	J137 DUV
DR 68	J368 GKH	DR 99	J599 DUV	DR 112	J112 DUV	DR 125	J125 DUV	DR 138	J138 DUV
DR 69	J369 GKH	DR 100	J610 DUV	DR 113	J113 DUV	DR 126	J126 DUV	DR 139	J139 DUV
DR 70	J370 GKH	DR 101	J101 DUV	DR 114	J114 DUV	DR 127	J127 DUV	DR 140	J140 DUV
DR 71	J371 GKH	DR 102	J102 DUV	DR 115	J115 DUV	DR 128	J128 DUV	DR 141	J141 DUV

DRL 96–108

Dennis Dart 9SDL3024 — Plaxton Pointer 9m — B34F — 1993
Ex London Buses, 1994

DRL 96	K96 SAG	DRL 99	K199 SAG	DRL 102	K102 SAG	DRL 105	K105 SAG	DRL 108	K108 SAG
DRL 97	K97 SAG	DRL 100	ALM 2B	DRL 103	K103 SAG	DRL 106	K106 SAG		
DRL 98	K98 SAG	DRL 101	K101 SAG	DRL 104	K104 SAG	DRL 107	K107 SAG		

DRL 159–171

Dennis Dart 9SDL3034 — Plaxton Pointer 9m — B28F — 1993/4
Ex London Buses, 1994

DRL 159	L159 XRH	DRL 162	L162 XRH	DRL 165	L165 YAT	DRL 168	L168 YAT	DRL 171	L171 CKH
DRL 160	L160 XRH	DRL 163	L163 XRH	DRL 166	L166 YAT	DRL 169	L169 YAT		
DRL 161	L161 XRH	DRL 164	L164 XRH	DRL 167	L167 YAT	DRL 170	L170 CKH		

DT 12

G512 VYE — Dennis Dart 8.5SDL3003 — Duple Dartline 8.5m — DP21F — 1990
Ex London Buses, 1994.

DWL 2–14

Dennis Dart 9SDL3002 — Wright Handybus 9m — B36F — 1990
Ex London Buses, 1994

DWL 2	JDW 2402	DWL 6	JDW 2406	DWL 8	JDW 2408	DWL 13	JDW 2413
DWL 5	JDW 2405	DWL 7	JDW 2407	DWL 9	JDW 2409	DWL 14	JDW 2414

L 293–305

Leyland Olympian ONCL10/1RZ — Leyland — H47/31F — 1989
Ex London Buses, 1994

L 293	G293 UYK	L 300	G300 UYK	L 303	G303 UYK
L 298	G298 UYK	L 302	G302 UYK	L 305	G305 UYK

L 308–310

Leyland Olympian ON2R50C13Z4 — Leyland — H47/31F — 1989
Ex London Buses, 1994

L 308	G308 UYK	L 309	G309 UYK	L 310	G310 UYK

LLW1–10

Dennis Lance SLF 11SDA3202 — Wright Pathfinder 320 — B34D — 1993/4
Ex London Buses, 1994

LLW 1	ODZ 8901	LLW 3	ODZ 8903	LLW 5	ODZ 8905	LLW 7	ODZ 8907	LLW 9	ODZ 8909
LLW 2	ODZ 8902	LLW 4	ODZ 8904	LLW 6	ODZ 8906	LLW 8	ODZ 8908	LLW 10	ODZ 8910

LS 153t	THX 153S	Leyland National 10351A/2R Ex West Midlands, 1995	Urban Bus (1996)	B38F	1977
LS 297t	YYE 297T	Leyland National 10351A/2R Ex London Buses, 1994	Urban Bus (1996)	B38F	1979
LS 405t	BYW 405V	Leyland National 10351A/2R Ex West Midlands, 1995	Urban Bus (1996)	B38F	1979
LS 431t	BYW 431V	Leyland National 10351A/2R Ex London Buses, 1994	Urban Bus (1996)	B38F	1979
M 30t	WYW 30T	MCW Metrobus DR101/8 Ex London Buses, 1994	MCW	H0/15D	1978
M 36t	WYW 36T	MCW Metrobus DR101/8 Ex London Buses, 1994	MCW	H0/15D	1978
M 46t	WYW 46T	MCW Metrobus DR101/8 Ex London Buses, 1994	MCW	H0/15D	1978
M 147t	BYX 147V	MCW Metrobus DR101/12 Ex London Buses, 1994	MCW	H0/15D	1980
M 157t	BYX 157V	MCW Metrobus DR101/12 Ex London Buses, 1994	MCW	H0/15D	1980
M 159u	BYX 159V	MCW Metrobus DR101/12 Ex London Buses, 1994	MCW	H0/15D	1980
M 203	BYX 203V	MCW Metrobus DR101/12 Ex London Buses, 1994	MCW	H43/28D	1980
M 204t	BYX 204V	MCW Metrobus DR101/12 Ex London Buses, 1994	MCW	H0/15D	1980
M 227w	BYX 227V	MCW Metrobus DR101/12 Ex London Buses, 1994	MCW	H43/28D	1980
M 687	KYV 687X	MCW Metrobus DR101/14 Ex London Buses, 1994	MCW	H43/28D	1981
M 835	OJD 835Y	MCW Metrobus DR101/16 Ex London Buses, 1994	MCW	H43/28D	1983
M 841	OJD 841Y	MCW Metrobus DR101/16 Ex London Buses, 1994	MCW	H43/28D	1983
M 844	OJD 844Y	MCW Metrobus DR101/16 Ex London Buses, 1994	MCW	H43/28D	1983
M 881	OJD 881Y	MCW Metrobus DR101/16 Ex London Buses, 1994	MCW	H43/28D	1983
M 960	A960 SYF	MCW Metrobus DR101/17 Ex London Buses, 1994	MCW	H43/28D	1984
M 962	A962 SYF	MCW Metrobus DR101/17 Ex London Buses, 1994	MCW	H43/28D	1984
M 967	A967 SYF	MCW Metrobus DR101/17 Ex London Buses, 1994	MCW	H43/28D	1984
M 1006–1029		MCW Metrobus DR101/18 Ex London Buses, 1994	MCW	H41/28D	1984

M 1006t	A706 THV	**M 1013**	A713 THV	**M 1019**t A719 THV	**M 1023**	A723 THV	**M 1028**t	A728 THV
M 1008w A708 THV		**M 1014**t	A714 THV	**M 1020** A720 THV	**M 1024**	A724 THV	**M 1029**t	A729 THV
M 1010	A710 THV	**M 1015**	A715 THV	**M 1021** A721 THV	**M 1026**t	A726 THV		
M 1011	A711 THV	**M 1016**	A716 THV	**M 1022**t A722 THV	**M 1027**t	A727 THV		

M 1030	A730 THV	MCW Metrobus DR101/17 Ex London Buses, 1994	MCW	H43/28D	1984
M 1039	A739 THV	MCW Metrobus DR101/17 Ex London Buses, 1994	MCW	H43/28D	1984
M 1048w A748 THV		MCW Metrobus DR101/19 Ex London Buses, 1994	MCW	H43/28D	1984
M 1050	A750 THV	MCW Metrobus DR101/19 Ex London Buses, 1994	MCW	H43/28D	1984

M 1069–1439 MCW Metrobus DR101/17 MCW H43/28D 1984/6
Ex London Buses, 1994

M 1069 B69 WUL	**M 1200** B200 WUL	**M 1262** B262 WUL	**M 1343** C343 BUV	**M 1360** C360 BUV
M 1172 B172 WUL	**M 1212** B212 WUL	**M 1266** B266 WUL	**M 1344** C344 BUV	**M 1361** C361 BUV
M 1178 B178 WUL	**M 1238** B238 WUL	**M 1269** B269 WUL	**M 1345** C345 BUV	**M 1363** C363 BUV
M 1184 B184 WUL	**M 1240** B240 WUL	**M 1270** B270 WUL	**M 1351** C351 BUV	**M 1368** C368 BUV
M 1188 B188 WUL	**M 1242** B242 WUL	**M 1271** B271 WUL	**M 1352** C352 BUV	**M 1374** C374 BUV
M 1190 B190 WUL	**M 1243** B243 WUL	**M 1272** B272 WUL	**M 1353** C353 BUV	**M 1381** C381 BUV
M 1191w B191 WUL	**M 1251** B251 WUL	**M 1336** C336 BUV	**M 1356** C356 BUV	**M 1439** C439 BUV
M 1194 B194 WUL	**M 1257** B257 WUL	**M 1341** C341 BUV	**M 1358** C358 BUV	

MV 1–8 MAN 11.190 Optare Vecta B42F 1995

MV 1 N281 DWY	**MV 3** N283 DWY	**MV 5** N285 DWY	**MV 7** N287 DWY
MV 2 N282 DWY	**MV 4** N284 DWY	**MV 6** N286 DWY	**MV 8** N288 DWY

RM 2033 ALM 33B AEC Routemaster R2RH Park Royal H36/28R 1964
Ex London Transport, 1997
RM 2078 ALM 78B AEC Routemaster R2RH Park Royal H36/28R 1964
Ex London Transport, 1997
RML 880 WLT 880 AEC Routemaster R2RH Park Royal H40/32R 1961
Ex London Buses, 1994 (Carries fleet number ER880)
RML 881 HSL 656 AEC Routemaster R2RH Park Royal H40/32R 1961
Ex London Buses, 1994 (Carries fleet number ER881)
RML 891 HSL 660 AEC Routemaster R2RH Park Royal H40/32R 1961
Ex London Buses, 1994

RML 2269–2757 AEC Routemaster R2RH/1 Park Royal H40/32R 1965–8
(RML 2404 and 2487 ex London Sovereign, 2001. Rest ex London Buses, 1994)

RML 2269 CUV 269C	**RML 2447** JJD 447D	**RML 2519** JJD 519D	**RML 2697** SMK 697F	**RML 2729** SMK 729S
RML 2293 CUV 293C	**RML 2455** JJD 455D	**RML 2600** NML 600E	**RML 2700** SMK 700F	**RML 2734** SMK 734F
RML 2298 CUV 298C	**RML 2463** JJD 463D	**RML 2621** NML 621E	**RML 2702** SMK 702F	**RML 2739** SMK 739F
RML 2349 CUV 349C	**RML 2464** JJD 464D	**RML 2622** NML 622E	**RML 2704** SMK 704F	**RML 2744** SMK 744F
RML 2353 CUV 353C	**RML 2485** JJD 485D	**RML 2645** NML 645E	**RML 2707** SMK 707F	**RML 2751** SMK 751F
RML 2404 JJD 404D	**RML 2487** JJD 487D	**RML 2646** NML 646E	**RML 2720** SMK 720F	**RML 2757** SMK 757F
RML 2414 JJD 414D	**RML 2489** JJD 489D	**RML 2650** NML 650E	**RML 2721** SMK 721F	
RML 2432 JJD 432D	**RML 2500** JJD 500D	**RML 2662** SMK 662F	**RML 2722** SMK 722F	

TA 201–203 *Dennis Trident 2 SFD113BR1YGX2 Alexander ALX400 9.9m H43/21D 2000
*(TA 202 is SFD123BR1YGX2)

TA 201 X201 UMS	**TA 202** X202 UMS	**TA 203**t X203 UMS

VA 1–10 Volvo Olympian YN2RV18Z4 Alexander RH H45/29F 1996

VA 1 N131 YRW	**VA 3** N133 YRW	**VA 5** N135 YRW	**VA 7** N137 YRW	**VA 9** N139 YRW
VA 2 N132 YRW	**VA 4** N134 YRW	**VA 6** N136 YRW	**VA 8** N138 YRW	**VA 10** N140 YRW

VA 11–54 Volvo Olympian OLY–4953 Alexander RH (Belfast) H47/25D 1997/8

VA 11 XDZ 5911	**VA 20** R920 WOE	**VA 29** R929 WOE	**VA 38** R938 YOV	**VA 47** R947 YOV
VA 12 XDZ 5912	**VA 21** R921 WOE	**VA 30** R930 WOE	**VA 39** R939 YOV	**VA 48** R948 YOV
VA 13 XDZ 5913	**VA 22** R922 WOE	**VA 31** R931 WOE	**VA 40** R940 YOV	**VA 49** R949 YOV
VA 14 XDZ 5914	**VA 23** R923 WOE	**VA 32** R932 YOV	**VA 41** R941 YOV	**VA 50** R950 YOV
VA 15 XDZ 5915	**VA 24** R924 WOE	**VA 33** R933 YOV	**VA 42** R942 YOV	**VA 51** R951 YOV
VA 16 XDZ 5916	**VA 25** R925 WOE	**VA 34** R934 YOV	**VA 43** R943 YOV	**VA 52** R952 YOV
VA 17 XDZ 5917	**VA 26** R926 WOE	**VA 35** R935 YOV	**VA 44** R944 YOV	**VA 53** R953 YOV
VA 18 R918 WOE	**VA 27** R927 WOE	**VA 36** R936 YOV	**VA 45** R945 YOV	**VA 54** R954 YOV
VA 19 R919 WOE	**VA 28** R928 WOE	**VA 37** R937 YOV	**VA 46** R946 YOV	

VA 60–104 Volvo B7TL Alexander ALX400 10.1m H43/20D 2000

VA 60	V176 OOE	**VA 69**	V185 OOE	**VA 78**	V194 OOE	**VA 87**	W117 EON	**VA 96**	W131 EON
VA 61	V177 OOE	**VA 70**	V186 OOE	**VA 79**	V202 OOE	**VA 88**	W118 EON	**VA 97**	W132 EON
VA 62	V178 OOE	**VA 71**	V187 OOE	**VA 80**	V203 OOE	**VA 89**	W119 EON	**VA 98**	W133 EON
VA 63	V179 OOE	**VA 72**	V188 OOE	**VA 81**	V204 OOE	**VA 90**	W122 EON	**VA 99**	W134 EON
VA 64	V180 OOE	**VA 73**	V189 OOE	**VA 82**	V205 OOE	**VA 91**	W124 EON	**VA 100**	W136 EON
VA 65	V181 OOE	**VA 74**	V190 OOE	**VA 83**	V206 OOE	**VA 92**	W126 EON	**VA 101**	W137 EON
VA 66	V182 OOE	**VA 75**	V191 OOE	**VA 84**	V207 OOE	**VA 93**	W127 EON	**VA 102**	W138 EON
VA 67	V183 OOE	**VA 76**	V192 OOE	**VA 85**	V208 OOE	**VA 94**	W128 EON	**VA 103**	W139 EON
VA 68	V184 OOE	**VA 77**	V193 OOE	**VA 86**	W116 EON	**VA 95**	W129 EON	**VA 104**	W141 EON

VP 105–130 Volvo B7TL Plaxton President 10m H41/21D 2000

VP 105	W448 BCW	**VP 111**	W457 BCW	**VP 117**	W464 BCW	**VP 123**	W471 BCW	**VP 129**	W477 BCW
VP 106	W449 BCW	**VP 112**	W458 BCW	**VP 118**	W465 BCW	**VP 124**	W472 BCW	**VP 130**	W478 BCW
VP 107	W451 BCW	**VP 113**	W459 BCW	**VP 119**	W466 BCW	**VP 125**	W473 BCW		
VP 108	W452 BCW	**VP 114**	W461 BCW	**VP 120**	W467 BCW	**VP 126**	W474 BCW		
VP 109	W453 BCW	**VP 115**	W462 BCW	**VP 121**	W468 BCW	**VP 127**	W475 BCW		
VP 110	W454 BCW	**VP 116**	W463 BCW	**VP 122**	W469 BCW	**VP 128**	W476 BCW		

XL 1–7 Optare Excel L1000 Optare B36F 1997

XL 1	P151 BUG	**XL 3**	P153 BUG	**XL 6**	P156 BUG
XL 2	P152 BUG	**XL 4**	P154 BUG	**XL 7**	P157 BUG

Special Liveries:

DP 18–22 carry Feltham Gateway livery.
DP 23–33 carry Heathrow Connection livery.
DT 12 carries all over adverts and livery for Marks & Spencer.
Training buses are red with either orange or yellow relief.

On Order:

45 x Dennis Dart 10.1m
22 x Dennis Trident/Alexander ALX400 for route 131 and 267.
3 x Volvo B7TL/Wright Eclipse Gemini due 2002.
13 x Dennis Dart 8.8m

Previous registrations:

ALM 2B	K210 SAG	**HSL 660**	WLT 891	**WLT 946**	J611 DUV
HSL 656	WLT 881	**J610 DUV**	VLT 23, J610 DUV		

241–248 *Dennis Dart SLF SFD212BR1VGW1 Plaxton Pointer 10m B35F 1998
Formerly numbered 741–748 *(246–8 are SFD212BR1WGW1)

241	R741 BMY	**243**	R743 BMY	**245**	R745 BMY	**247**	R747 FGX
242	R742 BMY	**244**	R744 BMY	**246**	R746 FGX	**248**	R748 FGX

301–308 Dennis Dart SLF SFD212BR1TGW1 Plaxton Pointer 10m B33F 1997
Ex Limebourne, SW8, 1999

301	P301 HDP	**303**	P303 HDP	**305**	P305 HDP	**307**	P307 HDP
302	P302 HDP	**304**	P304 HDP	**306**	P306 HDP	**308**	P308 HDP

312–319 Dennis Dart SLF SFD612BR1XGW1 Plaxton Pointer 2 8.8m B29F 1999–2000

312	T312 SMV	**314**	T314 SMV	**316**	T316 SMV	**319**	W319 VGX
313	T313 SMV	**315**	T315 SMV	**317**	W317 VGX		

322–331 Dennis Dart SLF SFD322BR1XGW1 Plaxton Pointer 2 10.7m B31D 1999

322	V322 KMY	**324**	V324 KMY	**326**	V326 KMY	**328**	V328 KMY	**330**	V330 KMY
323	V323 KMY	**325**	V325 KMY	**327**	V327 KMY	**329**	V329 KMY	**331**	V331 KMY

332–338 Dennis Dart SLF SFD322BR1YGW1 Plaxton Pointer 2 10.7m B31D 2000

332	W332 VGX	**335**	W335 VGX	**337**	W337 VGX
334	W334 VGX	**336**	W336 VGX	**338**	W338 VGX

339–343 Dennis Dart SLF SFD612BR1XGW1 Plaxton Pointer 2 8.8m B29F 2000

339	W339 VGX	**341**	W341 VGX	**342**	W342 VGX	**343**	W343 VGX

348–358 Dennis Dart SLF SFD612BR1YGW1 Plaxton Pointer 2 8.8m B29F 2001

348	Y348 HMY	**351**	Y351 HMY	**353**	Y353 HMY	**356**	Y356 HMY	**358**	Y358 HMY
349	Y349 HMY	**352**	Y352 HMY	**354**	Y354 HMY	**357**	Y357 HMY		

381–393 Dennis Dart SLF SFD612 Plaxton Pointer 2 8.8m B27F 2001

381	Y381 HKE	**384**	Y384 HKE	**387**	Y387 HKE	**391**	Y391 HKE
382	Y382 HKE	**385**	Y385 HKE	**388**	Y388 HKE	**392**	Y392 HKE
383	Y383 HKE	**386**	Y386 HKE	**389**	Y389 HKE	**393**	Y393 HKE

401–416 *Dennis Trident 2 SFD113BR1XGX1 East Lancs Lolyne 10m H45/24D 1999–2001
*(416 is SFD113BR21GX2)

401	T401 SMV	**405**	T405 SMV	**409**	T409 SMV	**413**	V413 KMY
402	T402 SMV	**406**	T406 SMV	**410**	T410 SMV	**414**	V414 KMY
403	T403 SMV	**407**	T407 SMV	**411**	T411 SMV	**415**	V415 KMY
404	T404 SMV	**408**	T408 SMV	**412**	V412 KMY	**416**	Y416 HMY

417–428 Dennis Trident SFD East Lancs Lolyne H 2001

417	LV51 YCC	**420**	LV51 YCF	**423**	LV51 YCJ	**426**	LV51 YCM
418	LV51 YCD	**421**	LV51 YCG	**424**	LV51 YCK	**427**	LV51 YCN
419	LV51 YCE	**422**	LV51 YCH	**425**	LV51 YCL	**428**	LV51 YCO

701–707			Dennis Dart 8.5SDL3010 *(701 is DP32F)			Reeve Burgess Pointer 8.5m			*B32F	1991
701	J701 EMX	703	J703 EMX	705	J705 EMX	707	J707 EMX			
702	J702 EMX	704	J704 EMX	706	J706 EMX					

733–739			Dennis Dart 9SDL3011 Ex Kentish Bus, 1996			Plaxton Pointer 9m			B35F	1992
733	J223 HGY	735	J225 HGY	737	J227 HGY	739	J229 HGY			
734	J224 HGY	736	J226 HGY	738	J228 HGY					

830–858			Volvo Olympian OLY–4953			East Lancs Pyoneer			H47/25D	1997–8
830	R830 MFR	836	R836 MFR	843	R843 MFR	849	S849 DGX	855	S855 DGX	
831	R831 MFR	837	R837 MFR	844	R844 MFR	850	S850 DGX	856	S856 DGX	
832	R832 MFR	838	R838 MFR	845	R845 MFR	851	S851 DGX	857	S857 DGX	
833	R833 MFR	839	R839 MFR	846	S846 DGX	852	S852 DGX	858	S858 DGX	
834	R834 MFR	841	R841 MFR	847	S847 DGX	853	S853 DGX			
835	R835 MFR	842	R842 MFR	848	S848 DGX	854	S854 DGX			

859–866			Volvo Olympian OLY–4953			Northern Counties Palatine I			H47/29F	1998
859	S859 DGX	861	S861 DGX	863	S863 DGX	865	S865 DGX			
860	S860 DGX	862	S862 DGX	864	S864 DGX	866	S866 DGX			

868–882			Volvo Olympian YN2RV18Z4 Ex London Central, 2001			Northern Counties Palatine I			*H48/27D	1996
868	N528 LHG	872	N532 LHG	877	N537 LHG	880	N540 LHG			
870	N530 LHG	873	N533 LHG	878	WLT 688	881	N541 LHG			
871	N531 LHG	875	N535 LHG	879	N539 LHG	882	N542 LHG			

901–906			Optare MetroRider MR13			Optare			B26F	1996
901	N901 HWY	903	N903 HWY	905	N905 HWY					
902	N902 HWY	904	N904 HWY	906	N906 HWY					

Previous Registration:

WLT 688   N538 LHG

METROLINE

(Metroline London Northern and
Metroline Travel)

AV 1–22			Volvo Olympian YN2RV18Z4			Alexander RH			H43/25D	1996
AV 1	585 CLT	AV 6	P486 MBY	AV 11	P491 MBY	AV 16	P476 MBY	AV 21	P474 MBY	
AV 2	P482 MBY	AV 7	P487 MBY	AV 12	P492 MBY	AV 17	P477 MBY	AV 22	P475 MBY	
AV 3	P483 MBY	AV 8	P488 MBY	AV 13	P493 MBY	AV 18	P478 MBY			
AV 4	P484 MBY	AV 9	P489 MBY	AV 14	P494 MBY	AV 19	P479 MBY			
AV 5	P485 MBY	AV 10	P490 MBY	AV 15	P495 MBY	AV 20	P480 MBY			

AV 23–38			Volvo Olympian OLY–4953			Alexander RH (Belfast)			H43/25D	1998
AV 23	S233 RLH	AV 27	S127 RLE	AV 31	S131 RLE	AV 35	S135 RLE			
AV 24	S124 RLE	AV 28	S128 RLE	AV 32	S132 RLE	AV 36	S136 RLE			
AV 25	S125 RLE	AV 29	S129 RLE	AV 33	S133 RLE	AV 37	S137 RLE			
AV 26	S126 RLE	AV 30	S130 RLE	AV 34	S134 RLE	AV 38	S138 RLE			

AV 39	M650 ELA	Volvo Olympian YN3RC16Z4 Ex Singapore Bus Services, 2000		Alexander 10.5m				H42/26D	1994

DL 1–21		Dennis Dart SLF SFD212BR1VGW1		Plaxton Pointer 10m				B36F	1997
DL 1	P201 OLX	**DL 6**	P206 OLX	**DL 11**	P211 OLX	**DL 16**	R116 RLY	**DL 21**	R121 RLY
DL 2	P202 OLX	**DL 7**	P207 OLX	**DL 12**	R112 RLY	**DL 17**	R117 RLY		
DL 3	P203 OLX	**DL 8**	P208 OLX	**DL 13**	R113 RLY	**DL 18**	R118 RLY		
DL 4	P204 OLX	**DL 9**	P209 OLX	**DL 14**	R114 RLY	**DL 19**	R119 RLY		
DL 5	P205 OLX	**DL 10**	P210 OLX	**DL 15**	R115 RLY	**DL 20**	R120 RLY		

DL 75–85		Dennis Dart SLF SFD212BR1WGW1		Plaxton Pointer 2 10.1m				B35F	1998
DL 75	R175 VLA	**DL 78**	R178 VLA	**DL 81**	R181 VLA	**DL 84**	R184 VLA		
DL 76	R176 VLA	**DL 79**	R179 VLA	**DL 82**	R182 VLA	**DL 85**	R185 VLA		
DL 77	R177 VLA	**DL 80**	R180 VLA	**DL 83**	R183 VLA				

DLD 22–53		Dennis Dart SLF SFD212BR1VGW1		Plaxton Pointer 2 10.1m				B30D	1997
DLD 22	R122 RLY	**DLD 29**	R129 RLY	**DLD 36**	R136 RLY	**DLD 43**	R143 RLY	**DLD 50**	R150 RLY
DLD 23	R123 RLY	**DLD 30**	R130 RLY	**DLD 37**	R137 RLY	**DLD 44**	R144 RLY	**DLD 51**	R151 RLY
DLD 24	R124 RLY	**DLD 31**	R131 RLY	**DLD 38**	R138 RLY	**DLD 45**	R145 RLY	**DLD 52**	R152 RLY
DLD 25	R125 RLY	**DLD 32**	R132 RLY	**DLD 39**	R139 RLY	**DLD 46**	R146 RLY	**DLD 53**	R153 RLY
DLD 26	R126 RLY	**DLD 33**	R133 RLY	**DLD 40**	R140 RLY	**DLD 47**	R147 RLY		
DLD 27	R127 RLY	**DLD 34**	R134 RLY	**DLD 41**	R141 RLY	**DLD 48**	R148 RLY		
DLD 28	R128 RLY	**DLD 35**	R135 RLY	**DLD 42**	R142 RLY	**DLD 49**	R149 RLY		

DLD 54–74		Dennis Dart SLF SFD212BR1WGW1		Plaxton Pointer 2 10.1m				B30D	1998
DLD 54	R154 VLA	**DLD 59**	R159 VLA	**DLD 64**	R164 VLA	**DLD 69**	R169 VLA	**DLD 74**	R174 VLA
DLD 55	R155 VLA	**DLD 60**	R160 VLA	**DLD 65**	R165 VLA	**DLD 70**	R170 VLA		
DLD 56	R156 VLA	**DLD 61**	R161 VLA	**DLD 66**	R166 VLA	**DLD 71**	R171 VLA		
DLD 57	R157 VLA	**DLD 62**	R162 VLA	**DLD 67**	R167 VLA	**DLD 72**	R172 VLA		
DLD 58	R158 VLA	**DLD 63**	R163 VLA	**DLD 68**	R168 VLA	**DLD 73**	R173 VLA		

DLD 86–100		Dennis Dart SLF SFD212AR1WGW1		Plaxton Pointer 2 10.1m				B25D	1998
DLD 86	S286 JLP	**DLD 89**	S289 JLP	**DLD 92**	S292 JLP	**DLD 95**	S295 JLP	**DLD 98**	S298 JLP
DLD 87	S287 JLP	**DLD 90**	S290 JLP	**DLD 93**	S293 JLP	**DLD 96**	S296 JLP	**DLD 99**	S299 JLP
DLD 88	S288 JLP	**DLD 91**	S291 JLP	**DLD 94**	S294 JLP	**DLD 97**	S297 JLP	**DLD 100**	S301 JLP

DLD 108–117		Dennis Dart SLF SFD212BR1XGW1		Plaxton Pointer 2 10.1m				B31D	1999
DLD 108	T48 KLD	**DLD 110**	T39 KLD	**DLD 112**	T52 KLD	**DLD 114**	T54 KLD	**DLD 116**	T56 KLD
DLD 109	T49 KLD	**DLD 111**	T51 KLD	**DLD 113**	T53 KLD	**DLD 115**	T35 KLD	**DLD 117**	T47 KLD

DLD 118–132		Dennis Dart SLF SFD212BR1XGW1		Plaxton Pointer 2 10.1m				B31D	1999
DLD 118	V118 GBY	**DLD 121**	V134 GBY	**DLD 124**	V124 GBY	**DLD 127**	V127 GBY	**DLD 130**	V130 GBY
DLD 119	V119 GBY	**DLD 122**	V122 GBY	**DLD 125**	V125 GBY	**DLD 128**	V128 GBY	**DLD 131**	V131 GBY
DLD 120	V120 GBY	**DLD 123**	V133 GBY	**DLD 126**	V126 GBY	**DLD 129**	V129 GBY	**DLD 132**	V132 GBY

DLD 133–149		Dennis Dart SLF SFD212AR1YGW1		Plaxton Pointer 2 10.1m				B31D	2000
DLD 133	W133 ULR	**DLD 137**	W137 ULR	**DLD 141**	W141 ULR	**DLD 145**	W153 ULR	**DLD 149**	W149 ULR
DLD 134	W134 ULR	**DLD 138**	W138 ULR	**DLD 142**	W142 ULR	**DLD 146**	W146 ULR		
DLD 135	W151 ULR	**DLD 139**	W139 ULR	**DLD 143**	W143 ULR	**DLD 147**	W147 ULR		
DLD 136	W136 ULR	**DLD 140**	W152 ULR	**DLD 144**	W144 ULR	**DLD 148**	W148 ULR		

DLD 161–197 Dennis Dart SLF SFD212AR11GW1 Plaxton Pointer 2 10.1m B30D 2001

DLD 161 Y661 NLO	**DLD 169** Y669 NLO	**DLD 177** Y237 NLK	**DLD 185** Y658 NLO	**DLD 193** Y263 NLK
DLD 162 Y662 NLO	**DLD 170** Y152 NLK	**DLD 178** Y238 NLK	**DLD 186** Y656 NLO	**DLD 194** Y264 NLK
DLD 163 Y663 NLO	**DLD 171** Y671 NLO	**DLD 179** Y239 NLK	**DLD 187** Y657 NLO	**DLD 195** Y265 NLK
DLD 164 Y664 NLO	**DLD 172** Y672 NLO	**DLD 180** Y158 NLK	**DLD 188** Y248 NLK	**DLD 196** Y159 NLK
DLD 165 Y665 NLO	**DLD 173** Y673 NLO	**DLD 181** Y659 NLO	**DLD 189** Y249 NLK	**DLD 197** Y157 NLK
DLD 166 Y161 NLK	**DLD 174** Y674 NLO	**DLD 182** Y652 NLO	**DLD 190** Y154 NLK	
DLD 167 Y667 NLO	**DLD 175** Y675 NLO	**DLD 183** Y653 NLO	**DLD 191** Y261 NLK	
DLD 168 Y668 NLO	**DLD 176** Y153 NLK	**DLD 184** Y654 NLO	**DLD 192** Y262 NLK	

DLM 150 X667 LLX Dennis Dart SLF SFD622AR1YGW1 Plaxton Pointer 2 8.8m B26F 2000
DLM 151 X668 LLX Dennis Dart SLF SFD622AR1YGW1 Plaxton Pointer 2 8.8m B26F 2000

DLM 152–160 Dennis Dart SLF SFD612AR11GW1 Plaxton Pointer 2 8.8m B29F 2001

DLM 152 Y252 NLK	**DLM 154** Y254 NLK	**DLM 156** Y256 NLK	**DLM 158** Y258 NLK	**DLM 160** Y151 NLK
DLM 153 Y253 NLK	**DLM 155** Y251 NLK	**DLM 157** Y257 NLK	**DLM 159** Y259 NLK	

DLS 1–7 Dennis Dart SLF SFD112BR1VGW1 Plaxton Pointer 9.2m B32F 1997

DLS 1 P101 OLX	**DLS 3** P103 OLX	**DLS 5** P105 OLX	**DLS 7** P107 OLX
DLS 2 P102 OLX	**DLS 4** P104 OLX	**DLS 6** P106 OLX	

DM 242t RIB 8431 Dennis Dart 9.8SDL3035 Marshall C37 B40F 1994
Ex MTL, London, 1998

DML 1–18 Dennis Dart SLF SFD212BR1VGW2 Marshall Capital 10.2m B28D 1998

DML 1 R681 MEW	**DML 5** R685 MEW	**DML 9** R689 MEW	**DML 13** R693 MEW	**DML 17** R697 MEW
DML 2 R682 MEW	**DML 6** R686 MEW	**DML 10** R690 MEW	**DML 14** R694 MEW	**DML 18** R698 MEW
DML 3 R683 MEW	**DML 7** R687 MEW	**DML 11** R691 MEW	**DML 15** R695 MEW	
DML 4 R684 MEW	**DML 8** R688 MEW	**DML 12** R692 MEW	**DML 16** R696 MEW	

DML 33–47 Dennis Dart SLF SFD212BR1WGW1 Marshall Capital 10.2m B28D 1998

DML 33 R863 MCE	**DML 36** R866 MCE	**DML 39** R869 MCE	**DML 42** R872 MCE	**DML 45** R875 MCE
DML 34 R864 MCE	**DML 37** R867 MCE	**DML 40** R870 MCE	**DML 43** R873 MCE	**DML 46** R876 MCE
DML 35 R865 MCE	**DML 38** R868 MCE	**DML 41** R871 MCE	**DML 44** R874 MCE	**DML 47** R877 MCE

DML 519–535 Dennis Dart SLF SFD212BR1WGW1 Marshall Capital 10.2m B31F 1998–9
(Originally numbered DML19–32)

DML 519 R619 VEG	**DML 523** R623 VEG	**DML 527** R627 VEG	**DML 531** R631 VEG	**DML 535** T65 KLD
DML 520 R620 VEG	**DML 524** R624 VEG	**DML 528** R638 VEG	**DML 532** R632 VEG	
DML 521 R621 VEG	**DML 525** R625 VEG	**DML 529** R629 VEG	**DML 533** T63 KLD	
DML 522 R622 VEG	**DML 526** R626 VEG	**DML 530** R630 VEG	**DML 534** T64 KLD	

DMS 1–12 Dennis Dart SLF SFD112BR1VGW1 Marshall Capital 9.3m B32F 1998

DMS 1 R701 MEW	**DMS 4** R704 MEW	**DMS 7** R707 MEW	**DMS 10** R710 MEW
DMS 2 R702 MEW	**DMS 5** R705 MEW	**DMS 8** R708 MEW	**DMS 11** R711 MEW
DMS 3 R703 MEW	**DMS 6** R706 MEW	**DMS 9** R709 MEW	**DMS 12** R699 MEW

DMS 13–29 Dennis Dart SLF SFD112BR1WGW1 Marshall Capital 9.3m *B32F 1998
*(DMS 28 is B27F)

DMS 13 S513 KFL	**DMS 17** S517 KFL	**DMS 21** S521 KFL	**DMS 25** S525 KFL	**DMS 29** S529 KFL
DMS 14 S514 KFL	**DMS 18** S518 KFL	**DMS 22** S522 KFL	**DMS 26** S526 KFL	
DMS 15 S515 KFL	**DMS 19** S519 KFL	**DMS 23** S523 KFL	**DMS 27** S527 KFL	
DMS 16 S516 KFL	**DMS 20** S520 KFL	**DMS 24** S524 KFL	**DMS 28** S528 KFL	

| DNL 101–120 | Dennis Dart 9SDL3034 Ex MTL, London, 1998 | Northern Counties Paladin 9m | B34F | 1994 |

DNL 101 L101 HHV	DNL 105 L105 HHV	DNL 109 L109 HHV	DNL 114 L114 HHV	DNL 118 L118 HHV
DNL 102 L102 HHV	DNL 106 L106 HHV	DNL 110 L110 HHV	DNL 115 L115 HHV	DNL 119 L119 HHV
DNL 103 L103 HHV	DNL 107 L107 HHV	DNL 112 L112 HHV	DNL 116 L116 HHV	DNL 120 L120 HHV
DNL 104 L104 HHV	DNL 108 L108 HHV	DNL 113 L113 HHV	DNL 117 L117 HHV	

| DP 234–239 | Dennis Dart 9SDL3011 Ex MTL, London, 1998 | Plaxton Pointer 9m | B35F | 1992 |

DP 234s K414 MGN	DP 236 K416 MGN	DP 238 K418 MGN
DP 235t RIB 5085	DP 237 K417 MGN	DP 239 K419 MGN

| DP 240 M498 ALP | Dennis Dart 9SDL3031 Ex MTL, London, 1998 | Plaxton Pointer 9m | B35F | 1995 |
| DP 241 M499 ALP | Dennis Dart 9SDL3031 Ex MTL, London, 1998 | Plaxton Pointer 9m | B35F | 1995 |

| DP 273–276 | Dennis Dart SFD212BR5VGD1 Ex MTL, London, 1998 | Plaxton Pointer 9m | B35F | 1997 |

DP 273 P673 MLE	DP 274 P674 MLE	DP 275 P675 MLE	DP 276 P676 MLE

| DR 81–148 | *Dennis Dart 8.5SDL3010 *(DR 142–8 are 8.5SDL3015) | Plaxton Pointer 8.5m | B28F | 1992 |

DR 81u J381 GKH	DR 90u J390 GKH	DR 94 J394 GKH	DR 144u K244 PAG	DR 147u K247 PAG
DR 86w J386 GKH	DR 92w J392 GKH	DR 96w J396 GKH	DR 145u K245 PAG	DR 148u K248 PAG
DR 89t J389 GKH	DR 93 J393 GKH	DR 97u J397 GKH	DR 146u K246 PAG	

| DRL 18–37 | Dennis Dart 9SDL3016 Ex MTL, London, 1998 | Plaxton Pointer 9m | B34F | 1992 |

DRL 18 K818 NKH	DRL 22 K822 NKH	DRL 26u K826 NKH	DRL 30 K430 OKH	DRL 34 K434 OKH
DRL 19 K819 NKH	DRL 23 K823 NKH	DRL 27u K827 NKH	DRL 31 K431 OKH	DRL 37s K437 OKH
DRL 20 K820 NKH	DRL 24 K824 NKH	DRL 28s K828 NKH	DRL 32 K432 OKH	
DRL 21 K821 NKH	DRL 25 K825 NKH	DRL 29 K429 OKH	DRL 33u K433 OKH	

| EDR 1–9 | Dennis Dart 9.8SDL3040 | Plaxton Pointer 9.8m | B39F | 1994 |

EDR 1 M101 BLE	EDR 3 M103 BLE	EDR 5 M105 BLE	EDR 7 M107 BLE	EDR 9 M109 BLE
EDR 2 M102 BLE	EDR 4 M104 BLE	EDR 6 M106 BLE	EDR 8 M108 BLE	

| EDR 10–44 | Dennis Dart SFD412BR5TGD1 | Plaxton Pointer 9.8m | B39F | 1996 |

EDR 10 P285 MLD	EDR 17 P292 MLD	EDR 24 P299 MLD	EDR 31 P307 MLD	EDR 38 P314 MLD
EDR 11 P286 MLD	EDR 18 P293 MLD	EDR 25 P301 MLD	EDR 32 P308 MLD	EDR 39 P315 MLD
EDR 12 P287 MLD	EDR 19 P294 MLD	EDR 26 P302 MLD	EDR 33 P309 MLD	EDR 40 P316 MLD
EDR 13 P288 MLD	EDR 20 P295 MLD	EDR 27 P303 MLD	EDR 34 P310 MLD	EDR 41 P317 MLD
EDR 14 P289 MLD	EDR 21 P296 MLD	EDR 28 P304 MLD	EDR 35 P311 MLD	EDR 42 P318 MLD
EDR 15 P290 MLD	EDR 22 P297 MLD	EDR 29 P305 MLD	EDR 36 P312 MLD	EDR 43 P319 MLD
EDR 16 P291 MLD	EDR 23 P298 MLD	EDR 30 P306 MLD	EDR 37 P313 MLD	EDR 44 P320 MLD

EDR 45	M503 ALP	Dennis Dart 9.8SDL3054	Plaxton Pointer 9.8m	B39F	1995
		Ex MTL, London, 1998 (Formerly DP 245)			
EDR 46	M504 ALP	Dennis Dart 9.8SDL3054	Plaxton Pointer 9.8m	B39F	1995
		Ex MTL, London, 1998 (Formerly DP 246)			
EDR 47	M505 ALP	Dennis Dart 9.8SDL3054	Plaxton Pointer 9.8m	B39F	1995
		Ex MTL, London, 1998 (Formerly DP 247)			
EDR 48	M506 ALP	Dennis Dart 9.8SDL3054	Plaxton Pointer 9.8m	B39F	1995
		Ex MTL, London, 1998 (Formerly DP 248)			
EDR 49	33 LUG	Dennis Dart 9.8SDL3017	Plaxton Pointer 9.8m	B39F	1992
		Ex MTL, London, 1998 (Formerly DPL 233)			

LLW 25–38		Dennis Lance SLF 11SDA3202	Wright Pathfinder 320	B34D	1993/4
		Ex London Buses, 1994			

LLW 25	L25 WLH	**LLW 28**	L28 WLH	**LLW 31**	L31 WLH	**LLW 34**	L34 WLH	**LLW 37**	L37 WLH
LLW 26	L26 WLH	**LLW 29**	L29 WLH	**LLW 32**	L32 WLH	**LLW 35**	L35 WLH	**LLW 38**	L38 WLH
LLW 27	L27 WLH	**LLW 30**	L21 WLH	**LLW 33**	L39 WLH	**LLW 36**	L36 WLH		

M 1–5		MCW Metrobus DR101/3	MCW	H43/28D	1978
		Ex London Buses, 1994			

M 1t	THX 101S	**M 3**t	THX 103S	**M 4**t	THX 104S	**M 5**t	THX 105S

M 102–166		MCW Metrobus DR101/8	MCW	H43/28D	1979
		Ex London Buses, 1994			

M 102t	BYX 102V	**M 111**t	BYX 111V	**M 151**w	BYX 151V	**M 166**w	BYX 166V

M 306–482		MCW Metrobus DR101/12	MCW	H43/28D	1980
		Ex London Buses, 1994			

M 306	BYX 306V	**M 367**t	GYE 367W	**M 409**t	GYE 409W	**M 449**	GYE 449W
M 324	EYE 324V	**M 373**	GYE 373W	**M 429**	GYE 429W	**M 455**s	GYE 455W
M 342	EYE 342V	**M 391**	GYE 391W	**M 432**	GYE 432W	**M 460**	GYE 460W
M 352	GYE 352W	**M 407**	GYE 407W	**M 446**t	GYE 446W	**M 482**t	GYE 482W

M 595	GYE 595W	MCW Metrobus DR101/14	MCW	H43/28D	1981
		Ex London Buses, 1994			
M 618	KYO 618X	MCW Metrobus DR101/14	MCW	H43/28D	1981
		Ex London Buses, 1994			
M 655	KYV 655X	MCW Metrobus DR101/14	MCW	H43/28D	1981
		Ex London Buses, 1994			
M 678t	KYV 678X	MCW Metrobus DR101/14	MCW	H43/28D	1981
		Ex MTL, London, 1998			

M 876–955		MCW Metrobus DR101/16	MCW	H43/28D	1983
		* Ex MTL, London, 1998 *(Ms 935, 937, 950, 955 are ex London Buses, 1994)			

M 876	OJD 876Y	**M 879**t	OJD 879Y	**M 921**	A921 SUL	**M 950**	A950 SUL
M 878t	OJD 878Y	**M 890**t	OJD 890Y	**M 935**	A935 SUL	**M 955**	A955 SUL

M 961–1042		MCW Metrobus DR101/17	MCW	H43/28D	1984
		*Ex London Buses, 1994 (*M 961, 964, 1032, 1042 ex MTL, London, 1998)			

M 961t	A961 SYF	**M 1004**	A704 THV	**M 1034**	A734 THV	**M 1042**	A742 THV
M 995t	A995 SYF	**M 1032**u	A732 THV	**M 1035**	A735 THV		

M 1045t	A745 THV	MCW Metrobus DR101/19 Ex MTL, London, 1998	MCW	DPH43/28D	1984
M 1047	A747 THV	MCW Metrobus DR101/19 Ex London Buses, 1994	MCW	H43/28D	1984

M 1058–1431 MCW Metrobus DR101/17 MCW *H43/28D 1985–6
Ex MTL, London, 1998 or ex London Buses, 1994(†) *(Ms 1185, 1236,1393 & 1396 are DPH43/28D)

M 1058u	B58 WUL	**M 1142**t	B142 WUL	**M 1197**†	B197 WUL	**M 1339**†	C339 BUV	**M 1395**	C395 BUV
M 1059	B59 WUL	**M 1147**	B147 WUL	**M 1198**†	B198 WUL	**M 1342**†	C342 BUV	**M 1396**t	C396 BUV
M 1060u	B60 WUL	**M 1148**	B148 WUL	**M 1204**†	B204 WUL	**M 1346**†	C346 BUV	**M 1397**	C397 BUV
M 1061t	B61 WUL	**M 1150**	B150 WUL	**M 1205**†	B205 WUL	**M 1349**†	C349 BUV	**M 1403**	C403 BUV
M 1065	B65 WUL	**M 1151**	B151 WUL	**M 1208**†	B208 WUL	**M 1350**†	C350 BUV	**M 1408**†	C408 BUV
M 1067t	B67 WUL	**M 1153**	B153 WUL	**M 1234**	B234 WUL	**M 1355**	C355 BUV	**M 1416**†	C416 BUV
M 1068†	B68 WUL	**M 1156**w	B156 WUL	**M 1236**†	B236 WUL	**M 1365**	C365 BUV	**M 1425**†	C425 BUV
M 1076	B76 WUL	**M 1157**	B157 WUL	**M 1250**	B250 WUL	**M 1366**†	C366 BUV	**M 1427**†	C427 BUV
M 1080	B80 WUL	**M 1158**	B158 WUL	**M 1273**†	B273 WUL	**M 1383**†	C383 BUV	**M 1428**†	C428 BUV
M 1081	B81 WUL	**M 1167**†	B167 WUL	**M 1274**†	B274 WUL	**M 1385**	C385 BUV	**M 1429**†	WLT 826
M 1111	B111 WUL	**M 1181**†	B181 WUL	**M 1287**	B287 WUL	**M 1390**t	C390 BUV	**M 1431**†	C431 BUV
M 1114	B114 WUL	**M 1185**†	B185 WUL	**M 1292**	B292 WUL	**M 1392**t	C392 BUV		
M 1118	B118 WUL	**M 1189**†	B189 WUL	**M 1325**	C325 BUV	**M 1393**t	C393 BUV		
M 1141	B141 WUL	**M 1193**†	B193 WUL	**M 1330**	C330 BUV	**M 1394**	C394 BUV		

MC 1w	P481 HEG	Marshall Minibus Ex MTL, London, 1998	Marshall	B29F	1996

MM 254–278 MAN 11.220 *Marshall C37 B38F 1996
Ex MTL, London, 1998 *(MM 270–278 are Marshall Capital)

MM 254	N121 XEG	**MM 259**	N126 XEG	**MM 264**	N131 XEG	**MM 270**	P470 JEG	**MM 275** P475 JEG
MM 255	N122 XEG	**MM 260**	N127 XEG	**MM 265**	N132 XEG	**MM 271**	P471 JEG	**MM 276** P476 JEG
MM 256	N123 XEG	**MM 261**	N128 XEG	**MM 266**	N133 XEG	**MM 272**	P472 JEG	**MM 277** P477 JEG
MM 257	N124 XEG	**MM 262**	N129 XEG	**MM 267**	N134 XEG	**MM 273**	P473 JEG	**MM 278** P478 JEG
MM 258	N125 XEG	**MM 263**	N130 XEG	**MM 268**	N135 XEG	**MM 274**	P474 JEG	

MMS 269	N161 YEG	Mercedes-Benz 811D Ex MTL, London, 1998	Marshall C16	B26F	1996
MR 87	F87 GGC	Mercedes-Benz 811D Ex MTL, London, 1998	Robin Hood	C29F	1989
MR 90	F90 GGC	Mercedes-Benz 811D Ex MTL, London, 1998	Robin Hood	C29F	1989
MRL 223	P448 SWX	Optare MetroRider MR13 Ex MTL, London, 1998	Optare	B29F	1997
MRL 224	P449 SWX	Optare MetroRider MR13 Ex MTL, London, 1998	Optare	B29F	1997

OM 243 M501 ALP		Optare MetroRider MR33 Ex MTL, London, 1998		Optare				B25F		1995
OM 244 M502 ALP		Optare MetroRider MR33 Ex MTL, London, 1998		Optare				B25F		1995
OM 279 P509 NWU		Optare MetroRider MR13 Ex MTL, London, 1998		Optare				B25F		1996

RM 268–1979   AEC Routemaster R2RH   Park Royal   *H36/28R   1959–65
Ex MTL, London, 1998 (RM 644 ex London Buses, 1994. RM 848 ex Reading Mainline, 2000)
*(RM 644 is O36/28RD)

RM 268 VLT 268	**RM 644** WLT 644	**RM 848** WLT 848	**RM 1799** 799 DYE	**RM 1979** ALD 979B
RM 446 WLT 446	**RM 646** WLT 646	**RM 1348** 348 CLT	**RM 1971** ALD 971B	

RMC 1513 513 CLT		AEC Routemaster R2RH Ex London Buses, 1994		Park Royal				O32/25RD		1962
RML 893 WLT 893		AEC Routemaster R2RH Ex London Buses, 1994		Park Royal				H40/32R		1961
RML 902 WLT 902		AEC Routemaster R2RH Ex London Buses, 1994		Park Royal				H40/32R		1961
RML 903 WLT 903		AEC Routemaster R2RH Ex MTL, London, 1998		Park Royal				H40/32R		1961

RML 2274–2755   AEC Routemaster R2RH/1   Park Royal   H40/32R   1965–8
(Ex London Buses, 1994 or [†] MTL, London, 1998 [‡]). (RML 2443, 2633 & 2659 ex London Transport, 1997)

RML 2274† CUV 274C	**RML 2367**‡ JJD 367D	**RML 2478**† JJD 478D	**RML 2599**† NML 599E	**RML 2698**† SMK 698F
RML 2282‡ CUV 282C	**RML 2368**† JJD 368D	**RML 2479**‡ JJD 479D	**RML 2603**‡ NML 603E	**RML 2699**‡ SMK 699F
RML 2284‡ CUV 284C	**RML 2377**† JJD 377D	**RML 2508**† JJD 508D	**RML 2620**‡ NML 620E	**RML 2701**† SMK 701F
RML 2285† CUV 285C	**RML 2384**† JJD 384D	**RML 2509**† JJD 509D	**RML 2633** NML 633E	**RML 2703**† SMK 703F
RML 2288† CUV 288C	**RML 2393**‡ JJD 393D	**RML 2511**‡ JJD 511D	**RML 2634**† NML 634E	**RML 2706**† SMK 706F
RML 2289† CUV 289C	**RML 2395**† JJD 395D	**RML 2532**† JJD 532D	**RML 2649**† NML 649E	**RML 2710**† SMK 710F
RML 2295‡ CUV 295C	**RML 2413**† JJD 413D	**RML 2537**† JJD 537D	**RML 2651**† NML 651E	**RML 2713**† SMK 713F
RML 2296‡ CUV 296C	**RML 2419**‡ JJD 419D	**RML 2547**† JJD 547D	**RML 2652**† NML 652E	**RML 2727**‡ SMK 727F
RML 2299† CUV 299C	**RML 2430**† JJD 430D	**RML 2558**† JJD 558D	**RML 2659** SMK 659F	**RML 2728**† SMK 728F
RML 2308† CUV 308C	**RML 2431**† JJD 431D	**RML 2561**‡ JJD 561D	**RML 2679**‡ SMK 679F	**RML 2731**‡ SMK 731F
RML 2310‡ CUV 310C	**RML 2439**† JJD 439D	**RML 2566**† JJD 566D	**RML 2681**† SMK 681F	**RML 2737**† SMK 737F
RML 2312† CUV 312C	**RML 2443** JJD 443D	**RML 2579**† JJD 579D	**RML 2689**† SMK 689F	**RML 2755**† SMK 755F
RML 2331† CUV 331C	**RML 2446**† JJD 446D	**RML 2585**† JJD 585D	**RML 2690**† SMK 690F	
RML 2348† CUV 348C	**RML 2471**† JJD 471D	**RML 2594**† JJD 594D	**RML 2695**† SMK 695F	

S 11–20   Scania N113DRB   Alexander RH   H47/31F   1991
Ex MTL, London, 1998

S 11	J811 HMC	**S 13**	J813 HMC	**S 15**	J815 HMC	**S 17**	J817 HMC	**S 19** J819 HMC
S 12	J812 HMC	**S 14**	J814 HMC	**S 16**	J816 HMC	**S 18**	J818 HMC	**S 20** J820 HMC

TA 66–117   Dennis Trident 2 SFD111BR1XGX1   Alexander ALX400 9.9m   H45/19D   1999

TA 66 T61 KLD	**TA 77** T87 KLD	**TA 88** T188 CLO	**TA 99** T199 CLO	**TA 110** V310 GLB
TA 67 T67 KLD	**TA 78** T78 KLD	**TA 89** T189 CLO	**TA 100** T218 CLO	**TA 111** V311 GLB
TA 68 T68 KLD	**TA 79** T79 KLD	**TA 90** T190 CLO	**TA 101** T201 CLO	**TA 112** V312 GLB
TA 69 T69 KLD	**TA 80** T89 KLD	**TA 91** T191 CLO	**TA 102** T202 CLO	**TA 113** V313 GLB
TA 70 T37 KLD	**TA 81** T38 KLD	**TA 92** T192 CLO	**TA 103** V303 GLB	**TA 114** V314 GLB
TA 71 T41 KLD	**TA 82** T182 CLO	**TA 93** T193 CLO	**TA 104** T204 CLO	**TA 115** V315 GLB
TA 72 T72 KLD	**TA 83** T183 CLO	**TA 94** T194 CLO	**TA 105** T205 CLO	**TA 116** V316 GLB
TA 73 T43 KLD	**TA 84** T184 CLO	**TA 95** T195 CLO	**TA 106** T206 CLO	**TA 117** V317 GLB
TA 74 T74 KLD	**TA 85** T185 CLO	**TA 96** T196 CLO	**TA 107** T207 CLO	
TA 75 T75 KLD	**TA 86** T186 CLO	**TA 97** T197 CLO	**TA 108** V308 GLB	
TA 76 T76 KLD	**TA 87** T187 CLO	**TA 98** T198 CLO	**TA 109** V309 GLB	

TAL 118–134

Dennis Trident 2 SFD311BR1YGX2   Alexander ALX400 10.5m   H45/24D   2000

TAL 118	X341 HLL	TAL 122	X322 HLL	TAL 126	X326 HLL	TAL 130	X342 HLL	TAL 134	X334 HLL
TAL 119	X319 HLL	TAL 123	X343 HLL	TAL 127	X327 HLL	TAL 131	X331 HLL		
TAL 120	X336 HLL	TAL 124	X324 HLL	TAL 128	X338 HLL	TAL 132	X332 HLL		
TAL 121	X337 HLL	TAL 125	X335 HLL	TAL 129	X329 HLL	TAL 133	X339 HLL		

TP 1–65

*Dennis Trident 2 SFD111BR1XGX2   Plaxton President 9.9m   *H41/21D   1999
*(TP 2–31 are SFD111BR1WGX2 and are also H45/22D)

TP 1	T101 KLD	TP 14	T114 KLD	TP 27	T127 KLD	TP 40	T140 CLO	TP 53	V753 HBY
TP 2	T102 KLD	TP 15	T115 KLD	TP 28	T128 KLD	TP 41	T141 CLO	TP 54	V754 HBY
TP 3	T103 KLD	TP 16	T116 KLD	TP 29	T129 KLD	TP 42	T142 CLO	TP 55	V755 HBY
TP 4	T104 KLD	TP 17	T117 KLD	TP 30	T97 KLD	TP 43	T143 CLO	TP 56	V756 HBY
TP 5	T105 KLD	TP 18	T118 KLD	TP 31	T98 KLD	TP 44	T144 CLO	TP 57	V757 HBY
TP 6	T106 KLD	TP 19	T119 KLD	TP 32	T132 CLO	TP 45	T145 CLO	TP 58	V758 HBY
TP 7	T107 KLD	TP 20	T120 KLD	TP 33	T133 CLO	TP 46	T146 CLO	TP 59	V759 HBY
TP 8	T108 KLD	TP 21	T71 KLD	TP 34	T134 CLO	TP 47	V307 GLB	TP 60	V760 HBY
TP 9	T109 KLD	TP 22	T122 KLD	TP 35	T135 CLO	TP 48	T148 CLO	TP 61	V761 HBY
TP 10	T110 KLD	TP 23	T73 KLD	TP 36	T136 CLO	TP 49	V749 HBY	TP 62	V762 HBY
TP 11	T81 KLD	TP 24	T124 KLD	TP 37	T137 CLO	TP 50	V750 HBY	TP 63	V763 HBY
TP 12	T112 KLD	TP 25	T125 KLD	TP 38	T138 CLO	TP 51	V751 HBY	TP 64	V764 HBY
TP 13	T113 KLD	TP 26	T126 KLD	TP 39	T139 CLO	TP 52	V752 HBY	TP 65	V765 HBY

V 201–217

Volvo Olympian YN2RV18Z4   Northern Counties Palatine II   H47/25D   1993/4
Ex MTL, London, 1998

V 201	L201 SKD	V 205	L205 SKD	V 209	L209 SKD	V 214	L214 TWM
V 202	L202 SKD	V 206	L206 SKD	V 210	L210 SKD	V 215	L215 TWM
V 203	L203 SKD	V 207	L207 SKD	V 212	L212 TWM	V 216	L216 TWM
V 204	L204 SKD	V 208	L208 SKD	V 213	L213 TWM	V 217	L217 TWM

VPL 135–236

Volvo B7TL   Plaxton President 10.6m   H43/24D   2001

VPL 135	X635 LLX	VPL 156	X656 LLX	VPL 177	Y177 NLK	VPL 198	Y148 NLK	VPL 219	LK51 XGO
VPL 136	X636 LLX	VPL 157	X657 LLX	VPL 178	Y178 NLK	VPL 199	Y199 NLK	VPL 220	LK51 XGP
VPL 137	X637 LLX	VPL 158	X658 LLX	VPL 179	Y179 NLK	VPL 200	Y149 NLK	VPL 221	LK51 XGR
VPL 138	X638 LLX	VPL 159	X659 LLX	VPL 180	Y197 NLK	VPL 201	Y201 NLK	VPL 222	LK51 XGS
VPL 139	X639 LLX	VPL 160	X662 LLX	VPL 181	Y181 NLK	VPL 202	Y202 NLK	VPL 223	LK51 XGT
VPL 140	X664 LLX	VPL 161	X661 LLX	VPL 182	Y182 NLK	VPL 203	Y203 NLK	VPL 224	LK51 XGU
VPL 141	X641 LLX	VPL 162	Y162 NLK	VPL 183	Y183 NLK	VPL 204	Y204 NLK	VPL 225	LK51 XGV
VPL 142	X642 LLX	VPL 163	Y163 NLK	VPL 184	Y184 NLK	VPL 205	LK51 XGD	VPL 226	LK51 XGW
VPL 143	X643 LLX	VPL 164	Y164 NLK	VPL 185	Y185 NLK	VPL 206	Y246 NLK	VPL 227	LK51 XGX
VPL 144	X644 LLX	VPL 165	Y165 NLK	VPL 186	Y186 NLK	VPL 207	Y207 NLK	VPL 228	LK51 XGY
VPL 145	X645 LLX	VPL 166	Y166 NLK	VPL 187	Y187 NLK	VPL 208	Y208 NLK	VPL 229	LK51 XGZ
VPL 146	X646 LLX	VPL 167	Y167 NLK	VPL 188	Y188 NLK	VPL 209	Y209 NLK	VPL 230	LK51 XHA
VPL 147	X647 LLX	VPL 168	Y168 NLK	VPL 189	Y189 NLK	VPL 210	Y143 NLK	VPL 231	LK51 XHB
VPL 148	X648 LLX	VPL 169	Y169 NLK	VPL 190	Y198 NLK	VPL 211	LK51 XGE	VPL 232	Y232 NLK
VPL 149	X649 LLX	VPL 170	Y196 NLK	VPL 191	Y191 NLK	VPL 212	LK51 XGF	VPL 233	Y233 NLK
VPL 150	X663 LLX	VPL 171	Y171 NLK	VPL 192	Y192 NLK	VPL 213	LK51 XGG	VPL 234	Y234 NLK
VPL 151	X651 LLX	VPL 172	Y172 NLK	VPL 193	Y193 NLK	VPL 214	LK51 XGH	VPL 235	Y235 NLK
VPL 152	X652 LLX	VPL 173	Y173 NLK	VPL 194	Y194 NLK	VPL 215	LK51 XGJ	VPL 236	Y236 NLK
VPL 153	X653 LLX	VPL 174	Y174 NLK	VPL 195	Y144 NLK	VPL 216	LK51 XGL		
VPL 154	X654 LLX	VPL 175	Y195 NLK	VPL 196	Y146 NLK	VPL 217	LK51 XGM		
VPL 155	X665 LLX	VPL 176	Y176 NLK	VPL 197	Y147 NLK	VPL 218	LK51 XGN		

Special Liveries:
DR 93, 94 and MM 273 all blue and carry dedicated adverts for Tesco.
M 409 allover advert for AA Roadwatch.
M 1393 allover advert for the Ultimate People Carrier.

Previous registrations:

33 LUG	J823 GGF	**B273 WUL**	WLT 902, B273 WUL	**WLT 646**	KFF 257, WLT 646
585 CLT	P481 MBY	**RIB 5085**	K415 MGN	**WLT 826**	C429 BUV
B185 WUL	WLT 893, B185 WUL	**RIB 8431**	L416 PAR	**WLT 893**	KFF 276, WLT 893
B236 WUL	WLT646, B236 WUL	**M650 ELA**	SBS 7251Y	**WLT 902**	ALC 464A, WLT 902

On order:
33 x Dennis Trident/Plaxton President 10.5m for routes 263 and C2.
10 x DLD Darts.

METROPOLITAN OMNIBUS

M 76	WYW 76T	MCW Metrobus DR101/9	MCW	H43/28F	1979
		Ex Metrobus, 1999			
M 231	BYX 231V	MCW Metrobus DR101/12	MCW	H43/28D	1980
		Ex London General, 1998			
M 235	BYX 235V	MCW Metrobus DR101/12	MCW	H43/28D	1980
		Ex London General, 1998			
M 259	BYX 259V	MCW Metrobus DR101/12	MCW	H43/28D	1980
		Ex London General, 1998			
M 262	BYX 262V	MCW Metrobus DR101/12	MCW	H43/28D	1980
		Ex Metrobus, 1999			
M 292	BYX 292V	MCW Metrobus DR101/12	MCW	H43/28D	1980
		Ex London General, 2000			
M 444	GYE 444W	MCW Metrobus DR101/12	MCW	H43/28D	1980
		Ex Frimley Coaches, Aldershot, 2001			
M 527	GYE 527W	MCW Metrobus DR101/14	MCW	H43/28D	1981
		Ex London General, 1998			
M 571	GYE 571W	MCW Metrobus DR101/14	MCW	H43/28D	1981
		Ex Metroline, 2000			
M 693	KYV 693X	MCW Metrobus DR101/14	MCW	H43/28D	1981
		Ex Metroline, 2000			
M 709	KYV 709X	MCW Metrobus DR101/14	MCW	H43/30F	1981
		Ex Arriva Croydon & North Surrey, 2001			
M 764	KYV 764X	MCW Metrobus DR101/14	MCW	H43/28D	1982
		Ex Metroline, 2000			
M 801	KYV 801X	MCW Metrobus DR101/14	MCW	H43/28D	1982
		Ex Metroline, 2000			

VS 501–515		Volvo B6BLE	East Lancs Spryte 10.9m	B35D	1999

VS 501	V501 EFR	**VS 504**	V504 EFR	**VS 507**	V507 EFR	**VS 510**	V510 EFR	**VS 513** V513 EFR
VS 502	V502 EFR	**VS 505**	V505 EFR	**VS 508**	V508 EFR	**VS 511**	V511 EFR	**VS 514** V514 EFR
VS 503	V503 EFR	**VS 506**	V506 EFR	**VS 509**	V509 EFR	**VS 512**	V512 EFR	**VS 515** V515 EFR

VS 516–521		Volvo B6BLE	East Lancs Spryte 10.9m	B34D	2000

VS 516	W516 CCK	**VS 517**	W517 CCK	**VS 518**	W518 CCK	**VS 519** W519 CCK	**VS 521** W521 CCK

MITCHAM BELLE   (Bus Fleet)

	Dennis Dart SLF SFD322BR1XGW1		Plaxton Pointer 2 10.7m	B33D	1999
T151 OGC	T153 OGC	T156 OGC	T158 OGC		
T152 OGC	T154 OGC	T157 OGC	T159 OGC		

	Dennis Dart SLF SFD322BR1XGW1		Plaxton Pointer 2 10.7m	B33D	1999
T875 HGT	T876 HGT	T877 HGT	T880 HGT		

	Dennis Dart SLF SFD212BR1YGW1		Plaxton Pointer 2 10.1m	B31D	2000
W112 WGT	W119 WGT	W128 WGT	W137 WGT	W144 WGT	
W114 WGT	W122 WGT	W132 WGT	W138 WGT	W146 WGT	
W116 WGT	W124 WGT	W133 WGT	W141 WGT	W147 WGT	
W117 WGT	W126 WGT	W134 WGT	W142 WGT	W149 WGT	
W118 WGT	W127 WGT	W136 WGT	W143 WGT		

	Optare Solo M850		Optare	B29F	2001
KX51 UCS	KX51 UCT	KX51 UCU	KX51 UCV		

On order:
New vehicles for route 152. Details not confirmed at time of going to press.

SOVEREIGN BUSES (London)   (LBSL fleet)

RM 23	JFO 256	AEC Routemaster R2RH	Park Royal	H36/28R	1959
		Ex Reading Mainline, 2000			
RM 45	ATS 415A	AEC Routemaster R2RH	Park Royal	H36/28R	1959
		Ex Reading Mainline, 2000			
RM 121	SSL 806	AEC Routemaster R2RH	Park Royal	H36/28R	1959
		Ex First Capital, 2000			
RM 180	XVS 830	AEC Routemaster R2RH	Park Royal	H36/28R	1960
		Ex Reading Mainline, 2000			
RM 191	ATS 416A	AEC Routemaster R2RH	Park Royal	H36/28R	1960
		Ex Reading Mainline, 2000			
RM 324	WLT 324	AEC Routemaster R2RH	Park Royal	H36/28R	1960
		Ex Halifax Joint Committee, 2000			
RM 329	MFF 578	AEC Routemaster R2RH	Park Royal	H36/28R	1960
		Ex preservation, 2000			
RM 441	LDS 341A	AEC Routemaster R2RH	Park Royal	H36/28R	1960
		Ex preservation, 2000			
RM 659	KFF 239	AEC Routemaster R2RH	Park Royal	H36/28R	1961
		Ex Halifax Joint Committee, 2000			
RM 931	MFF 580	AEC Routemaster R2RH	Park Royal	H36/28R	1961
		Ex Reading Mainline, 2000			
RM 1005	ALC 290A	AEC Routemaster R2RH	Park Royal	H36/28R	1962
		Re-acquired ex London Buses, 2000			
RM 1018	PVS 828	AEC Routemaster R2RH	Park Royal	H36/28R	1962
		Ex Reading Mainline, 2000			
RM 1204	204 CLT	AEC Routemaster R2RH	Park Royal	H36/28R	1962
		Ex Halifax Joint Committee, 2000			
RM 1218	218 CLT	AEC Routemaster R2RH	Park Royal	H36/28R	1962
		Ex preservation, 2000			

RM 1568 BNK 324A	AEC Routemaster R2RH Ex MTL, London, 2000		Park Royal			H36/28R		1963
RM 1627 627 DYE	AEC Routemaster R2RH Ex Reading Mainline, 2000		Park Royal			H36/28R		1963
RM 1735 735 DYE	AEC Routemaster R2RH Ex Reading Mainline, 2000		Park Royal			H36/28R		1963
RM 1913 ALD 913B	AEC Routemaster R2RH Ex private owner, 2000		Park Royal			H36/28R		1964
RM 1933 ALD 933B	AEC Routemaster R2RH Ex Stagecoach Cumberland, 2000		Park Royal			H36/28R		1964
RM 2071 ALM 71B	AEC Routemaster R2RH Ex Reading Mainline, 2000		Park Royal			H36/28R		1964
RM 2089 ALM 89B	AEC Routemaster R2RH Ex Reading Mainline, 2000		Park Royal			H36/28R		1964

24–29 DAF DE02DB250LF Ex Arriva London, 2001 Optare Spectra H40/21D 1999

24	T124 AUA	26	T126 AUA	28	T128 AUA
25	T125 AUA	27	T127 AUA	29	T129 AUA

30–39 DAF DE02DB250LF Ex Arriva London, 2001 Plaxton President 10.5m H45/19D 1999

30	T130 AUA	32	T132 AUA	34	T134 AUA	36	T136 AUA	38	T138 AUA
31	T131 AUA	33	T133 AUA	35	T135 AUA	37	T137 AUA	39	T139 AUA

37t BPF 137Y Leyland Olympian ONTL11/1R Roe H43/29F 1983

48–52 Leyland Olympian ON2R50C13Z4 Ex BTS, Borehamwood, 1998 Northern Counties H47/30F 1991

48	H148 GGS	49	H149 GGS	50	H150 GGS	52	H152 GGS

53–64 Volvo Olympian OLY–4953 Northern Counties Palatine 1 H43/29F 1998

53	S53 VNM	56	S56 VNM	58	S58 VNM	63	S63 WNM
54	S54 VNM	57	S57 VNM	59	S59 VNM	64	S64 WNM

457–461 Mercedes-Benz 811D Plaxton Beaver 2 B31F 1995

457	M457 UUR	458	M458 UUR	459	M459 UUR	460	M460 UUR	461	M461 UUR

503–557 Dennis Dart SLF SFD212BR1XGW1 Plaxton Pointer 2 10.1m B31D 1999

503	T503 JPP	515	V515 JBH	526	V526 JBH	537	V537 JBH	549	V549 JBH
504	T504 JPP	516	V516 JBH	527	V527 JBH	538	V538 JBH	550	V550 JBH
506	V506 JBH	517	V517 JBH	528	V528 JBH	539	V539 JBH	551	V551 JBH
507	V507 JBH	518	V518 JBH	529	V529 JBH	540	V540 JBH	552	V552 JBH
508	V508 JBH	519	V519 JBH	530	V530 JBH	542	V542 JBH	553	V553 JBH
509	V509 JBH	520	V520 JBH	531	V531 JBH	543	V543 JBH	554	V554 JBH
510	V510 JBH	521	V521 JBH	532	V532 JBH	544	V544 JBH	556	V556 JBH
511	V511 JBH	522	V522 JBH	533	V533 JBH	545	V545 JBH	557	V557 JBH
512	V512 JBH	523	V523 JBH	534	V534 JBH	546	V546 JBH		
513	V513 JBH	524	V524 JBH	535	V535 JBH	547	V547 JBH		
514	V514 JBH	525	V525 JBH	536	V536 JBH	548	V548 JBH		

558–562 Dennis Dart SLF SFD112BR1XGW1 Plaxton Pointer 2 9.3m B29F 1999

558	V558 JBH	559	V559 JBH	560	V560 JBH	561	V561 JBH	562	V562 JBH

2717–2733		Volvo B7TL			Plaxton President 10.6m			H43/24D	2001
2717	LN51 AZA	**2721**	LN51 AZF	**2725**	LN51 AZP	**2729**	LN51 AZV	**2733**	LN51 AZZ
2718	LN51 AZB	**2722**	LN51 AZG	**2726**	LN51 AZR	**2730**	LN51 AZW		
2719	LN51 AZC	**2723**	LN51 AZJ	**2727**	LN51 AZT	**2731**	LN51 AZX		
2720	LN51 AZD	**2724**	LN51 AZL	**2728**	LN51 AZU	**2732**	LN51 AZY		

Previous registrations:

ALC 290A	5 CLT	**KFF 239**	WLT 659	**S63 VNM**	S63 WNM
ATS 415A	VLT 45	**LDS 341A**	WLT 441	**S64 VNM**	S64 WNM
ATS 416A	VLT 191	**MFF 578**	WLT 329	**SSL 806**	VLT 121
BNK 324A	568 CLT	**MFF 580**	WLT 931	**XVS 830**	VLT 180
JFO 256	VLT 23, LGH 31T	**PVS 828**	18 CLT		

STAGECOACH IN LONDON

DA 10t	G684 KNW	DAF SB220LC550 Ex London Buses, 1994		Optare Delta				B40D	1989

DA 11–35		DAF SB220LC550		Optare Delta				B40D	1992/3
		(DA 13 & 15 ex Stagecoach South, 2000, the rest ex London Buses, 1994)							
DA 11t	J711 CYG	**DA 16**t	J716 CYG	**DA 21**t	J721 CYG	**DA 26**t	J726 CYG	**DA 31**t	K631 HWX
DA 12t	J712 CYG	**DA 17**t	J717 CYG	**DA 22**t	J722 CYG	**DA 27**t	J727 CYG	**DA 32**t	K632 HWX
DA 13t	J713 DAP	**DA 18**t	J718 CYG	**DA 23**t	J723 CYG	**DA 28**t	J728 CYG	**DA 33**t	K633 HWX
DA 14t	J714 CYG	**DA 19**t	J719 CYG	**DA 24**t	J724 CYG	**DA 29**t	J729 CYG	**DA 34**t	K634 HWX
DA 15t	J715 DAP	**DA 20**t	J720 CYG	**DA 25**t	J725 CYG	**DA 30**t	K630 HWX	**DA 35**t	K635 HWX

DRL 126–134		Dennis Dart 9SDL3024 Ex London Buses, 1994		Plaxton Pointer 9m				B34F	1993
DRL 126w	K126 SRH	**DRL 130**w	K130 SRH	**DRL 133**w	K133 SRH	**DRL 134**w	K134 SRH		

DT 618	P618 PGP	Dennis Dart SFD412BR5TGD1		Alexander Dash 9.8m				B36F	1996
DT 619	P619 PGP	Dennis Dart SFD412BR5TGD1		Alexander Dash 9.8m				B36F	1996
DT 634	P634 PGP	Dennis Dart SFD412BR5TGD1		Alexander Dash 9.8m				B36F	1996

LCY 1–7		Dennis Dart SLF SFD212BR1TGW1		Alexander ALX 200 10.2m				B29D	1997
LCY 1	P801 NJN	**LCY 3**	P803 NJN	**LCY 5**	P805 NJN	**LCY 7**	P807 NJN		
LCY 2	P802 NJN	**LCY 4**	P804 NJN	**LCY 6**	P806 NJN				

LCY 8–11		*Dennis Dart SLF SFD212BR1VGW1		Alexander ALX 200 10.2m				B29D	1998
		*(LCY 10 & 11 are SFD212BR1WGW1)							
LCY 8	R208 XNO	**LCY 9**	R209 XNO	**LCY 10**	S410 TNO	**LCY 11**	S411 TNO		

LV 8u	L208 YAG	Dennis Lance 11SDA3108		Plaxton Verde				B42D	1994

MB 1–18		Mercedes-Benz 814 Vario				Plaxton Beaver 2		B29F	1997
MB 1	R501 YWC	**MB 5**	R505 YWC	**MB 9**	R509 YWC	**MB 13**	R513 YWC	**MB 17**	R517 YWC
MB 2	R502 YWC	**MB 6**	R506 YWC	**MB 10**	R510 YWC	**MB 14**	R514 YWC	**MB 18**	R518 YWC
MB 3	R503 YWC	**MB 7**	R507 YWC	**MB 11**	R511 YWC	**MB 15**	R515 YWC		
MB 4	R504 YWC	**MB 8**	R508 YWC	**MB 12**	R512 YWC	**MB 16**	R516 YWC		

PD 1–18		Dennis Dart SFD412BR5VGD1				Plaxton Pointer 9.8m		B37D	1997
PD 1	R701 YWC	**PD 5**	R705 YWC	**PD 9**	R709 YWC	**PD 13**	R713 YWC	**PD 17**	R717 YWC
PD 2	R702 YWC	**PD 6**	R706 YWC	**PD 10**	R710 YWC	**PD 14**	R714 YWC	**PD 18**	R718 YWC
PD 3	R703 YWC	**PD 7**	R707 YWC	**PD 11**	R711 YWC	**PD 15**	R715 YWC		
PD 4	R704 YWC	**PD 8**	R708 YWC	**PD 12**	R712 YWC	**PD 16**	R716 YWC		

PD 63–102		Dennis Dart 9.8SDL3054 Ex Stagecoach Oxford, 1998				Plaxton Pointer 9.8m		B37D	1995
PD 63	M63 VJO	**PD 91**	M91 WBW	**PD 96**	M96 WBW	**PD 98**	M98WBW	**PD 102**	M102 WBW
PD 64	M64 VJO	**PD 92**	M92 WBW	**PD 97**	M97WBW	**PD 101**	M101 WBW		

PD 715–722		Dennis Dart 9.8SDL3035 Ex Stagecoach Oxford, 1998				Plaxton Pointer 9.8m		B37D	1994
PD 715	L715 JUD	**PD 717**	L717 JUD	**PD 719**w	L719 JUD	**PD 721**	L721 JUD		
PD 716	L716 JUD	**PD 718**	L718 JUD	**PD 720**	L720 JUD	**PD 722**	L722 JUD		

RM 613	WLT 613	AEC Routemaster R2RH Ex London Buses, 1994	Park Royal	H36/28R	1960
RM 980	USK 625	AEC Routemaster R2RH Ex Stagecoach Bluebird Buses, 1997	Park Royal	H36/28R	1961
RM 1289	XSL 596A	AEC Routemaster R2RH Ex Stagecoach Bluebird Buses, 1997	Park Royal	H36/28R	1962
RM 1527	527 CLT	AEC Routemaster R2RH Ex London Buses, 1994	Park Royal	H36/28R	1963
RM 1599	YTS 820A	AEC Routemaster R2RH Ex Stagecoach Bluebird Buses, 1997	Park Royal	H36/28R	1963
RMC 1456	LFF 875	AEC Routemaster R2RH Ex London Buses, 1994	Park Royal	H32/25RD	1962
RMC 1461	461 CLT	AEC Routemaster R2RH Ex London Buses, 1994	Park Royal	H32/25RD	1962
RMC 1485	485 CLT	AEC Routemaster R2RH Ex London Buses, 1994	Park Royal	H32/25RD	1962
RML 886	WLT 886	AEC Routemaster R2RH Ex London Buses, 1994	Park Royal	H40/32R	1961
RML 890	XFF 814	AEC Routemaster R2RH Ex London Buses, 1994	Park Royal	H40/32R	1961
RML 898	XFF 813	AEC Routemaster R2RH Ex London Buses, 1994	Park Royal	H40/32R	1961

RML 2272–2760	AEC Routemaster R2RH/1	Park Royal	H40/32R	1965–68

(Ex London Buses, 1994 except RML 2527, 2668, 2719 ex London Sovereign, 2001)

RML 2272	CUV 272C	**RML 2429**	JJD 429D	**RML 2470**	JJD 470D	**RML 2550**	JJD 550D	**RML 2641**	NML 641E
RML 2286	CUV 286C	**RML 2435**	JJD 435D	**RML 2481**	JJD 481D	**RML 2565**	JJD 565D	**RML 2642**	NML 642E
RML 2300	CUV 300C	**RML 2437**	JJD 437D	**RML 2488**	JJD 488D	**RML 2581**	JJD 581D	**RML 2657**	NML 657E
RML 2303	CUV 303C	**RML 2444**	JJD 444D	**RML 2493**	JJD 493D	**RML 2592**	JJD 592D	**RML 2661**	SMK 661F
RML 2311	CUV 311C	**RML 2445**	JJD 445D	**RML 2495**	JJD 495D	**RML 2607**	NML 607E	**RML 2665**	SMK 665F
RML 2392	JJD 392D	**RML 2450**	JJD 450D	**RML 2496**	JJD 496D	**RML 2610**	NML 610E	**RML 2668**	SMK 668F
RML 2399	JJD 399D	**RML 2451**	JJD 451D	**RML 2497**	JJD 497D	**RML 2616**	NML 616E	**RML 2670**	SMK 670F
RML 2402	JJD 402D	**RML 2456**	JJD 456D	**RML 2527**	JJD 527D	**RML 2624**	NML 624E	**RML 2671**	SMK 671F
RML 2415	JJD 415D	**RML 2462**	JJD 462D	**RML 2541**	JJD 541D	**RML 2639**	NML 639E	**RML 2696**	SMK 696F

RML 2705 SMK 705F	**RML 2719** SMK 719F	**RML 2738** SMK 738F	**RML 2748** SMK 748F	**RML 2760** SMK 760F
RML 2709 SMK 709F	**RML 2723** SMK 723F	**RML 2743** SMK 743F	**RML 2749** SMK 749F	

SLD 21–29 Dennis Dart SLF SFD212BR1VGW1 Alexander ALX 200 10.2mB33F 1997

SLD 21 R121 VPU	**SLD 23** R123 VPU	**SLD 25** R125 VPU	**SLD 27** R127 VPU	**SLD 29** R129 VPU
SLD 22 R122 VPU	**SLD 24** R124 VPU	**SLD 26** R126 VPU	**SLD 28** R128 VPU	

SLD 30–41 Dennis Dart SLF SFD212BR1VGW1 Alexander ALX 200 10.2m B30D 1998

SLD 30 R930 FOO	**SLD 33** R933 FOO	**SLD 36** R936 FOO	**SLD 39** R939 FOO
SLD 31 R931 FOO	**SLD 34** R934 FOO	**SLD 37** R937 FOO	**SLD 40** R940 FOO
SLD 32 R932 FOO	**SLD 35** R935 FOO	**SLD 38** R938 FOO	**SLD 41** R941 FOO

SLD 42–58 Dennis Dart SLF SFD112BR1WGW1 Alexander ALX 200 9.4m B29F 1998

SLD 42 R942 FOO	**SLD 46** R946 FOO	**SLD 50** R950 FOO	**SLD 54** R454 FVX	**SLD 58** R458 FVX
SLD 43 R943 FOO	**SLD 47** R947 FOO	**SLD 51** R451 FVX	**SLD 55** R455 FVX	
SLD 44 R944 FOO	**SLD 48** R948 FOO	**SLD 52** R452 FVX	**SLD 56** R456 FVX	
SLD 45 R945 FOO	**SLD 49** R949 FOO	**SLD 53** R453 FVX	**SLD 57** R457 FVX	

SLD 59–78 Dennis Dart SLF SFD212BR1WGW1 Alexander ALX 200 10.2m B33F 1998/9

SLD 59 S459 BWC	**SLD 63** S463 BWC	**SLD 67** S467 BWC	**SLD 71** S471 BWC	**SLD 75** S475 BWC
SLD 60 S460 BWC	**SLD 64** S464 BWC	**SLD 68** S468 BWC	**SLD 72** S472 BWC	**SLD 76** S476 BWC
SLD 61 S461 BWC	**SLD 65** S465 BWC	**SLD 69** S469 BWC	**SLD 73** S473 BWC	**SLD 77** S477 BWC
SLD 62 S462 BWC	**SLD 66** S466 BWC	**SLD 70** S470 BWC	**SLD 74** S474 BWC	**SLD 78** S478 BWC

SLD 79–88 Dennis Dart SLF SFD112BR1WGW1 Alexander ALX 200 9.4m B29F 1998

SLD 79 S479 BWC	**SLD 81** S481 BWC	**SLD 83** S483 BWC	**SLD 85** S485 BWC	**SLD 87** S487 BWC
SLD 80 S480 BWC	**SLD 82** S482 BWC	**SLD 84** S484 BWC	**SLD 86** S486 BWC	**SLD 88** S488 BWC

SLD 89–95 Dennis Dart SLF SFD212BR1WGW1 Alexander ALX 200 10.2m *B33F 1999
*(SLD 89 is B29F, SLD 90 is B31F)

SLD 89 S489 BWC	**SLD 91** S491 BWC	**SLD 93** S493 BWC	**SLD 95** S495 BWC
SLD 90 S490 BWC	**SLD 92** S492 BWC	**SLD 94** S494 BWC	

SLD 96–106 Dennis Dart SLF SFD112BR1WGW1 Alexander ALX 200 9.4m B29F 1999

SLD 96 S496 BWC	**SLD 99** S499 BWC	**SLD 102** S102 WHK	**SLD 105** S105 WHK
SLD 97 S497 BWC	**SLD 100** WLT 898	**SLD 103** S103 WHK	**SLD 106** S106 WHK
SLD 98 S498 BWC	**SLD 101** S101 WHK	**SLD 104** S104 WHK	

SLD 107–138 Dennis Dart SLF SFD212BR1XGW1 Plaxton Pointer 2 10.1m *B33F 1999
*(SLD 111–138 are B31D)

SLD 107 V107 MVX	**SLD 114** V114 MVX	**SLD 121** V174 MVX	**SLD 128** V128 MVX	**SLD 135** V135 MVX
SLD 108 V108 MVX	**SLD 115** V115 MVX	**SLD 122** V122 MVX	**SLD 129** V129 MVX	**SLD 136** V136 MVX
SLD 109 V109 MVX	**SLD 116** V116 MVX	**SLD 123** V175 MVX	**SLD 130** V130 MVX	**SLD 137** V137 MVX
SLD 110 V110 MVX	**SLD 117** V117 MVX	**SLD 124** V124 MVX	**SLD 131** V131 MVX	**SLD 138** V138 MVX
SLD 111 V173 MVX	**SLD 118** V118 MVX	**SLD 125** V125 MVX	**SLD 132** V132 MVX	
SLD 112 V112 MVX	**SLD 119** V119 MVX	**SLD 126** V126 MVX	**SLD 133** V133 MVX	
SLD 113 V113 MVX	**SLD 120** V120 MVX	**SLD 127** V127 MVX	**SLD 134** V134 MVX	

SLD 139-172 Dennis Dart SLF SFD112BR1XGW1 Plaxton Pointer 2 9.3m B27D 1999–2000

SLD 139 V139 MVX	**SLD 146** V146 MVX	**SLD 153** V153 MVX	**SLD 160** V160 MVX	**SLD 167** V167 MVX
SLD 140 V140 MVX	**SLD 147** V147 MVX	**SLD 154** V154 MVX	**SLD 161** V161 MVX	**SLD 168** V168 MVX
SLD 141 V141 MVX	**SLD 148** V148 MVX	**SLD 155** V155 MVX	**SLD 162** V162 MVX	**SLD 169** V169 MVX
SLD 142 V142 MVX	**SLD 149** V149 MVX	**SLD 156** V156 MVX	**SLD 163** V163 MVX	**SLD 170** V170 MVX
SLD 143 V143 MVX	**SLD 150** V150 MVX	**SLD 157** V157 MVX	**SLD 164** V164 MVX	**SLD 171** V171 MVX
SLD 144 V144 MVX	**SLD 151** V151 MVX	**SLD 158** V158 MVX	**SLD 165** V165 MVX	**SLD 172** V172 MVX
SLD 145 V145 MVX	**SLD 152** V152 MVX	**SLD 159** V159 MVX	**SLD 166** V166 MVX	

SLD 173–203 Dennis Dart SLF SFD212BR1YGW1 Plaxton Pointer 2 10.1m B31D 2000

SLD 173 W173 DNO	**SLD 180** W227 DNO	**SLD 187** W187 DNO	**SLD 194** W194 DNO	**SLD 201** W201 DNO
SLD 174 W174 DNO	**SLD 181** W181 DNO	**SLD 188** W188 DNO	**SLD 195** W195 DNO	**SLD 202** W202 DNO
SLD 175 W224 DNO	**SLD 182** W182 DNO	**SLD 189** W189 DNO	**SLD 196** W196 DNO	**SLD 203** W203 DNO
SLD 176 W176 DNO	**SLD 183** W183 DNO	**SLD 190** W231 DNO	**SLD 197** W197 DNO	
SLD 177 W177 DNO	**SLD 184** W184 DNO	**SLD 191** W191 DNO	**SLD 198** W198 DNO	
SLD 178 W178 DNO	**SLD 185** W185 DNO	**SLD 192** W192 DNO	**SLD 199** W199 DNO	
SLD 179 W226 DNO	**SLD 186** W186 DNO	**SLD 193** W193 DNO	**SLD 200** W233 DNO	

SLD 204–223 Dennis Dart SLF SFD112BR1YGW1 Plaxton Pointer 2 9.3m *B27D 2000
*(SLD 212–223 are B30F)

SLD 204 W204 DNO	**SLD 208** W208 DNO	**SLD 212** W212 DNO	**SLD 216** W216 DNO	**SLD 220** W235 DNO
SLD 205 W228 DNO	**SLD 209** W209 DNO	**SLD 213** W213 DNO	**SLD 217** W234 DNO	**SLD 221** W221 DNO
SLD 206 W229 DNO	**SLD 210** W232 DNO	**SLD 214** W214 DNO	**SLD 218** W218 DNO	**SLD 222** W236 DNO
SLD 207 W207 DNO	**SLD 211** W211 DNO	**SLD 215** W215 DNO	**SLD 219** W219 DNO	**SLD 223** W223 DNO

SLD 224–236 Dennis Dart SLF SFD467BR1YGW3 Plaxton Pointer 2 11.3m B38D 2001

SLD 224 X224 WNO	**SLD 227** X227 WNO	**SLD 230** X238 WNO	**SLD 233** X233 WNO	**SLD 236** X236 WNO
SLD 225 X237 WNO	**SLD 228** X228 WNO	**SLD 231** X231 WNO	**SLD 234** X234 WNO	
SLD 226 X226 WNO	**SLD 229** X229 WNO	**SLD 232** X232 WNO	**SLD 235** X235 WNO	

SLD 237–253 Dennis Dart SLF SFD612BR11GW1 Alexander ALX200 8.9m B28F 2001

SLD 237 Y237 FJN	**SLD 241** Y241 FJN	**SLD 245** Y348 FJN	**SLD 249** Y249 FJN	**SLD 253** Y253 FJN
SLD 238 Y238 FJN	**SLD 242** Y242 FJN	**SLD 246** Y246 FJN	**SLD 250** Y349 FJN	
SLD 239 Y239 FJN	**SLD 243** Y243 FJN	**SLD 247** Y247 FJN	**SLD 251** Y251 FJN	
SLD 240 Y347 FJN	**SLD 244** Y244 FJN	**SLD 248** Y248 FJN	**SLD 252** Y252 FJN	

SLD 254–327 Dennis Dart SLF SFD212BR11GW6 Alexander ALX200 10.2m B30D 2001

SLD 254 Y254 FJN	**SLD 269** Y269 FJN	**SLD 284** Y284 FJN	**SLD 299** Y299 FJN	**SLD 314** LX51 FGP
SLD 255 Y351 FJN	**SLD 270** Y353 FJN	**SLD 285** Y285 FJN	**SLD 300** LX51 FPJ	**SLD 315** LX51 FGU
SLD 256 Y256 FJN	**SLD 271** Y271 FJN	**SLD 286** Y286 FJN	**SLD 301** Y301 FJN	**SLD 316** LX51 FGZ
SLD 257 Y257 FJN	**SLD 272** Y272 FJN	**SLD 287** Y287 FJN	**SLD 302** Y302 FJN	**SLD 317** LX51 FHG
SLD 258 Y258 FJN	**SLD 273** Y273 FJN	**SLD 288** Y671 JSG	**SLD 303** LX51 FGA	**SLD 318** LX51 FHB
SLD 259 Y259 FJN	**SLD 274** Y274 FJN	**SLD 289** Y289 FJN	**SLD 304** LX51 FGF	**SLD 319** LX51 FHA
SLD 260 Y352 FJN	**SLD 275** Y354 FJN	**SLD 290** LX51 FFW	**SLD 305** LX51 FGE	**SLD 320** LX51 FHC
SLD 261 Y261 FJN	**SLD 276** Y276 FJN	**SLD 291** Y291 FJN	**SLD 306** LX51 FGD	**SLD 321** LX51 FHD
SLD 262 Y262 FJN	**SLD 277** Y277 FJN	**SLD 292** Y292 FJN	**SLD 307** LX51 FGG	**SLD 322** LX51 FHE
SLD 263 Y263 FJN	**SLD 278** LX51 FPE	**SLD 293** Y293 FJN	**SLD 308** LX51 FGM	**SLD 323** LX51 FHF
SLD 264 Y264 FJN	**SLD 279** Y279 FJN	**SLD 294** Y294 FJN	**SLD 309** LX51 FGK	**SLD 324** LX51 FHK
SLD 265 Y265 FJN	**SLD 280** Y356 FJN	**SLD 295** Y295 FJN	**SLD 310** LX51 FGV	**SLD 325** LX51 FHL
SLD 266 Y266 FJN	**SLD 281** Y281 FJN	**SLD 296** Y296 FJN	**SLD 311** LX51 FGJ	**SLD 326** LX51 FHH
SLD 267 Y267 FJN	**SLD 282** Y282 FJN	**SLD 297** Y297 FJN	**SLD 312** LX51 FGN	**SLD 327** LX51 FHJ
SLD 268 Y268 FJN	**SLD 283** Y283 FJN	**SLD 298** Y298 FJN	**SLD 313** LX51 FGO	

SLD 328–346 — Dennis Dart SLF SFD322BR1YGW1 — Alexander ALX200 10.8m — B33D — 2001

SLD 328 Y371 FJN	SLD 332 Y332 FJN	SLD 336 Y336 FJN	SLD 340 Y374 FJN	SLD 344 Y344 FJN
SLD 329 Y329 FJN	SLD 333 Y373 FJN	SLD 337 Y337 FJN	SLD 341 LX51 FOO	SLD 345 Y376 FJN
SLD 330 Y372 FJN	SLD 334 Y334 FJN	SLD 338 Y338 FJN	SLD 342 Y342 FJN	SLD 346 Y346 FJN
SLD 331 Y331 FJN	SLD 335 Y335 FJN	SLD 339 Y339 FJN	SLD 343 Y343 FJN	

SLW 15–30 — Scania N113CRL — Wright Pathfinder 320 — B37D — 1994
Ex London Buses, 1994

SLW 15 RDZ 6115	SLW 19 RDZ 6119	SLW 23 RDZ 6123	SLW 27 RDZ 6127
SLW 16 RDZ 6116	SLW 20 RDZ 6120	SLW 24 RDZ 6124	SLW 28 RDZ 6128
SLW 17 RDZ 6117	SLW 21 RDZ 6121	SLW 25 RDZ 6125	SLW 29 RDZ 6129
SLW 18 RDZ 6118	SLW 22 RDZ 6122	SLW 26 RDZ 6126	SLW 30 RDZ 6130

T 1sp — THX 401S — Leyland Titan TNLXB2RRsp — Park Royal — H44/24D — 1978
Ex London Buses, 1994

TA 1–98 — Dennis Trident 2 SFD311BR1WGX2 — Alexander ALX 400 10.5m — H51/22D — 1999

TA 1 S801 BWC	TA 21 S821 BWC	TA 41 T641 KPU	TA 61 T661 KPU	TA 82 T682 KPU
TA 2 S802 BWC	TA 22 S822 BWC	TA 42 T642 KPU	TA 62 T662 KPU	TA 83 T683 KPU
TA 3 S803 BWC	TA 23 S823 BWC	TA 43 T643 KPU	TA 63 T663 KPU	TA 84 T684 KPU
TA 4 S804 BWC	TA 24 S824 BWC	TA 44 T644 KPU	TA 64 T664 KPU	TA 85 T685 KPU
TA 5 S805 BWC	TA 25 S825 BWC	TA 45 T645 KPU	TA 65 T665 KPU	TA 86 T686 KPU
TA 6 S806 BWC	TA 26 S826 BWC	TA 46 T646 KPU	TA 66 T699 KVX	TA 87 T687 KPU
TA 7 S807 BWC	TA 27 S827 BWC	TA 47 T647 KPU	TA 67 T667 KPU	TA 88 T688 KPU
TA 8 S808 BWC	TA 28 S828 BWC	TA 48 T648 KPU	TA 68 T668 KPU	TA 89 T689 KPU
TA 9 S809 BWC	TA 29 S829 BWC	TA 49 T649 KPU	TA 69 T669 KPU	TA 90 T690 KPU
TA 10 S810 BWC	TA 30 S830 BWC	TA 50 T650 KPU	TA 70 T670 KPU	TA 91 T691 KPU
TA 11 S811 BWC	TA 31 S831 BWC	TA 51 T651 KPU	TA 71 T671 KPU	TA 92 T692 KPU
TA 12 S812 BWC	TA 32 S832 BWC	TA 52 T652 KPU	TA 72 T672 KPU	TA 93 T693 KPU
TA 13 S813 BWC	TA 33 S833 BWC	TA 53 T653 KPU	TA 73 T673 KPU	TA 94 T694 KPU
TA 14 S814 BWC	TA 34 S834 BWC	TA 54 T654 KPU	TA 75 T675 KPU	TA 95 T695 KPU
TA 15 S815 BWC	TA 35 S835 BWC	TA 55 T655 KPU	TA 76 T676 KPU	TA 96 T696 KPU
TA 16 S816 BWC	TA 36 S836 BWC	TA 56 T656 KPU	TA 77 T677 KPU	TA 97 T697 KPU
TA 17 S817 BWC	TA 37 S837 BWC	TA 57 T657 KPU	TA 78 T678 KPU	TA 98 T698 KPU
TA 18 S818 BWC	TA 38 S838 BWC	TA 58 T658 KPU	TA 79 T679 KPU	
TA 19 S819 BWC	TA 39 S839 BWC	TA 59 T659 KPU	TA 80 T680 KPU	
TA 20 S820 BWC	TA 40 T640 KPU	TA 60 T660 KPU	TA 81 T681 KPU	

TA 99–222 — Dennis Trident 2 SFD311BR1XGX2 — Alexander ALX 400 10.5m — H47/24D — 1999–2000

TA 99 VLT 14	TA 118 V118 MEV	TA 137 V137 MEV	TA 156 V156 MEV	TA 175 V175 MEV
TA 100 WLT 491	TA 119 V119 MEV	TA 138 V138 MEV	TA 157 V157 MEV	TA 176 V176 MEV
TA 101 WLT 461	TA 120 V120 MEV	TA 139 V139 MEV	TA 158 V158 MEV	TA 177 V177 MEV
TA 102 V102 MEV	TA 121 V478 KJN	TA 140 V140 MEV	TA 159 V159 MEV	TA 178 V178 MEV
TA 103 V103 MEV	TA 122 V122 MEV	TA 141 V141 MEV	TA 160 V160 MEV	TA 179 V179 MEV
TA 104 V104 MEV	TA 123 V479 KJN	TA 142 V142 MEV	TA 161 V161 MEV	TA 180 W187 CNO
TA 105 V105 MEV	TA 124 V124 MEV	TA 143 V143 MEV	TA 162 V162 MEV	TA 181 V181 MEV
TA 106 V106 MEV	TA 125 V125 MEV	TA 144 V144 MEV	TA 163 V163 MEV	TA 182 V182 MEV
TA 107 V107 MEV	TA 126 V126 MEV	TA 145 V145 MEV	TA 164 V164 MEV	TA 183 V183 MEV
TA 108 V108 MEV	TA 127 V127 MEV	TA 146 V146 MEV	TA 165 V165 MEV	TA 184 V184 MEV
TA 109 V109 MEV	TA 128 V128 MEV	TA 146 V147 MEV	TA 166 V166 MEV	TA 185 V185 MEV
TA 110 V476 KJN	TA 129 V129 MEV	TA 148 V148 MEV	TA 167 V167 MEV	TA 186 V186 MEV
TA 111 V477 KJN	TA 130 V130 MEV	TA 149 V149 MEV	TA 168 V168 MEV	TA 187 V362 OWC
TA 112 V112 MEV	TA 131 V131 MEV	TA 150 V150 MEV	TA 169 V169 MEV	TA 188 V188 MEV
TA 113 V113 MEV	TA 132 V132 MEV	TA 151 V151 MEV	TA 170 V170 MEV	TA 189 V189 MEV
TA 114 V114 MEV	TA 133 V133 MEV	TA 152 V152 MEV	TA 171 V171 MEV	TA 190 V190 MEV
TA 115 V115 MEV	TA 134 V134 MEV	TA 153 V153 MEV	TA 172 V172 MEV	TA 191 V191 MEV
TA 116 V116 MEV	TA 135 V135 MEV	TA 154 V154 MEV	TA 173 V173 MEV	TA 192 V192 MEV
TA 117 V117 MEV	TA 136 V136 MEV	TA 155 V155 MEV	TA 174 V174 MEV	TA 193 V193 MEV

TA 194	V194 MEV	TA 200	V363 OWC	TA 206	V206 MEV	TA 212	V212 MEV	TA 218	V218 MEV
TA 195	V195 MEV	TA 201	V201 MEV	TA 207	V207 MEV	TA 213	V213 MEV	TA 219	V219 MEV
TA 196	V196 MEV	TA 202	V202 MEV	TA 208	V208 MEV	TA 214	V214 MEV	TA 220	V220 MEV
TA 197	V197 MEV	TA 203	V203 MEV	TA 209	V209 MEV	TA 215	V215 MEV	TA 221	V221 MEV
TA 198	V198 MEV	TA 204	V204 MEV	TA 210	V210 MEV	TA 216	V216 MEV	TA 222	V364 OWC
TA 199	V199 MEV	TA 205	V205 MEV	TA 211	V211 MEV	TA 217	V217 MEV		

TA 261–358 Dennis Trident 2 SFD311BR1YGX2 Alexander ALX 400 10.5m *H45/24D 2000–1
*(TA 261–267 are H47/24D)

TA 261	X261 NNO	TA 281	X281 NNO	TA 301	X301 NNO	TA 321	X388 NNO	TA 341	X341 NNO
TA 262	X262 NNO	TA 282	X282 NNO	TA 302	X302 NNO	TA 322	X322 NNO	TA 342	X342 NNO
TA 263	X263 NNO	TA 283	X283 NNO	TA 303	X303 NNO	TA 323	X389 NNO	TA 343	X343 NNO
TA 264	X264 NNO	TA 284	X284 NNO	TA 304	X304 NNO	TA 324	X324 NNO	TA 344	X344 NNO
TA 265	X265 NNO	TA 285	X285 NNO	TA 305	X382 NNO	TA 325	X391 NNO	TA 345	X396 NNO
TA 266	X266 NNO	TA 286	X286 NNO	TA 306	X383 NNO	TA 326	X326 NNO	TA 346	X346 NNO
TA 267	X267 NNO	TA 287	X287 NNO	TA 307	X307 NNO	TA 327	X327 NNO	TA 347	X347 NNO
TA 268	X268 NNO	TA 288	X288 NNO	TA 308	X308 NNO	TA 328	X392 NNO	TA 348	X348 NNO
TA 269	X269 NNO	TA 289	X289 NNO	TA 309	X309 NNO	TA 329	X329 NNO	TA 349	X349 NNO
TA 270	X376 NNO	TA 290	X379 NNO	TA 310	X384 NNO	TA 330	X393 NNO	TA 350	X397 NNO
TA 271	X271 NNO	TA 291	X291 NNO	TA 311	X311 NNO	TA 331	X331 NNO	TA 351	X351 NNO
TA 272	X272 NNO	TA 292	X292 NNO	TA 312	X312 NNO	TA 332	X332 NNO	TA 352	X352 NNO
TA 273	X273 NNO	TA 293	X293 NNO	TA 313	X313 NNO	TA 333	X394 NNO	TA 353	X353 NNO
TA 274	X274 NNO	TA 294	X294 NNO	TA 314	X314 NNO	TA 334	X334 NNO	TA 354	X354 NNO
TA 275	X377 NNO	TA 295	X295 NNO	TA 315	X315 NNO	TA 335	X335 NNO	TA 355	X398 NNO
TA 276	X276 NNO	TA 296	X296 NNO	TA 316	X385 NNO	TA 336	X336 NNO	TA 356	X356 NNO
TA 277	X277 NNO	TA 297	X297 NNO	TA 317	X317 NNO	TA 337	X337 NNO	TA 357	X357 NNO
TA 278	X278 NNO	TA 298	X298 NNO	TA 318	X386 NNO	TA 338	X338 NNO	TA 358	X358 NNO
TA 279	X279 NNO	TA 299	X299 NNO	TA 319	X319 NNO	TA 339	X339 NNO		
TA 280	X378 NNO	TA 300	X381 NNO	TA 320	X387 NNO	TA 340	X395 NNO		

TA 359–435 *Dennis Trident 2 SFD31BBR21GX2 Alexander ALX 400 10.5m H45/23D 2000–1
*(TA 401–435 are SFD317BR21GX2)

TA 359	Y359 NHK	TA 375	Y511 NHK	TA 391	Y391 NHK	TA 408	LX51 FHU	TA 424	LX51 FJV
TA 360	Y508 NHK	TA 376	Y376 NHK	TA 392	Y392 NHK	TA 409	Y409 NHK	TA 425	LX51 FJY
TA 361	Y361 NHK	TA 377	Y377 NHK	TA 393	Y393 NHK	TA 410	LX51 FHV	TA 426	LX51 FJZ
TA 362	Y362 NHK	TA 378	Y378 NHK	TA 394	LX51 FHN	TA 411	LX51 FHW	TA 427	LX51 FKA
TA 363	Y363 NHK	TA 379	Y379 NHK	TA 395	Y395 NHK	TA 412	LX51 FHY	TA 428	LX51 FKB
TA 364	Y364 NHK	TA 380	Y512 NHK	TA 396	LX51 FHO	TA 413	LX51 FHZ	TA 429	Y429 NHK
TA 365	Y365 NHK	TA 381	Y381 NHK	TA 397	Y397 NHK	TA 414	LX51 FJA	TA 430	LX51 FKD
TA 366	Y366 NHK	TA 382	Y382 NHK	TA 398	Y398 NHK	TA 415	LX51 FJC	TA 431	LX51 FKE
TA 367	Y367 NHK	TA 383	LX51 FPF	TA 399	LX51 FHP	TA 416	LX51 FJD	TA 432	LX51 FKF
TA 368	Y368 NHK	TA 384	Y384 NHK	TA 400	Y514 NHK	TA 417	LX51 FJE	TA 433	LX51 FKG
TA 369	Y369 NHK	TA 385	Y385 NHK	TA 401	Y401 NHK	TA 418	LX51 FJF	TA 434	Y434 NHK
TA 370	Y509 NHK	TA 386	Y386 NHK	TA 403	LX51 FHS	TA 419	LX51 FJJ	TA 435	LX51 FKJ
TA 371	Y371 NHK	TA 387	LX51 FPC	TA 404	Y404 NHK	TA 420	LX51 FJK		
TA 372	Y372 NHK	TA 388	Y388 NHK	TA 405	LX51 FHT	TA 421	LX51 FJN		
TA 373	Y373 NHK	TA 389	Y389 NHK	TA 406	Y517 NHK	TA 422	LX51 FJO		
TA 374	Y374 NHK	TA 390	LX51 FPD	TA 407	Y407 NHK	TA 423	LX51 FJP		

TAS 223–260 Dennis Trident 2 SFD111BR1YGX2 Alexander ALX 400 9.9m H43/21D 2000

TAS 223	X361 NNO	TAS 231	X231 NNO	TAS 239	X239 NNO	TAS 247	X247 NNO	TAS 255	X373 NNO
TAS 224	X362 NNO	TAS 232	X232 NNO	TAS 240	X368 NNO	TAS 248	X248 NNO	TAS 256	X256 NNO
TAS 225	X363 NNO	TAS 233	X233 NNO	TAS 241	X241 NNO	TAS 249	X249 NNO	TAS 257	X257 NNO
TAS 226	X364 NNO	TAS 234	X234 NNO	TAS 242	X242 NNO	TAS 250	X372 NNO	TAS 258	X258 NNO
TAS 227	X365 NNO	TAS 235	X235 NNO	TAS 243	X243 NNO	TAS 251	X251 NNO	TAS 259	X259 NNO
TAS 228	X366 NNO	TAS 236	X236 NNO	TAS 244	X369 NNO	TAS 252	X252 NNO	TAS 260	WLT 575
TAS 229	X229 NNO	TAS 237	X237 NNO	TAS 245	X371 NNO	TAS 253	X253 NNO		
TAS 230	X367 NNO	TAS 238	X238 NNO	TAS 246	X246 NNO	TAS 254	X254 NNO		

TAS 436–534   *Dennis Trident 2 SFD111BR21GX2   Alexander ALX 400 9.9m   H43/19D   2001
* A number of this batch have differing chassis designations which could not be confirmed at time of going to press

TAS 436 Y436 NHK	**TAS 456** Y527 NHK	**TAS 476** LX51 FLM	**TAS 496** LX51 FMV	**TAS 516** LX51 FNU
TAS 437 Y437 NHK	**TAS 457** LX51 FKT	**TAS 477** LX51 FLN	**TAS 497** LX51 FMY	**TAS 517** LX51 FNV
TAS 438 Y438 NHK	**TAS 458** Y458 NHK	**TAS 478** LX51 FLP	**TAS 498** LX51 FMZ	**TAS 518** LX51 FNW
TAS 439 LX51 FKL	**TAS 459** LX51 FKU	**TAS 479** LX51 FLR	**TAS 499** LX51 FNA	**TAS 519** LX51 FNY
TAS 440 Y522 NHK	**TAS 460** Y529 NHK	**TAS 480** LX51 FLV	**TAS 500** LX51 FNC	**TAS 520** LX51 FNZ
TAS 441 Y441 NHK	**TAS 461** LX51 FKW	**TAS 481** LX51 FLW	**TAS 501** LX51 FND	**TAS 521** LX51 FOA
TAS 442 Y442 NHK	**TAS 462** Y462 NHK	**TAS 482** LX51 FLZ	**TAS 502** LX51 FNE	**TAS 522** LX51 FOC
TAS 443 Y443 NHK	**TAS 463** LX51 FKZ	**TAS 483** LX51 FMA	**TAS 503** LX51 FNF	**TAS 523** LX51 FOD
TAS 444 LX51 FKO	**TAS 464** Y464 NHK	**TAS 484** LX51 FMC	**TAS 504** LX51 FNG	**TAS 524** LX51 FOF
TAS 445 Y445 NHK	**TAS 465** LX51 FLB	**TAS 485** LX51 FMD	**TAS 505** LX51 FNM	**TAS 525** LX51 FOH
TAS 446 Y446 NHK	**TAS 466** LX51 FLC	**TAS 486** LX51 FME	**TAS 506** LX51 FNJ	**TAS 526** LX51 FOJ
TAS 447 Y447 NHK	**TAS 467** LX51 FLD	**TAS 487** LX51 FMF	**TAS 507** LX51 FNK	**TAS 527** LX51 FOK
TAS 448 Y448 NHK	**TAS 468** LX51 FLE	**TAS 488** LX51 FMG	**TAS 508** LX51 FNL	**TAS 528** LX51 FOM
TAS 449 Y449 NHK	**TAS 469** LX51 FLF	**TAS 489** LX51 FMJ	**TAS 509** LX51 FNH	**TAS 529** LX51 FON
TAS 450 Y524 NHK	**TAS 470** Y531 NHK	**TAS 490** LX51 FMK	**TAS 510** LX51 FNN	**TAS 530** LX51 FOP
TAS 451 LX51 FKR	**TAS 471** LX51 FLG	**TAS 491** LX51 FML	**TAS 511** LX51 FNO	**TAS 531** LX51 FOT
TAS 452 Y452 NHK	**TAS 472** Y472 NHK	**TAS 492** LX51 FMM	**TAS 512** LX51 FNP	**TAS 532** LX51 FOU
TAS 453 Y453 NHK	**TAS 473** LX51 FLJ	**TAS 493** LX51 FMO	**TAS 513** LX51 FNR	**TAS 533** LX51 FOV
TAS 454 Y454 NHK	**TAS 474** LX51 FLK	**TAS 494** LX51 FMP	**TAS 514** LX51 FNS	**TAS 534** LX51 FOA
TAS 455 Y526 NHK	**TAS 475** LX51 FLL	**TAS 495** LX51 FMU	**TAS 515** LX51 FNT	

VA 44–81   Volvo Olympian OLY–56   Alexander RL   H51/28D   1997

VA 44 P644 SEV	**VA 52** R152 VPU	**VA 60** R160 VPU	**VA 68** R168 VPU	**VA 76** R176 VPU
VA 45 P645 SEV	**VA 53** R153 VPU	**VA 61** R161 VPU	**VA 69** R169 VPU	**VA 77** R177 VPU
VA 46 P646 SEV	**VA 54** R154 VPU	**VA 62** R162 VPU	**VA 70** R170 VPU	**VA 78** R178 VPU
VA 47 R747 XAR	**VA 55** R155 VPU	**VA 63** R163 VPU	**VA 71** R171 VPU	**VA 79** R179 VPU
VA 48 R148 VPU	**VA 56** R156 VPU	**VA 64** R164 VPU	**VA 72** R172 VPU	**VA 80** R180 VPU
VA 49 R149 VPU	**VA 57** R157 VPU	**VA 65** R165 VPU	**VA 73** R173 VPU	**VA 81** R181 VPU
VA 50 R150 VPU	**VA 58** R158 VPU	**VA 66** R166 VPU	**VA 74** R174 VPU	
VA 51 R151 VPU	**VA 59** R159 VPU	**VA 67** R167 VPU	**VA 75** R175 VPU	

VA 122–148   Volvo Olympian OLY–50   Alexander RL   H51/28D   1998

VA 122 R122 EVX	**VA 128** R128 EVX	**VA 134** R134 EVX	**VA 140** R140 EVX	**VA 146** R146 EVX
VA 123 R123 EVX	**VA 129** R129 EVX	**VA 135** R135 EVX	**VA 141** R141 EVX	**VA 147** R147 EVX
VA 124 R124 EVX	**VA 130** R130 EVX	**VA 136** R136 EVX	**VA 142** R142 EVX	**VA 148** R148 EVX
VA 125 R125 EVX	**VA 131** R131 EVX	**VA 137** R137 EVX	**VA 143** R143 EVX	
VA 126 R126 EVX	**VA 132** R132 EVX	**VA 138** R138 EVX	**VA 144** R144 EVX	
VA 127 R127 EVX	**VA 133** R133 EVX	**VA 139** R139 EVX	**VA 145** R145 EVX	

VN 1	P801 GMU	Volvo Olympian YN3RV16V3	Northern Counties Palatine I	H49/31F	1996
VN 2	P802 GMU	Volvo Olympian YN3RV16V3	Northern Counties Palatine I	H49/31F	1996
VN 3	P803 GMU	Volvo Olympian YN3RV16V3	Northern Counties Palatine I	H49/31F	1996

VN 35–43   Volvo Olympian YN3RV16V3   Northern Counties Palatine I   H49/25D   1996

VN 35 P535 HMP	**VN 37** P537 HMP	**VN 39** P539 HMP	**VN 41** P541 HMP	**VN 43** P543 HMP
VN 36 P536 HMP	**VN 38** P538 HMP	**VN 40** P540 HMP	**VN 42** P542 HMP	

VN 82–110 Volvo Olympian OLY–4953 Northern Counties Palatine I H45/23D 1997/8

VN 82	R82 XNO	**VN 88u**	R188 XNO	**VN 94**	R94 XNO	**VN 100**	R210 XNO	**VN 106**	R206 XNO
VN 83	R83 XNO	**VN 89**	R89 XNO	**VN 95**	R95 XNO	**VN 101**	R101 XNO	**VN 107**	R107 XNO
VN 84	R84 XNO	**VN 90**	R190 XNO	**VN 96**	R96 XNO	**VN 102**	R102 XNO	**VN 108**	R108 XNO
VN 85	R85 XNO	**VN 91**	R91 XNO	**VN 97**	R97 XNO	**VN 103**	R103 XNO	**VN 109**	R109 XNO
VN 86	R86 XNO	**VN 92**	R92 XNO	**VN 98**	R98 XNO	**VN 104**	R104 XNO	**VN 110**	S110 SHJ
VN 87	R87 XNO	**VN 93**	R93 XNO	**VN 99**	R207 XNO	**VN 105**	R105 XNO		

VN 111–121 Volvo Olympian OLY–5639 Northern Counties Palatine I H49/27D 1998

VN 111	R311 XNO	**VN 114**	R114 XNO	**VN 117**	R117 XNO	**VN 120**	R120 XNO
VN 112	R112 XNO	**VN 115**	R115 XNO	**VN 118**	R118 XNO	**VN 121**	R121 XNO
VN 113	R113 XNO	**VN 116**	R116 XNO	**VN 119**	R119 XNO		

VN 149–178 Volvo Olympian OLY–5639 Northern Counties Palatine I H49/27D 1998

VN 149	R149 HHK	**VN 155**	R155 HHK	**VN 161**	R161 HHK	**VN 168**	R168 HHK	**VN 174**	R174 HHK
VN 150	R150 HHK	**VN 156**	R156 HHK	**VN 162**	R162 HHK	**VN 169**	R169 HHK	**VN 175**	R175 HHK
VN 151	R151 HHK	**VN 157**	R157 HHK	**VN 163**	R163 HHK	**VN 170**	R170 HHK	**VN 176**	R176 HHK
VN 152	R152 HHK	**VN 158**	R158 HHK	**VN 165**	R165 HHK	**VN 171**	R171 HHK	**VN 177**	R177 HHK
VN 153	R153 HHK	**VN 159**	R159 HHK	**VN 166**	R166 HHK	**VN 172**	R172 HHK	**VN 178**	R178 HHK
VN 154	R154 HHK	**VN 160**	R160 HHK	**VN 167**	R167 HHK	**VN 173**	R173 HHK		

VN 301–352 Volvo Olympian YN2RC16V3 Northern Counties Palatine I H45/23D 1995

VN 301	M301 DGP	**VN 314**	M314 DGP	**VN 322**	N322 HGK	**VN 330**	N330 HGK	**VN 346**	N346 HGK
VN 302	M302 DGP	**VN 315**	M315 DGP	**VN 323**	N323 HGK	**VN 338**	N338 HGK	**VN 347**	N347 HGK
VN 305	M305 DGP	**VN 316**	M316 DGP	**VN 324**	N324 HGK	**VN 339**	N339 HGK	**VN 348**	N348 HGK
VN 307	M307 DGP	**VN 317**	M317 DGP	**VN 325**	N325 HGK	**VN 340**	N340 HGK	**VN 350**	N350 HGK
VN 309	M309 DGP	**VN 318**	M318 DGP	**VN 326**	N326 HGK	**VN 341**	N341 HGK	**VN 351**	N351 HGK
VN 310	M310 DGP	**VN 319**	M319 DGP	**VN 327**	N327 HGK	**VN 342**	N342 HGK	**VN 352**	N352 HGK
VN 312	M312 DGP	**VN 320**	M320 DGP	**VN 328**	N328 HGK	**VN 343**	N343 HGK		
VN 313	M313 DGP	**VN 321**	N321 HGK	**VN 329**	N329 HGK	**VN 345**	N345 HGK		

VP 4	630 DYE	Volvo B10M–60 Ex Willetts, Yorkley, 1995	Plaxton Paramount 3500 III	C49FT	1991
VP 5	WLT 890	Volvo B10M–60 Ex Wallace Arnold, 1995	Plaxton Paramount 3500 III	C49FT	1991
VP 6	CSU 992	Volvo B10M–62 Ex Stagecoach Devon General, 2001	Plaxton Premiere 350	C53F	1995
VP 7	SYC 852	Volvo B10M–62 Ex Stagecoach Devon General, 2001	Plaxton Premiere 350	C53F	1995

Previous registrations:

CSU 992	M409 BFG	**USK 625**	WLT 980	**WLT 898**	S210 WHK
630 DYE	H659 UWR, H654 UWR	**VLT 14**	V473 KJN	**XFF 813**	WLT 898
J713 DAP	472 YMF, J713 CYG	**WLT 461**	V475 KJN	**XFF 814**	WLT 890
J715 DAP	YLJ 332, J715 CYG	**WLT 491**	V474 KJN	**XSL 596A**	289 CLT
LFF 875	456 CLT	**WLT 575**	X374 NNO	**YTS 820A**	599 CLT
SYC 852	M407 BFG	**WLT 890**	H660 UWR, H655 UWR		

Special Liveries:

All LCYs and SLD 30 and 31 carry blue livery for London City Airport service.
SLD 32–34 carry green livery for Canning Town–London City Airport Shuttle service.
RMC 1461 carries full Green Line livery.

TELLINGS-GOLDEN MILLER (Bus fleet)

D141 TMR	Mercedes-Benz L307D Ex Stone, Wilton, 1997	Whittaker	M12	1987
E460 ANC	Mercedes-Benz 507D Ex Spirit of London, Hounslow, 1996	Made-to-Measure	M16	1988
E834 EUT	Mercedes-Benz L307D Ex Capital, West Drayton, 1997	Yeates	M8	1987
E231 FLDt	Scania K112DRB Ex Capital, West Drayton, 1997	Van Hool Alizee	B30C	1987
F34 CWY	Mercedes-Benz 811D Ex Bridge, Paisley, 1997	Optare StarRider	B26F	1988
F46 CWY	Mercedes-Benz 811D Ex Bridge, Paisley, 1997	Optare StarRider	B26F	1988
F71 SJX	Mercedes-Benz 709D Ex South Lancs, St.Helens, 1996	Onyx	DP24F	1989
H837 GLD	Mercedes-Benz 609D Ex Marton, West Drayton, 1992	North Western Coach Sales	C13F	1991
L204 ULX	Mercedes-Benz 709D	Plaxton Beaver	B18FL	1993
L205 ULX	Mercedes-Benz 709D	Plaxton Beaver	B18FL	1993
L206 ULX	Mercedes-Benz 709D	Plaxton Beaver	B18FL	1993
M70 TGM	Mercedes-Benz 709D	Plaxton Beaver	B23F	1995
M80 TGM	Mercedes-Benz 709D	Plaxton Beaver	B23F	1995
M90 TGM	Mercedes-Benz 709D	Plaxton Beaver	B23F	1995
M7 TUB	Dennis Dart 9.8SDL3054 Ex Midland Choice, 2001	Northern Counties Paladin 9.8m	B39F	1995
M26 XEH	Dennis Dart 9.8SDL3054 Ex Midland Choice, 2000	Northern Counties Paladin 9.8m	B39F	1995
M541 XFY	Mercedes-Benz 208D Ex Capital, West Drayton, 1997	Concept Coachcraft	M8	1995
M544 XFY	Mercedes-Benz 208D Ex Capital, West Drayton, 1997	Concept Coachcraft	M8	1995
N305 DHE	Dennis Dart SLF SFD323BR1SGW1 Ex Country Lion, Northampton, 2001	Plaxton Pointer 10.6m	B41F	1996
N70 TGM	Mercedes-Benz 709D	Plaxton Beaver	B23F	1996
P701 LCF	Mercedes-Benz 814 Vario	Plaxton Beaver 2	B31F	1997
P702 LCF	Mercedes-Benz 814 Vario	Plaxton Beaver 2	B31F	1997
P703 LCF	Mercedes-Benz 814 Vario	Plaxton Beaver 2	B31F	1997
P704 LCF	Mercedes-Benz 814 Vario	Plaxton Beaver 2	B31F	1997
P255 MLE	Mercedes-Benz 711D	Plaxton Beaver	B20FL	1997
P456 MLE	Mercedes-Benz 711D	Plaxton Beaver	B20FL	1997
P70 TGM	Mercedes-Benz 709D	Plaxton Beaver	B27F	1997

	Dennis Dart SLF SFD322BR1VGW1 On temporary loan from Arriva Southern Counties.	Plaxton Pointer 10.6m	B39F	1997
P290 FPK	P292 FPK	P294 FPK	P296 FPK	
P291 FPK	P293 FPK	P295 FPK		

	Optare Excel L1000 Ex Capital Logistics, 2000	Optare	B33F	1998
R985 EWU	R988 EWU	R990 EWU	R992 EWU	
R986 EWU	R989 EWU	R991 EWU	R993 EWU	

R705 MJH	Mercedes-Benz 814 Vario	Plaxton Beaver 2	B31F	1997
R706 MJH	Mercedes-Benz 814 Vario	Plaxton Beaver 2	B31F	1997

	Dennis Dart SLF SFD322BR1VGW1		Plaxton Pointer 10.6m	B36F	1997
R501 SJM	R504 SJM	R507 SJM	R510 SJM	R513 SJM	
R502 SJM	R505 SJM	R508 SJM	R511 SJM	R514 SJM	
R503 SJM	R506 SJM	R509 SJM	R512 SJM		

S548 BNV	Mercedes-Benz 814 Vario*		Plaxton Beaver 2	B31F	1998
S549 BNV	Mercedes-Benz 814 Vario*		Plaxton Beaver 2	B31F	1998
S554 BNV	Mercedes-Benz 814 Vario*		Plaxton Beaver 2	B31F	1998
S557 BNV	Mercedes-Benz 814 Vario*		Plaxton Beaver 2	B31F	1998
S515 JJH	Dennis Dart SLF SFD322BR1WGW1		Plaxton Pointer 2 10.7m	B39F	1998
S516 JJH	Dennis Dart SLF SFD322BR1WGW1		Plaxton Pointer 2 10.7m	B39F	1998
S517 JJH	Dennis Dart SLF SFD322BR1WGW1		Plaxton Pointer 2 10.7m	B39F	1998
S707 JJH	Mercedes-Benz 814 Vario		Plaxton Beaver 2	B31F	1998
S708 TCF	Mercedes-Benz 814 Vario		Plaxton Beaver 2	B31F	1999
S518 TCF	Dennis Dart SLF SFD322BR1WGW1		Plaxton Pointer 2 10.7m	B39F	1999
S519 TCF	Dennis Dart SLF SFD322BR1WGW1		Plaxton Pointer 2 10.7m	B39F	1999
	* Ex Pink Elephant, 1999				

	Dennis Dart SLF SFD612BR1XGW1		Plaxton Pointer 2 8.8m	B27F	2000
V301 MDP	V303 MDP	V305 MDP	V307 MDP	V309 MDP	
V302 MDP	V304 MDP	V306 MDP	V308 MDP		

	Dennis Dart SLF SFD212BR1YGW1		Plaxton Pointer 2 10.1m	B31D	2000
W401 UGM	W403 UGM	W407 UGM	W409 UGM	W412 UGM	
W402 UGM	W404 UGM	W408 UGM	W411 UGM	W413 UGM	

	Dennis Dart SLF SFD322BR1YGW1		Plaxton Pointer 2 10.7m	B35D	2000
W601 UGM	W604 UGM	W607 UGM	W611 UGM		
W602 UGM	W605 UGM	W608 UGM	W612 UGM		
W603 UGM	W606 UGM	W609 UGM			

	Volvo B10BLE		Alexander ALX300 12m	B44F	2000
W901 UJM	W903 UJM	W905 UJM	W907 UJM		
W902 UJM	W904 UJM	W906 UJM			

	Dennis Dart SLF SFD612BR1YGW1		Plaxton Pointer 2 8.8m	B27F	2001
X311 KRX	X313 KRX	X315 KRX	X319 KRX		
X312 KRX	X314 KRX	X317 KRX	X322 KRX		

Y40 TGM	Dennis Dart SLF SFD322BR1YGW1		Caetano Nimbus 10.7 m	B30D	2001
Y50 TGM	Dennis Dart SLF SFD322BR1YGW1		Caetano Nimbus 10.7 m	B30D	2001

323	1068 MW	Dennis Dart SLF SFD612BR11GW1	Plaxton Pointer 2 8.8m	B29F	2001	

414–420		Dennis Dart SLF SFD212BR11GW1	Plaxton Pointer 2 10.1m	B30D	2001
414	RX51 FGG	**416** RX51 FGJ	**418** RX51 FGN	**420** RX51 FGP	
415	RX51 FGK	**417** RX51 FGM	**419** RX51 FGO		

On order: 7 x Dennis Dart/Caetano Nimbus 10.1m for route H25.

Special liveries: P290–296 FPK are in green. 515–7 and 707 carry Kingston University livery.

THORPES

DLF 9	R309 NGM	Dennis Dart SLF212BR1VGW1		Plaxton Pointer 10m	B33F	1997
		Ex Limebourne, 1998				

DLF 29–40		Dennis Dart SLF SFD212BR1WGW1		Plaxton Pointer 2 10.2m	B29D	1998

DLF 29	S529 JLM	**DLF 32**	S532 JLM	**DLF 35**	S535 JLM	**DLF 38**	S538 JLM
DLF 30	S530 JLM	**DLF 33**	S533 JLM	**DLF 36**	S536 JLM	**DLF 39**	S539 JLM
DLF 31	S531 JLM	**DLF 34**	S534 JLM	**DLF 37**	S537 JLM	**DLF 40**	S540 JLM

DLF 41	P41 MLE	Dennis Dart SLF SFD112BR1SGW2	Plaxton Pointer 9.2m	B27D	1996
		Currently on loan from London Transport			

DLF 63–79		Dennis Dart SLF SFD212AR1YGW1		Plaxton Pointer 2 10.1m	B29D	2000/1

DLF 63	W963 TRP	**DLF 66**	W966 TRP	**DLF 69**	W969 TRP	**DLF 73**	W973 TRP	**DLF 76**	W976 TRP
DLF 64	W964 TRP	**DLF 67**	W967 TRP	**DLF 71**	W971 TRP	**DLF 74**	W974 TRP	**DLF 77**	W977 TRP
DLF 65	W965 TRP	**DLF 68**	W968 TRP	**DLF 72**	W972 TRP	**DLF 75**	W975 TRP	**DLF 79**	X179 BNH

ML 514	J514 WTW	Mercedes-Benz 709D	Wadham Stringer Wessex	B19FL	1991
		Ex Javelin, Wandsworth, 1997			
ML 520	J520 WTW	Mercedes-Benz 709D	Wadham Stringer Wessex	B20FL	1991
		Ex Javelin, Wandsworth, 1997			
ML 529	J529 WTW	Mercedes-Benz 709D	Wadham Stringer Wessex	B23FL	1991
		Ex Javelin, Wandsworth, 1997			
ML 530	J530 WTW	Mercedes-Benz 709D	Wadham Stringer Wessex	B15FL	1991
		Ex Javelin, Wandsworth, 1997			
OSL 1	YJ51 JWY	Optare Solo M850	Optare	B17F	2001
OSL 2	YJ51 JWZ	Optare Solo M850	Optare	B17F	2001
XL 100	N100 FET	Optare Excel L960	Optare	B27F	1996
XL 200	N200 FET	Optare Excel L960	Optare	B27F	1996
XL 300	N300 FET	Optare Excel L960	Optare	B27F	1996
XL 400	N400 FET	Optare Excel L960	Optare	B27F	1996
XL 845	R845 FWW	Optare Excel L960	Optare	B28F	1997
		Acquired 2001			
XL 846	R846 FWW	Optare Excel L960	Optare	B28F	1997
		Acquired 2001			
	GOG 208W	MCW Metrobus DR102/18	MCW	H43/30F	1981
		Ex Travel West Midlands, 2001			
	GYE 415W	MCW Metrobus DR101/12	MCW	H43/28D	1980
		Ex London United, 2000			
	OJD 815Y	MCW Metrobus DR101/16	MCW	H43/28D	1983
		Ex London United, 2000			
	OJD 864Y	MCW Metrobus DR101/16	MCW	H43/28D	1983
		Ex London United, 2000			
	OJD 889Y	MCW Metrobus DR101/16	MCW	H43/28D	1983
		Ex London United, 2000			
	POG 524Y	MCW Metrobus DR102/27	MCW	H43/30F	1982
		Ex Travel West Midlands, 2001			
	A700 UOE	MCW Metrobus DR102/27	MCW	H43/30F	1983
		Ex Travel West Midlands, 2001			
	B875 DOM	MCW Metrobus DR102/27	MCW	H43/30F	1985
		Ex Travel West Midlands, 2001			
	K2 FET	Mercedes-Benz 709D	Alexander AM (Belfast)	B16FL	1993
	K3 FET	Mercedes-Benz 709D	Alexander AM (Belfast)	B16FL	1993
	M191 TEV	Mercedes-Benz 709D	Wadham Stringer Wessex II	B20FL	1994
		Ex Javelin, Wandsworth, 1997			

Special liveries: The XL class carry dedicated Stationlink route branding and the Mercedes-Benz minibuses are dedicated LT mobility buses. Most of the DLF class for route 210 carry a red and yellow livery.

WING'S   (Bus fleet)

WB 1–3		Dennis Dart SLF SFD212BR1XGW1	East Lancs Spryte 10.5m	B30D	1999
WB 1 V336 MBV	**WB 2** V337 MBV	**WB 3** V338 MBV			

WB 4–7		Dennis Dart SLF SFD222AR1YGW1	East Lancs Spryte 10.5m	B29D	2000
WB 4 W435 CRN	**WB 5** W436 CRN	**WB 6** W437 CRN	**WB 7** W438 CRN		

Liveries:
WB 1–3 are in orange, yellow and white livery, WB 4–7 in green Trainlink colours.

TRANSPORT FOR LONDON (TfL)

AEC Routemaster R2RH being refurbished for further use

RM 548	SVS 618	Ex Marie Curie Cancer Project	Park Royal	H36/28R	1960
RM 652	WLT 652	Ex preservation, 2001	Park Royal	H36/28R	1961
RM 909	WTS 418A	Ex preservation, 2001	Park Royal	H36/28R	1961
RM 1145	LDS 402A	Ex Hallamshire, Sheffield, 2001	Park Royal	H36/28R	1962
RM 1164	NSG 636A	Ex preservation, 2001	Park Royal	H36/28R	1961
RM 1185	XYJ 427	Ex MTL, London, 2001	Park Royal	H36/28R	1962
RM 1562	562 CLT	Ex London's Transport Museum, 2001	Park Royal	H36/28R	1963
RM 1776	776 DYE	Ex private owner, 2001	Park Royal	H36/28R	1963
RM 1968	ALD 968B	Ex preservation, 2001	Park Royal	H36/28R	1964
RM 2050	ALM 50B	Ex London's Transport Museum, 2001	Park Royal	H36/28R	1964
RM 2060	ALM 60B	Ex KD Coach Hire, Dyserth, 2000	Park Royal	H36/28R	1964
RM 2122	CUV 122C	Ex KD Coach Hire, Dyserth, 2000	Park Royal	H36/28R	1965

Previous registrations:

LDS 402A	145 CLT	**NSG 636A**	164 CLT	**WTS 418A**	WLT 909	**XYJ 427**	185 CLT